MILITARY
COMMANDERS
THE 100 GREATEST
THROUGHOUT HISTORY

MILITARY
COMMANDERS
THE 100 GREATEST
THROUGHOUT HISTORY

NIGEL CAWTHORNE

Enchanted Lion Books
New York

CONTENTS

THE ANCIENTS

THE ANGLO-SAXONS & VIKINGS

THE MIDDLE AGES

THE ENGLISH CIVIL WAR

First American Edition published in 2004 by
Enchanted Lion Books, 115 West 18th Street, New York, NY 10011

Copyright © 2004 Arcturus Publishing Limited

26/27 Bickels Yard, 151–153 Bermondsey Street, London SE1 3HA

Printed in China

A CIP record is available from the Library of Congress

ISBN 1-59270-029-2

Editor: Paul Whittle
Cover design: Stünkel Studio
Cover image: *Napoleon Crossing The Alps at the St Bernard Pass,
20th May 1800* by Jacques Louis David, Musée Nationale du Chateau
de Malmaison, Rueil-Malmaison, France / Bridgeman Art Library

MILITARY
COMMANDERS
THE 100 GREATEST
THROUGHOUT HISTORY

LEONIDAS OF SPARTA

DIED 480 BC

CHRONOLOGY

494 BC The Persians put down the Greek revolt in Ionia.
492 Persian invasion fleet sunk by storm.
490 Persians beaten at Marathon.
489 Leonidas crowned king of Sparta.
480 Battle of Thermopylae; Leonidas dies.

L EONIDAS WAS THE military king of Sparta who defended southern Greece against the Persians. His small force fought to the death at Thermopylae, earning Leonidas the reputation of being the embodiment of Spartan courage. The name Leonidas means 'he who has the spirit of the lion'. A statue of Leonidas still stands near the site of the battle. Another stands at the heart of the city of Sparti, in the modern Greek province of Laconia in the Peloponnese.

It is not known when Leonidas was born, but he was the son of Anaxandridas II, King of Sparta. In 489, he succeeded his half-brother Cleomenes, who had gone insane and committed suicide. Leonidas I married Gorgo, Cleomenes' daughter. It is thought that Leonidas had backed Cleomenes' earlier attacks on Athens, though not his reluctance to fight the Persians. The war between the Persians and the Greeks had its origin in 546 BC, when the Persians took over the Greek city-state of Ionia in Anatolia, in modern-

day Turkey. In 500 BC, the Ionian Greeks revolted. Although the Ionian revolt was put down in 494 BC, the Athenians had sent a small fleet to support the rebels and the Persian Emperor Darius used this as an excuse to invade the mainland. In 492 BC, as the Persians moved towards Europe, their fleet was sunk by a storm. Two years later, in 490 BC, Darius landed 25,000 men on the mainland at Marathon. Athens appealed to Sparta to help them repel the invader, but the Spartans were delayed by a religious festival, leaving just 10,000 Athenians and 1,000 men from Plataea to face the Persians. However while the Persian cavalry was otherwise occupied, the Greek general Miltiades seized the opportunity to attack. The Athenians won a decisive victory, losing only 192 men to the Persians' 6,400.

▶ THE PERSIANS RETURN

After their defeat at Marathon the Persians went home, but returned in even greater numbers ten years later, under Xerxes who had succeeded his father Darius in 486 BC. This huge force moved slowly, giving the Greeks time to prepare. A Greek alliance against Persia was established in 481 BC. Command of the army was given to Sparta, that of the navy to Athens. An initial plan to defend Thessaly was abandoned as unrealistic. Instead the Greeks fell back on the narrow pass at Thermopylae.

To prevent their army from being outflanked by sea, the Greek fleet of 271 ships was stationed at Artemisium, commanding the straits between

'We shall fight them in the shade'

the island of Sciathos and the mainland. A detachment of 200 Persian ships attempted to surprise them, but the Greeks had been fore-warned and held back to engage the main Persian fleet. That night a tremendous storm destroyed the Persian fleet while the Greeks were safe in port. Meanwhile at Thermopylae Leonidas faced a force of 200,000 men.

Thermopylae means 'hot gates' and the pass derives its name from the hot sulphur springs nearby. With the sea on one side and high cliffs on the other, the pass is the perfect defensive position from which to control the strategic route between northern and southern Greece. Against Xerxes' formidable force, which was said to include 20,000 Libyan charioteers, Leonidas had just 4,000 Peloponnesians, including 300 full Spartan citizens, his elite royal guard. A contingent of *helots*, Greek serfs, may have brought their numbers up to 6,000 or 7,000.

▸ HOLDING THE PASS

The Battle of Thermopylae took place over three days in August 480 BC. Despite being vastly out-numbered, Leonidas' men easily repulsed the initial attacks by the Persian force. Xerxes then sent in a huge force of his elite 'Immortals'. But their great numbers were of no advantage in the confined space of the pass. The Greeks were armed with longer spears which prevented the Immortals engaging them at close quarters and it seemed as if the Greeks could hold the pass indefinitely. But on the second day of the battle,

a Greek deserter named Ephialtes told Xerxes that he could outflank the Greeks by following a path though the mountains. Some 10,000 Immortals set out at night under the command of Hydarnes. On the way, they met a detachment of 1,000 Phocian Greeks whom Leonidas had sent to guard the path. These men assumed that the Persians had come to fight them, and retreated to high ground, preparing to face death, but the Persians simply passed them by.

When the Greeks heard that they had been outflanked, some urged Leonidas to retreat. Others simply decamped. But Sparta did not retreat. Leonidas dismissed anyone who wanted to go, and he stayed to fight on in the pass with his 300 Spartans, 400 Thebans and 700 Thespians. Leonidas was killed and his men massacred. Leonidas's sacrifice allowed the other Greeks time to make an orderly retreat. By the time the Persians reached Athens and burnt it, the city had been evacuated.

Although, Leonidas would certainly have craved the glory of such an heroic death, there may have been another reason for his suicidal stand. An oracle had foretold that either Sparta would perish or one of her kings would perish – Sparta traditionally had two kings at any one time. By his death, Leonidas saved his city. After the Persians took Athens, they were defeated by the Greek navy at the Battle of Salamis, putting an end to Xerxes' imperial Greece. Leonidas and Gorgo's son, Pleistarchus, went on to become King of Sparta.

THE PASS AT THERMOPYLAE

- *Leonidas's stand at Thermopylae made a huge impression on the Greeks and helped give rise to the heroic Spartan ideal. When the Immortals arrived behind them, the remaining Greeks retreated to a small hillock. There they formed a circle and fought on until every man was cut down.*

- *While Leonidas was preparing to make his stand, a Persian envoy arrived, who explained the futility of trying to resist the huge Persian army. 'Our archers are so numerous,' said the envoy, 'that the flight of their arrows darkens the sun.' 'So much the better,' said Leonidas, 'we shall fight them in the shade.'*

SUN TZU

C. 400–330 BC

CHRONOLOGY Fourth century BC: Serves in army of king of Wu; writes *The Art of War* • AD 760 *The Art of War* translated into Japanese • 1722 French edition appears • 1782 New French edition thought to have been read by Napoleon • 1930s–1940s Used by Mao Tsetung in Communist takeover of China • 1950s–1970s Used by General Giap in defeating the French and the Americans in Indochina.

SUN TZU WAS A WRITER who used his experience fighting in wars in China to write *The Art of War*, one of the earliest treatises on military theory. It stresses the relationship between politics and warfare and the need for good intelligence and flexible tactics and strategies – and it warns of the dangerous unpredictability of war. It has become the standard textbook on warfare and is studied by many modern commanders.

▶ **SUN TZU IN BATTLE**

Some Chinese historians place Sun Tzu as early as the sixth century BC. But *The Art of War* is more likely to originate in the fourth century when, it is thought, Sun Tzu served as a general

'Know the enemy and know yourself, and you can fight a hundred battles without defeat'

and military strategist in the state of Wu in what is called the late Spring and Autumn period in China, from 770 to 476 BC. Clues in the text indicate that it was written early in the Warring States period – from 475 to 221 BC – when China was divided into six or seven warring states who were fighting for supremacy.

He is named as the military leader who captured Ying, the capital of Chu'u. Other accounts say he defeated the northern states of Chin and Chi'i. And it is said that he used hundreds of Wu's concubines to demonstrate drills and military manoeuvres.

The Art of War was widely used as a textbook on warfare by the Chinese and Mongols. In AD 760, the first complete translation appeared in Japanese. Then in 1722, it was brought to the West by Father J.J.M. Arniot, a Jesuit missionary to Peking, who published it in translation in Paris. Since then it has become widely available in numerous languages.

▶ WAR AS AN ART

To Sun Tzu, war is not an exact science, but an art the outcome of which is unpredictable. However, there are certain rules for success. The military leader should prepare defences that can repel any attack and be constantly on the lookout for ways to defeat the enemy. These are not necessarily military. In fact, Sun Tzu considered the use of military force a last resort and advocated the use of bribery, the spreading of false rumours in the enemy camp, the co-opting of the political opposition in the enemy state and otherwise undermining the enemy's capabilities and morale.

'The skilful strategist should be able to subdue the enemy's army without engaging it, take his cities without besieging them and overthrow his state without bloodying swords,' he wrote.

If military conflict became the only option, he insisted on obtaining detailed information about the enemy's forces and their disposition – as well as one's own. 'Know the enemy and know yourself, and you can fight a hundred battles with no danger of defeat,' Sun Tzu tells us. He required such detail on the disposition of the enemy that he was able to write several chapters on the nine kinds of battlefield terrain.

Further recommendations included: 'Avoid strength, attack weakness.' Wars should be short and decisive as 'No country ever benefited from a protracted war.' He also said that successful commanders 'defend when strength is inadequate and attack when strength is abundant'.

Although many of his axioms of warfare seem obvious, numerous military commanders who have followed them have won the day – and countless commanders who have ignored them have lost.

THE ART OF WAR

- *It is thought that Napoleon read* The Art of War *when a new edition was published in Paris in 1782. It was also picked up by two great military theorists who studied his methods – Antoine Henri Jomini who wrote* Summary of the Art of War *and Karl von Clausewitz, who wrote* On War. *However, modern military theorists find Jomini and von Clausewitz too parochially European and too nineteenth century. Only Sun Tzu has* stood the test of time.
- *Because of its emphasis on the political aspect of warfare,* The Art of War *was adopted as a handbook on guerrilla warfare by Mao Tsetung, Vo Nguyen Giap and Fidel Castro. However, it also influenced the pre-World War II theorists of armoured warfare General John Fuller and B.H. Liddell Hart – and, consequently, the German Panzer leaders who devoured their work.*

ALEXANDER THE GREAT

356–323 BC

A LEXANDER THE GREAT never lost a battle and by the time he died at the age of just 33 had conquered most of the known world. Fighting against numerically superior forces, he had defeated one of the greatest empires of the ancient world and spread Greek culture through Persia into Central Asia and India.

When Alexander was a boy, his father Philip II, King of Macedonia, told him, 'My son, look out for a kingdom worthy of yourself, for Macedonia is too small.' Indeed Macedonia was too small for Philip himself. After restoring order to his fragmented kingdom, he reformed the Macedonian army, fusing cavalry, highly mobile infantry and disciplined pikemen armed with 14-foot *sarissa* – twice as long as standard Greek spears. He went on to dominate the whole of Greece.

▸ THE PHILOSOPHER'S PUPIL

Born in 356 BC at Pella in Macedonia, Alexander was groomed for power. From the age of 13 to 16 his tutor was the philosopher Aristotle, who gave him an interest in philosophy, medicine and science, and taught that all non-Greeks should be slaves. Left in charge of Macedonia in 340 while Philip attacked Byzantium, Alexander defeated the Maedi, a Thracian people. Two years later he commanded the left flank at the Battle of Chaeronea, where Philip defeated the Greek states, displaying great personal courage.

Alexander fell out with his father when Philip divorced Alexander's mother and married again, threatening Alexander's position as his heir. When he expressed his contempt at his father's failing leadership at a party, Philip came to silence him but, being drunk, fell. 'There lies the man who is preparing to cross from Europe to Asia,' sneered Alexander, 'and he cannot even cross from one couch to another.'

In 336, Philip was assassinated by one of his own bodyguards and the 20-year-old Alexander succeeded him with the support of the army. They swept aside all opposition and marched south to take command of the Greek League. At Corinth, he was appointed the leader of the expedition to conquer Asia Minor (Turkey) which his father had already been planning, and returned to Macedonia via Delphi, where the Pythian priestess dubbed him 'invincible'.

Inspired by the *Iliad*, he landed in Asia Minor at Troy with 5,000 cavalry and 30,000 foot soldiers. Meeting elements of the Persian army at the Grancius River in 334, he found he was outnumbered by several thousand. But he crossed the river undetected and led his cavalry élite to

'My son, look out for a kingdom worthy of yourself, for Macedonia is too small'

victory. He moved quickly through Asia Minor, denying its ports to the Persian navy.

At Issus in northeastern Syria, he met the Persian main force under the command of King Darius III. Alexander found his supply lines cut. Outnumbered three to one, he attempted the flanking movement employed by his father, but it failed. Rallying his troops, Alexander led them directly at Darius, who was forced to flee. Though Darius's troops were winning elsewhere, they followed him.

Alexander then headed south, laying siege to Tyre for seven months. When it fell in July 332, he moved on to Gaza, occupied Egypt and established the new imperial city of Alexandria at the mouth of the Nile.

Now Alexander had fulfilled his father's plans. Believing himself to be a god, he moved swiftly across the Syrian desert to Mesopotamia. Once again, Alexander faced an army much greater than his own at Gaugamela. Again he led the attack and defeated the enemy, taking the Persian capital Persepolis and looting the royal treasury. The fleeing Darius was killed by his own commanders.

▶ EMPEROR ALEXANDER

Alexander was now master of a vast Asian empire. For the next six years, he led his men eastwards, through the mountains of Afghanistan into Central Asia. At the Hydaspes River, he defeated the Indian king Porus, whose army boasted 200 war elephants. Alexander wanted to go on but his men, worn out after eight years of fighting, persuaded him to go home. Leaving his conquests in the hands of trusted men, he headed westwards. In an attempt to unite east and west, he took a Persian wife and conducted a mass wedding between 10,000 Macedonian soldiers and Persian women. But his imperial dreams were to be shortlived. In 323, after a prolonged bout of eating and drinking, he died of fever in Babylon. His body was returned to Alexandria where it was placed in a golden coffin. With no heir to succeed him, his empire broke up into warring factions.

ALEXANDER'S BATTLES

- At the Battle of Granicus (334), the Persian plan to lure Alexander across the river and kill him almost succeeded, but the Persian line broke. Darius's Greek mercenaries were massacred, while 2,000 survivors were sent back to Macedonia in chains.
- After the Battle of Issus (333), Alexander captured Darius's entire family. Previously he had massacred all those who opposed him. Now he ordered that they be treated according to their station and offered captured soldiers the opportunity to change sides. Darius offered to pay a huge ransom and cede all his lands west of the Euphrates. 'I would accept, were I Alexander,' said Alexander's general Parmenio. 'I too, were I Parmenio,' retorted Alexander.

- At Tyre (332), Alexander used triremes carrying battering rams to pound the walls. When it fell, the men were massacred and the women and children sent into slavery.
- Before the Battle of Gaugamela (331) Darius had the battleground in northern Iraq levelled for his chariots. But by use of superior tactics, Alexander ended the Persian Empire established 180 years earlier.
- Facing Porus's army across the unfordable river Hydaspes in modern-day Pakistan, Alexander crossed the stream above the enemy's camp. During the Battle of Hydaspes (326), Alexander forced Porus's left wing back into the path of elephants that threatened the effectiveness of his cavalry. The elephants panicked and stampeded into the Indian ranks.

HANNIBAL

247–183 BC

HANNIBAL IS BEST KNOWN for taking the Carthaginian army, including men mounted on elephants, over the Alps to attack Rome. This was a tactical triumph. However, despite holding his own against the forces of Rome for fifteen years, it may have been a strategic blunder which led to the defeat of Carthage. Nevertheless he is still known as the 'father of military strategy' and is studied by students of military history to this day.

▶ HANNIBAL IN COMMAND

Born in Carthage in 247 BC, Hannibal learnt the military arts at the knee of his father, the Carthaginian general Hamilcar Barca. Hannibal accompanied his father to the Carthaginian province of Spain in the First Punic War (264–241 BC) where he swore eternal hostility towards Rome. He was given command by Hamilcar's son-in-law and successor Hasdrubal and, when Hasdrubal was assassinated in 221, Hannibal took command of the Carthaginian forces in the Iberian Peninsula. He then went on a two-year rampage, taking over the rest of

Spain in breach of all agreements between Rome and Carthage. In 218, the Romans declared war and demanded that Hannibal be handed over. So Hannibal went on the offensive. He left his brother, also named Hasdrubal, in command of the armies in Spain and North Africa and headed off across the Pyrenees with forty thousand men and some forty elephants.

They met stiff resistance from the Pyrenean tribes, but were supported by some Gaulish tribes. Others harassed him on his Alpine crossing. He also faced harsh weather and rock falls, and Hannibal descended into the Po Valley with 20,000 infantry, 6,000 cavalry and only a few of his elephants. This much reduced force was inadequate to suppress Rome. However, at the Ticino River, Hannibal's superior cavalry got the better of the Roman forces, which included his nemesis **Scipio**. This victory brought more tribes to his side, but a severe winter slowed his progress and cost him an eye due to infection.

A series of land victories at Trebia, Lake Trasimere and Cannae, made Hannibal master of

'He never required others to do what he could not and would not do himself'

the Italian peninsular. But he was not strong enough to besiege Rome and passed within three miles of the city. Cut off from Carthage by the Roman navy, he lived off the land. His brother Hasdrubal led an army from Spain to help him, but was stopped at the Metaurus River in 207. Hasdrubal's head was sent to Hannibal as a symbol of his defeat.

Starved of reinforcements, Hannibal's hope lay in the defection of the regions from the Italic confederacy, but the Romans took steps to hold on to the cities, which tied up Hannibal in southern Italy. Then in 204, Scipio landed in north Africa and attacked Carthage. This forced Hannibal to return to defend his homeland.

▸ A VICTIM OF TREACHERY

However, Carthage's ally the Massaesylian Numidians, who provided many of Hannibal's horsemen, changed sides and at the Battle of Zama in March 202, Scipio beat Hannibal, earning himself the title 'Africanus'. Hannibal lost 20,000 men, but escaped. When a treaty was signed between Carthage and Rome, Hannibal fled to Syria where he tried to get Antiochus III in Ephesus to take up arms against Rome. When they were defeated in 190, Hannibal found himself on the run again.

He either fled to the court of King Prusias of Bithynia, or he joined the rebel forces in Armenia, but eventually took refuge with Prusias, who was at war with Rome's ally, King Eumenes II of Pergamum. He served Prusias and, it is said, gained a victory at sea by throwing pots of snakes into enemy ships.

The Romans finally cornered Hannibal in the Bithynian village of Libyssa in 183, and he poisoned himself rather than be taken. Now in his sixties, he said before he died, 'Let us release the Romans from their long anxiety, since they think it too long to wait for the death of an old man.'

No Carthaginian record of Hannibal's exploits survived. The only record comes from the Romans who admired him as much as they feared him, for his tactical ability and willingness to share the hardships of his men. As one Roman chronicler wrote, 'He never required others to do what he could not and would not do himself.'

CROSSING THE ALPS

- When Hannibal crossed the Alps in 218, hostile Gallic tribes rolled rocks down on his army, causing men and animals to panic and lose their footing on the narrow paths. At the summit of the pass snow was falling and the descent was treacherous in the icy conditions. A landslide held them up for a day while it was cleared. He lost nearly half of the force he had set off from Spain with, but still beat the Romans on their home territory.
- Hannibal's crossing of the Alps forced Gaius Flaminius's army into open combat in 217. As it passed between the shores of Lake Trasimene and the nearby hills, he attacked from prepared positions, killing thousands and driving the rest into the lake where they drowned. When some 4,000 cavalry under Gaius Centenius rode to the rescue, they were intercepted and destroyed. But the Carthaginian troops were then too weary to march on the undefended Rome.
- At Cannae in southern Italy in 216, Hannibal let his well-trained Carthaginian foot soldiers fall back, drawing the Romans forward, while his cavalry on the flanks encircled them. The Roman army suffered its worst defeat, losing 60,000 dead. It was a classic enveloping movement which was to enter military textbooks.

SCIPIO AFRICANUS

236–183 BC

CHRONOLOGY

236 BC Born in Italy to patrician family.
218 Rescues father at the Ticino River.
216 Serves as military tribune at Cannae, but escapes the disaster.
209 Lands in Spain and seizes New Carthage.
206 Defeats Carthaginian army at Ilipa.
204 Invades North Africa.
202 Defeats Hannibal at the Battle of Zama.
190 Goes to fight in Syria.
180 Retires to farm in Liternum, Italy
183 Dies in Liternum.

eclipsed by that of Hannibal, as Field Marshal Bernard **Montgomery** pointed out, 'Hannibal's strategy in Italy was a failure. The only occasion when Scipio and Hannibal faced each other in battle, Scipio won.'

Born in 236 BC in Liternum, Campania (now Patria, Italy) Publius Scipio was the son of one of the great patrician families of Rome. His father, grandfather and great-grandfather had all been consuls. In 218, when Hannibal crossed the Alps into Italy, the young Scipio saw his father wounded and cut off by the enemy at the battle on the Ticino River and charged forward to save him. He served as a military tribune at the Battle of Cannae in 216. After the defeat there, he escaped to Canusium, where he thwarted a plot of some of the 4,000 survivors to desert Rome.

▶ SCIPIO IN SPAIN

In 211, his father and uncle were killed fighting the Carthaginians in Spain. His brother and father-in-law were also casualties of the Punic War and Scipio was set on vengeance. He led an army of 28,000 infantrymen and 3,000 cavalry to Spain and seized New Carthage (now Cartagena) the enemy base there. This denied the enemy their supplies and reinforcements, their arsenal and the local silver mines, and he freed

THE ROMAN GENERAL Scipio Africanus defeated **Hannibal** at the Battle of Zama in 202 BC, giving victory to Rome in the Second Punic War. Although Scipio's reputation has since been

'The only occasion when Scipio and Hannibal faced each other in battle, Scipio won'

the local chiefs that the Carthaginians held hostage. Then he set about retraining his army, abandoning the old Roman formations and perfecting the enveloping tactics that he had seen Hannibal use. His officers were taught to act independently on the battlefield and his men were equipped with the finest Spanish steel.

From 208 to 206, he fought a series of successful battles across Spain. Although he allowed Hasdrubal, Hannibal's brother, to escape, Scipio finished off the rest of the Carthaginian army at Ilipia, near Seville, in 206. Along the way he was hailed as '*imperator*' -- emperor: the first time this honour had been accorded a Roman general.

▶ MARCHING TO CARTHAGE

Scipio returned to Rome, where he was elected consul in 205. He decided not to confront Hannibal in Italy, but rather to attack his home-

land Carthage. After training an army in Sicily and making a treaty with the Numidians, Hannibal's north African allies, he landed in north Africa, winning the Battle of Bagbrades, near Utica, in 204. This forced Hannibal to return to defend his homeland, where he was defeated by Scipio at the Battle of Zama in 202. In honour of this victory, Scipio was given the title of 'Africanus'.

He became head of the Senate and in 190 accompanied his brother Lucius on his campaign against Antiochus III in Syria. Scipio was too ill to take part in Lucius's victory at Magnesia which earned him the title 'Asiagenus'. Back in Rome he found himself under political attack and withdrew to Liternum in 187 where he lived in a modest farmhouse until his death in 183. He is said to have asked to be buried at Liternum rather than in Rome in his family tomb.

SCIPIO'S BATTLES

- *When Scipio faced the Carthaginian army at Ilipa, his forces were outnumbered. To compensate, he staged an early morning raid on the Carthaginian camp. Then he reversed the Carthaginian order of battle. They put their strongest African troops in the center, with their Spanish allies on the flanks. He kept his Spanish troops in the middle, with Roman cavalrymen and legionnaires on either side. While his Spanish troops held the Carthaginians in the center, the Romans on his flanks pushed the Spaniards back, encircling them.*
- *At the Battle of Bagbrades (204), he put the Numidian and Roman cavalry on the flanks, refining his order of battle by using a screen of spearmen in the center. Behind them the infantry could manoeuvre independently to follow up on the gains made by the cavalry. Victory there forced Hannibal back to Africa.*
- *At the Battle of Zama (202), Scipio faced*

Hannibal, the master of the tactics he had employed with such success. Again Scipio was outnumbered and his formation was disrupted when Hannibal sent eighty elephants into the Roman ranks and the Numidian cavalry chased after the Carthaginians. Scipio had no alternative but to push forward in the center. His men crushed the first two lines of the Carthaginian defence, but they were exhausted when they came up against the third line, made up of hardened veterans from Hannibal's Italian campaign. But in the nick of time, the Numidian cavalry, having seen off the Carthaginian horsemen, returned, attacking the Carthaginian infantry from the rear. Fifteen thousand Carthaginians were killed and the rest of the army captured for the loss of 6,000 Romans. Hannibal and a handful of survivors escaped to Carthage, but were forced to make peace.

GAIUS MARIUS

157–86 BC

▶ A 'NEW MAN'

GAIUS MARIUS WAS A *novus homo* – a man from the Italian countryside with no senatorial forebears – who rose to prominence because of his military skills. Despite periods of political exile, he was elected consul seven times.

Born in 157 BC, in Cereatae in south Latium, he joined the staff of Scipio Aemilianus as an officer-cadet in the Numantine War in Spain, along with Jugurtha, later king of Numidia in north Africa. Enjoying the political backing of several noble families, he became tribune of the people in 119 BC and married the aunt of Julius Caesar. When Quintus Metellus was sent to fight Jugurtha who, as king of Numidia, sought to free his country from Roman rule, Marius accompanied him as a subordinate. Jugurtha was beaten by Metellus in a pitched battle, but continued guerrilla actions. Marius returned to Rome, got himself elected consul and returned to take over the army, for the first time enrolling volunteers from outside the propertied classes.

After a successful campaign, Jugurtha was captured by the ambitious aristocrat Sulla. He was taken to Rome and executed after being paraded in Marius's triumphal march. Marius was elected consul again – though having a second term was formally illegal. By this time, Rome was under attack from the north by the Germanic tribes of the Teutons and Cimbri. While Quintus Lutatius Catulus held the Brenner pass, Marius annihilated the Teutons at Aquae Sextiae – modern-day Aix-en-Provence in France. But Catulus failed to hold the Cimbri at bay, and they marched into northern Italy. Marius then joined forces with Catulus and defeated them at Vercellae, near Rovigo in the Po valley.

▶ INTO CIVIL WAR

Marius claimed the entire credit for the victory and was very popular in Rome, but he had made

Contrary to law and custom he enrolled in his army poor men with no property qualifications

powerful enemies in Metellus, Catulus and Sulla. Marius then made the mistake of plunging into party politics. In the resulting struggle two of Marius's allies, the tribune Lucius Appuleius Saturninus and Gaius Servilius Glaucia, seized the Capitoline Hill. The Senate called on Marius to save the republic. Saturninus and Glaucia surrendered to Marius, who locked them in the Senate house. Their enemies tore off the roof and stoned them to death, leaving Marius with the reputation of a man who betrayed his friends as well as his enemies.

Metellus returned from exile, while Marius sought refuge in the east. Civil war – known as the Social War, Italic War or Marsic War (90–88 BC) – ensued. Marius fought under the consul Rutilius Lupus, but Sulla was victorious, seizing Rome in 88. Marius escaped to Africa, but in 87 he returned and, with the dismissed consul Lucius Cornelius Cinna, captured Rome. Cinna and Marius were elected consuls for 86 BC – Marius for the seventh time. Prominent opponents were slaughtered. Marius died that year and his son was killed in further fighting with Sulla, who became dictator of Rome in 82 BC. He unexpectedly stepped down in 79 BC. Marius's widow survived until 69 BC, when she received a public funeral oration by her nephew Julius Caesar. Later Caesar restored Marius's trophies to the Capitol, which Sulla had removed.

MARIUS MOVES

- In 105 BC, Jugurtha, King of Numidia, had found refuge with his father-in-law Bocchus, king of Mauretania. Worried by the encroaching Romans, Bocchus betrayed Jugurtha. It was Sulla, Marius's quaestor, who made the hazardous journey to take Jugurtha, but Marius took credit for winning the Numidian War.

- While Marius was in north Africa in 105 BC, the Cimbri and the Teutons, both migrating German tribes, destroyed two Roman armies on the Rhône, killing some 80,000. This left Italy open to invasion from the north. However, the Cimbri marched into Spain and the Teutons stayed in northern Gaul, giving Marius time to prepare a new army. It was only in 102 that they advanced on Rome, with the Cimbri coming over the Alps from the northwest, via the Brenner Pass, and the Teutons advancing along the Mediterranean coast, while the Tigurini, an allied Celtic tribe who had defeated another Roman army in 107 BC, attacked from the northeast. Marius marched out to meet the Teutons, first refusing to give battle at a place of the Teutons' choosing, then withdrawing to Aix, where he blocked their path. The Germans' leading contingent then foolishly attacked without waiting for reinforcements, losing 30,000 men. Marius then hid 3,000 men so that they could attack the German main force from behind. The Teuton army was wiped out and over 100,000 died.

- Catulus allowed the Cimbri to enter Italy in late 102 BC. Marius marched north to join Catulus as they met the enemy at Vercellae in the summer of 101 BC. Again the discipline of Roman troops overcame greater numbers and between 65,000 and 100,000 Cimbri were killed, the rest enslaved. This persuaded the Tigurini to withdraw. Again Marius took credit for the victory, making an enemy of Catulus.

- With Sulla in power in Rome in 88 BC, Marius withdrew to Africa where he re-established himself. He landed in Etruria, the area north of Rome, in 87 BC and raised an army of veterans. They sacked Ostia, the port of Rome. Cinna joined forces with Marius and together they marched on Rome itself.

POMPEY

106–48 BC

CHRONOLOGY

106 BC Born in Rome 29 September.

81 Enters Rome in triumph after victories in Sicily and Egypt.

77 Helps drive Lepidus from Italy.

76 Fights in Spain.

72 Helps put down Spartacus's slave revolt.

70 Elected consul.

67 Begins campaign against pirates in Mediterranean.

66–62 Reorganizes the Middle East.

60 Joins First Triumvirate.

52 Given sole consulship.

49 Caesar crosses the Rubicon, starting civil war.

48 Defeated at Pharsalus; flees to Egypt where he is assassinated.

Pompey switched sides, fighting with distinction for Sulla in Picenum, eastern Italy, and in Sicily and Africa, ruthlessly executing Marian leaders who surrendered to him. Refusing to disband his army, he entered Rome in triumph as Gnaeus Pompeius Magnus – Pompey the Great.

When Sulla abdicated, he supported Marcus Lepidus as consul in 78 BC. But when Lepidus attempted a revolution, he helped drive Lepidus from Italy. Then in 76 BC, he went to Spain to fight the remnants of the Marians led by Sertorius. Having pacified Spain, southern Gaul and northern Italy, he returned to Italy in 72 BC and helped to end the slave revolt of Spartacus. Returning to Rome in triumph, he was elected consul in 70 BC, although not legally eligible, promising reforms at home and abroad.

P OMPEY WAS ONE OF THE GREAT generals of the late Roman republic. His skill as a commander led his troops to call him Magnus ('the Great'), and earned him a place in the First Triumvirate.

Born Gnaeus Pompeius in Rome in 106 BC, he was the son of Gnaeus Pompeius Strabo, consul in 89. In the Civil War (88–87 BC) between the rival generals Lucius Sulla and Gaius **Marius**, Strabo supported Marius. But when Strabo died,

▸ CHASING PIRATES

In 67 BC, he was commissioned by the Senate to stamp out piracy which was hampering trade. He assembled a fleet of 270 ships and swept through the Mediterranean. Although many pirates were successfully resettled as farmers, the campaign

Pompey's military career was the equal of any general of his day, earning him three Triumphs

climaxed in a major sea battle off the coast of Anatolia. He went on to defeat Mithradates VI in northern Anatolia and Tigranes in Armenia, and establish a number of protectorates in the southern Caucasus. He next annexed Syria, but left Judea as a dependent state.

Pompey returned to Rome in triumph for the third time in 61. He may have been a great general, but Pompey was no politician. He was forced into an alliance with Julius **Caesar**, who was already eroding his power base. The First Triumvirate was established in 60, with Marcus Licinius Crassus, Caesar and Pompey as the rulers of Rome. Pompey secured the deal by marrying Caesar's daughter Julia. In 53, Crassus was killed at the Battle of Carrhae in southern Anatolia, ending the triumvirate. And the following year Julia died, breaking the tie between Pompey and Caesar.

Caesar offered him another marriage alliance. Pompey refused. Rome was now descending into anarchy and the Senate called on Pompey to restore order. They made him sole consul, though not dictator as he craved. Caesar, who was in Gaul, refused to disband his army and return to Rome, where he was promised a consulship. Instead, he marched on Italy. The Senate decreed a state of war on 7 January 49 BC. Four days later Caesar crossed the Rubicon.

▶ POMPEY VS. CAESAR

Pompey's strategy was to abandon Rome and Italy to Caesar. With the navy and the east under his command, he planned to starve Caesar into submission. As Caesar raced south, Pompey escaped to Dyrrhachium, now Durres in Albania. In pursuit, Caesar made a hazardous crossing of the Adriatic and found himself cut off from his base in Italy by sea and facing superior land forces. But Pompey eventually had to abandon his naval blockade of Brundisium and more of Caesar's forces joined him. Pompey repelled an attack on his camp at Dyrrhachium and Caesar moved eastwards into Thessaly. Pompey was now in pursuit. He joined forces with the Senate's army. Up to this point Caesar had not shown himself to be a military genius, so Pompey attacked. He suffered a disastrous defeat on the plain of Pharsalus in 48 BC. As his camp was stormed, he escaped.

All was not lost, however. He still had enough support in Spain, Africa and the East to tie up Caesar in fighting for three more years. Pompey himself fled southwards to Cilicia, Cyprus, and then Egypt to seek the help of Ptolemy who marched down to the coast to welcome him. However, Ptolemy could not risk offending the victorious Caesar. As Pompey stepped ashore on 28 September 48, he was struck down and killed.

CAREER HIGHLIGHTS

- *Pompey's military career was the equal of any general of his day, fighting victoriously across the entire Roman world and entering Rome in triumph three times. But history largely remembers him for losing to Caesar in the civil war. This is at least partly because Caesar wrote the history, inflating his own reputation and damaging that of his great adversary.*

- *Pompey's reorganization of the Middle East with a series of defensive borders remained almost unchanged for 500 years.*
- *Pompey's military campaigns made him the wealthiest man of his age. He invested his millions carefully and his estates were spread throughout Italy in units that were easy to manage.*

JULIUS CAESAR

100–44 BC

A LTHOUGH AN EXTREMELY able general, Julius Caesar was no tactical genius: he was first and foremost a politician, who used his skills in oratory to inspire his men. His conquests spread Roman law, customs and language through Europe and secured the ascendancy of its empire for five hundred years, winning himself a considerable reputation in the process.

▶ LUCK AND LEADERSHIP

Caesar himself, however, ascribed his victories in Gaul, the Roman Civil War and in Asia Minor to two things – luck and leadership. In his *Commentaries on the Gallic War*, written in the third person, he wrote, 'The situation was critical and as no reserves were available, Caesar seized a shield from a soldier in the rear and made his way to the front line, ordering [the troops] to push forward and open their ranks so they could use their swords more easily. His coming gave them fresh heart and hope'.

CHRONOLOGY

100 BC Born 12 or 13 July (disputed).
59 Forms First Triumvirate.
58–51 Conquers Gaul.
56 Crosses English Channel.
49 Crosses the Rubicon, beginning Civil War.
48 Battle of Pharsalus; goes to Egypt and begins affair with Cleopatra.
47 Battle of Zela.
46 Becomes dictator of Rome.
44 Assassinated on the Ides of March (15th)
42 Declared a god.

Born in 100 BC to a patrician family, Caesar devoted his early life to politics. However, after his marriage into a radical family, he found it advisable to withdraw from a Rome ruled by the dictator Lucius Cornelius Sulla and do military service in Asia Minor. Returning to Rome in 78 BC, he became a prosecuting lawyer. On his way to study oratory in Rhodes he was captured by pirates. He raised money to ransom himself, then raised a naval force, captured the pirates and had them crucified, all as a private citizen. When Mithradates VI Eupators, king of Pontus, attacked Rome, he raised an army to fight him.

Back in Rome, Caesar moved relentlessly up the political ladder. In 61 BC, he had his first taste of military command, fighting the Celtiberians in Spain. In 59 BC the First Triumvirate was formed with **Pompey** holding Rome, Crassus in control in the east and Caesar governing Cisalpine Gaul (northern Italy), Illyricum (Yugoslavia) and Nabonese Gaul (southern France). Realizing that the Celtic tribes of Gaul would not unite against him, Caesar picked them off piecemeal. Over seven years, he subdued the entire region as far as the Rhine and the English Channel, which he crossed in 56 BC. His campaign culminated with the defeat of the Gallic chieftain Vercingetorix. In all, it is estimated that he fought more than three million men in ten years in Gaul.

'I came, I saw, I conquered.'

▶ CROSSING THE RUBICON

His victories made him a political threat to the other two members of the Triumvirate and in 49 BC the Senate ordered him to lay down his command. He refused and crossed the Rubicon into the area of Italy held by Pompey, effectively a declaration of war, and Caesar knew it. As his troops crossed the river, Julius is said to have remarked, '*Alea jacta est*' – 'the die is cast', meaning he was now irrevocably committed. The Roman Empire was thrown into Civil War. Pompey fled to Greece. Instead of pursuing him there, Caesar first attacked Pompey's legions in Spain, saying, 'I set forth to fight an army without a leader so as later to fight a leader without an army.'

Pompey's leaderless legions were forced to surrender at Ilerda, before Caesar crushed the remains of Pompey's army at the Battle of Pharsalus. Pompey fled to Egypt, but by the time Caesar caught up with him he had already been assassinated. Caesar fought a brief local war and celebrated his victory with his famous liaison with the Egyptian queen Cleopatra.

On his way back to Rome he defeated Mithradates VI Eupators' son, Pharnaces II, at the Battle of Zela after a five-day campaign, reporting his victory with the famous words, '*Veni, vidi, vici*' – 'I came, I saw, I conquered'. Rewarded with the title of dictator, he spent a further two years crushing the remains of Pompey's army which had now rallied in Spain and Africa.

When his dictatorship was converted into a lifelong office, Romans began to fear that Caesar might try and make himself emperor. Cassius, who Caesar had allowed to retain power after being on the wrong side in the Civil War, and Brutus, a trusted subordinate, hatched a plot to assassinate him with sixty co-conspirators. On 14 March 44 BC, he was stabbed to death on the steps of the Senate. Shakespeare put the words '*Et tu, Brute*' – 'You too, Brutus' on his lips. He actually said to Brutus in Greek: '*Kai su, technon*' – 'You too, my child'. It is thought that Brutus was Caesar's illegitimate son. But the new ascendancy of the aristocracy Caesar had started could not be halted. In 42 BC, Julius Caesar was declared to be a god and in 27 BC his adopted son Augustus was proclaimed the first Roman Emperor, taking supreme power. With this the name Caesar later became synonymous.

FROM SOLDIER TO EMPEROR

- *From a small base in southern France, in the years 58 to 51 BC, Caesar conquered the whole of Gaul, which comprised France, Belgium, Holland, Switzerland and parts of Germany, even though his army was vastly outnumbered. It was not until 52 that the peoples of central Gaul found a leader, Vercingetorix, king of the Arverni, who led an uprising. He held the hill-fort of Gergovia against Caesar, but a subsequent attack failed. Vercingetorix was defeated at Alesia and taken to Rome in chains. Six years later he was executed.*
- *On 10–11 January 49 BC, Caesar crossed the River Rubicon, between Cisalpine Gaul and*

  Italy proper – an act of war. It took Caesar's battle-hardened legions just sixty-six days to drive Pompey and the Senate out of Italy.
- *At the end of 49, Caesar transported seven legions across the Adriatic to Dyrrhachium The following year at Pharsalus, Caesar's 22,000 men met Pompey's 45,000. Caesar threw his reserves against Pompey's superior cavalry with orders to use their javelins as pikes, rather than throwing them. Caesar himself led the third line of legionnaires through the first two, dealing the final blow. Losing fewer than 1,200, Caesar killed 6,000 Pompeians and captured the rest of Pompey's army.*

MARCUS AGRIPPA

C. 63–12 BC

MARCUS AGRIPPA was the loyal deputy of the first Roman emperor, **Augustus**, and without Agrippa it is unlikely that Augustus would ever have come to the throne.

▶ HUMBLE BEGINNINGS

Little is known of his birth, background or early life. However, it is known that his beginnings were humble as he was looked down on by the Roman aristocracy. Agrippa was at military school with Octavian, Julius **Caesar's** adopted son, and at Apollonia (now in Albanian) in 44 BC when Caesar was murdered. Together they returned to Rome to stake Octavian's claim as Caesar's political heir. Agrippa became tribune of the people and prosecuted Cassius, the chief conspirator in the assassination of Caesar, who had fled to Syria.

During the ensuing struggle for power, Agrippa served Octavian as a military commander. He fought Mark Antony's brother Lucius and helped negotiate a settlement with Mark Antony at Brundisium (Brindisi) dividing the Roman world between them. After two years fighting in Aquitania in Gaul and along the Rhine, Agrippa returned to Rome to become consul in 37 BC. Meanwhile Octavian had been having trouble fighting the navy of Sextus Pompeius, son of the republican general Gnaeus **Pompey**. Agrippa took over, building a naval base at Puteoli in the Bay of Naples and winning

Without Agrippa, it is unlikely that Augustus would ever have come to the throne

decisive victories at Mylae and Naulochus, ending any further threat from Pompeius. In 35–34 BC he fought under Octavian in Dalmatia, modern Croatia.

▸ TAKING CONTROL IN ROME

In 33 BC, Agrippa became head of public works in Rome, building aqueducts, sewers, and baths – later he completed the Pantheon – which won favour for Octavian. Agrippa then commanded the Roman fleet that defeated Mark Antony at the Battle of Actium. While Octavian went on to conquer Egypt, causing the death of Cleopatra and Mark Antony and murdering Cleopatra's son by Caesar, Ptolemy XV Caesar, Agrippa ran Rome with the diplomat Maecenas. When Octavian returned in 29 BC, they purged the Senate of political enemies. In 28 BC and 27 BC, Agrippa and Octavian were consuls. With Octavian changing his named to Caesar Augustus, he gradually took imperial powers.

When Augustus fell ill in 23 BC, he gave Agrippa his ring, signifying that he should take over as emperor if Augustus were to die. To consolidate their bond, Agrippa divorced his second wife and married Augustus's daughter. Then he went to Mytilene on the island of Lesbos, where he administered the Eastern empire.

Soon Agrippa was back in Rome to work on behalf of the emperor. Then in 19, he went to Spain to suppress the Cantabrians. In 17 BC, he participated in the Secular Games in Rome which had not been celebrated since 146 BC. In 15 BC, he accepted an invitation from Herod the Great to visit Judea. Together they settled an uprising in the Bosporan kingdom on the Black Sea.

In 13 BC, Agrippa went to settle troubles in Pannonia, Augustus's new Roman province covering western Hungary, eastern Austria, Slovenia and northern Yugoslavia. However, the severe winter put a strain on his health and he died on 12 March. Augustus delivered his funeral oration.

AGRIPPA'S BATTLES

- *A traditional enemy of Caesar, Sextus Pompeius and his fleet supported Mark Antony after the assassination of Caesar. When Antony and Octavian made peace in 39, he was to become governor of Sicily and Achaea on the north coast of the Peloponnese, south of the Gulf of Corinth. But when peace was not forthcoming, Pompeius went back to war, winning some notable actions against Octavian. Nevertheless, Agrippa finished him off at Naulochus near Messina in 36. Fleeing to Asia Minor, he was captured and executed by the Roman general Marcus Titius.*
- *At the Battle of Actium on 2 September 31 BC, Mark Antony, with 70,000 infantry and 500 ships, faced Octavian, with 80,000 infantry and 400 ships under the command*

of Agrippa. Antony followed Cleopatra's advice and decided to fight at sea. He lined up his ships outside the bay, facing westwards, with Cleopatra's Egyptian galleys behind him. In the hotly contested naval battle, each side tried to outflank the other. Suddenly, Cleopatra fled. Antony set off after her with a few ships. Leaderless, the rest of his fleet surrendered. The land forces surrendered a week later, making Octavian the undisputed master of the Roman world.
- *Living in the Cantabrian mountains along the coast of northern Spain, the Cantabri were considered the fiercest people in the Iberian Peninsula. The Romans had been fighting them since 200 BC. Agrippa subdued them in 19 BC, completing the subjugation of Spain.*

AUGUSTUS OCTAVIAN

63 BC–AD 14

CHRONOLOGY

63 BC Born 23 September.
51 Delivers funeral speech for his grandmother, Julia, Julius Caesar's sister.
46 Accompanies Caesar on his triumphal process after victory in Civil War.
44 Caesar assassinated; Octavian returns to Rome to take up his inheritance.
43 Octavian, Mark Antony and Lepidus form triumvirate.
42 Julius Caesar declared a god, so Octavian becomes son of god; wins two battles of Philippi against Brutus and Cassius.
36 Removes Lepidus from power, taking the entire western empire.
31 Victory over Mark Antony at Battle of Actium.
30 Annexes Egypt.
27 Takes name Caesar Augustus.
20 Takes control of Armenia.
17 Holds Secular Games to purify Roman people.
16–15 Crosses Alps, extending frontier to the Danube.
12 Becomes chief priest '*pontifex maximus*'.
9 Frontier extended to the Elbe.
AD 6 Annexes Judea.
AD 14 Dies on 19 August.

AUGUSTUS OCTAVIAN BECAME the first emperor of Rome, gradually establishing himself in power through a a series of key campaigns after his great-uncle and adoptive father Julius **Caesar** had destroyed the republic. He went on to overhaul every aspect of life in the Roman world and considerably expanded the territory under the control of Rome.

▸ **FAMILY CONNECTIONS**

Born in 63 BC to a rich family in Velitrae, southeast of Rome, he was originally named Gaius Octavius. When he was seventeen, he accompanied Caesar on the triumphal procession after his victory in Africa made him dictator and, the following year, went with him to Spain.

Octavian, as he was generally known, was finishing his academic and military training in Apollonia in present-day Albania when Caesar was killed. With his schoolmate **Agrippa**, he returned to Italy, where he learnt that before Caesar had died he had adopted him and made him his heir. This immediately brought Octavian into conflict with Mark Antony, Caesar's chief lieutenant, who believed he was Caesar's heir and refused to hand over Caesar's possessions. Octavian raised money to pay Caesar's debts and held games to win favour with the populace.

With the Senate's support, Octavian joined the campaign against Antony at Mutina, modern-day Modena. After Antony was defeated and forced to withdraw to Gaul, Octavian used his troops to force the Senate to confer a vacant consulship on

'He subjected the whole wide earth to the rule of the Roman people'

him. He now called himself Gaius Julius Caesar, and was acknowledged as Caesar's son.

Antony and Octavian crossed the Adriatic to defeat Brutus and Cassius, Caesar's two principal assassins at the two battles of Philippi; both committed suicide. While Antony returned to Gaul, Octavian defeated his brother and wife in the Perusine War. Sextus Pompeius, son of Caesar's enemy **Pompey** the Great, then sided with Mark Antony, but Antony made a fresh agreement with Octavian limiting Lepidus's territory to Africa. Pompeius fought on alone, but was defeated by Agrippa.

To seal the deal, Antony, who had already spent the winter with Cleopatra, was to marry Octavian's sister Octavia. But the balance of power was already changing. Octavian deprived Lepidus of his remaining territory and now commanded the whole of the west. The situation was further inflamed when Antony divorced Octavia to marry Cleopatra.

Octavian declared war – not on Antony but on Cleopatra. Antony and Cleopatra responded by taking their combined force to Actium on the west coast of Greece, where they were defeated in 31. Octavian pursued the doomed couple and, after their deaths, annexed Egypt. He was now master of the Greco-Roman world.

▶ **THE FIRST EMPEROR**

Back in Rome, he established a Praetorian guard to maintain his absolute control and added the 'Augustus' to his name to become Caesar Augustus. He continued to rule by a succession of consulships, conferred by a cowed Senate, assuming the powers of a tribune, an office formerly elected annually, for life.

With Agrippa as his deputy, Octavian travelled east, where he took Armenia as a protectorate. Meanwhile Agrippa subjugated Spain. To mark the beginning of a new age, seventeen Secular Games were held in Rome. Augustus now centralized the administration of the empire and sent armies northwards to extend the empire into Switzerland, Austria and Germany. Three legions were lost to an uprising led by the German warlord **Arminius**, halting the expansion. Nevertheless, with the growth of commerce, a new system of taxation and peace at home, the empire grew rich.

Augustus spent the rest of his life as an administrator. He died on 19 August AD 14, and became a god on 17 September. He was succeeded by his adopted son Tiberius.

FOLLOWING CAESAR

- *Five months after the assassination of Julius Caesar, Brutus and Cassius were forced by Mark Antony to leave Rome for Macedonia, where they raised an army against him. In February 43 BC the Senate granted them supreme command in the east. They were camped in Philippi when the armies of Octavian and Mark Antony arrived in October 42 BC. Brutus defeated Octavian in the first engagement of the Battle of Philippi, but Cassius was defeated by Mark Antony and ordered his freedman to slay him. Brutus was defeated by the combined forces of* Antony and Octavian three weeks later. Recognizing that the republican cause was lost, he committed suicide.

- *After Cleopatra fled at the Battle of Actium (31), Antony tried to extricate his ships, hoping to continue the fight elsewhere. But only a quarter of their fleet got away. Antony and Cleopatra fled to Egypt. Octavian pursued them and they committed suicide when he captured the country the next year. He executed Cleopatra's son by Julius Caesar, Ptolemy XV Caesar, and used her treasure to pay off his soldiers.*

ARMINIUS

C. 18 BC–AD 19

Arminius was the German tribal leader who defeated the Roman army under Publius Quinctilius Varus and thwarted Germanicus Caesar, putting an end to the Emperor **Augustus's** plans for the conquest of Germany.

▸ HERMANN THE GERMAN

Arminius's German name was Hermann and he was the son of Sigimer, chief of the Cherusci. Although the German tribes were happy to trade with the Romans, they also made frequent raids into Roman-occupied Gaul. In 12 BC, Augustus ordered his legions under his nephew Drusus across the Rhine. In 11 BC, Drusus crossed the River Weser. He erected a statue to Augustus at the site of present-day Cologne, and reached the Elbe in the same year.

When Drusus died in an accident he was replaced by his older brother Tiberius, later to become emperor, who was recalled to Rome in 7 BC. When Tiberius returned in 4 BC, he advanced to the Elbe again, intending to subdue the Marcomanni. Hearing of trouble in Illyricum, the northern Balkans, however, he instead made an alliance with the Marcomanni.

The young Arminius was impressed by the Romans and he and his brother Flavus joined the Roman auxiliary forces. Arminius command-ed the Cherusci, became a Roman citizen and served under Tiberius in the province of Pannonia to the south.

▸ MASSACRE IN THE TEUTOBERG FOREST

When Publius Quinctilius Varus, husband of the grand-niece of Augustus and former governor of Syria, was appointed legate of Germania in AD 9, he treated the Germans like a subjugated people and imposed harsh taxes. Arminius pretended to be a loyal ally and was entertained in the Roman camp, even though Varus was warned that Arminius was plotting a rebellion. Varus was told that a distant tribe was in revolt and set off with his legions to put down the uprising. In the Teutoburg Forest Arminius turned on Varus and massacred his legions. Varus himself fell on his sword. His head was sent to Marobodus, but instead of joining forces with Arminius, Marobodus sent the head to Augustus who cried: 'Varus, give me back my legions.'

In AD 14, Augustus died and was succeeded by Tiberius. The following year Germanicus Caesar, the son of Drusus and nephew of Tiberius, moved against the Chatti, slaughtering women, children and the elderly. Arminius sought to aid the Chatti, but his father-in-law Segestes called for Germanicus's help in a family dispute. Germanicus rescued Segestes, capturing Arminius's pregnant wife, Thusnelda. She refused to betray her husband, and brought up their son Thumelicus in Ravenna, spurning Arminius.

'My fighting has been open, not treacherous, and against men, not women'

The war continued, with Arminius telling the Cherusci, 'My fighting has been open, not treacherous and it has been against armed men and not pregnant women. The groves of Germany still display the Roman Eagles and standards which I hung there in honour of the gods of our fathers.' And he gave his people a stark choice, 'Follow Segestes to shameful slavery [or] follow Arminius to glory and freedom.'

Germanicus sent a detachment which recovered the Eagle of the lost XIX Legion. With a reconnaissance mission sent ahead, he marched into the Teutoburg Forest where they found the whitening bones of the Romans slaughtered six years before. They pursued Arminius deep into the forest. But Arminius withdrew to draw in the enemy, then used hidden troops to envelope him. Germanicus only averted disaster by sending in the cavalry, and the battle broke off without a victor.

As the Romans withdrew to their winter quarters, Arminius caught their rearguard in a swamp and mauled it badly, but did not win a decisive victory because his men turned prematurely to looting. Arminius faced the Romans several times more, often with his brother on the other side, but failed to defeat them conclusively.

Germanicus ordered his men not to take prisoners, believing that only the total destruction of the Cherusci would end the war. But the stalemate was ended in AD 17 when Germanicus was recalled by Tiberius, believing the Cherusci had been punished enough and the German tribes could now be left to their own internal rivalries.

He was right. Arminius was soon at war with Marobodus and the Marcomanni, who he swiftly defeated. Marobodus went into exile in Ravenna, leaving Arminius master of the German forests.

Adgandes, a Chatti chieftain, offered to poison Arminius, but Tiberius would not countenance such foul play. However, it seems likely that Arminius was killed by one of his distrustful allies when he died in AD 19, at the age of 37.

THE LOST LEGIONS

- In AD 9, Arminius led Varus's three legions – XVII, XVIII, and XIX – some 18,000 to 30,000 men, into the Teutoburg Forest. The column was spread for miles. When the Germans began probing attacks, Arminius joined the attackers. The Romans burnt their baggage and marched on in close order, while the Germans harried them. Near modern Bielefeld in Westphalia, the Germans felled trees to block the path. The morning brought a raging storm. Disoriented by howling winds and lashing rain, and unable to manoeuvre in the mud, the Romans were cut down, and the disgraced Varus committed suicide. Of the legions three Eagle standards, two were captured, the third lost in a swamp.
- In AD 15, Arminius caught up with the Roman rearguard led by Aulus Caecina Severus crossing a swamp. The heavily armed Romans lost their footing in the mud and were saved from annihilation by nightfall. They had just buried their dead in Teutoburg Forest and the Germans shouted and sang all night. Caecina had a nightmare in which the blood-drenched Varus rose from the swamp. Next day his horse was slain beneath him. Victory was near, but the Germans turned to looting and the Romans escaped to firm ground. That night a horse broke loose, causing panic in the Roman camp. Meanwhile the Germans quarrelled. Arminius wanted to lure the Romans back into the swamp and destroy them, while his uncle Inguiomerus wanted prisoners and undamaged loot. So they surrounded the camp and attacked at dawn. This time on firm ground, the Romans were ready. The Germans were defeated, but Arminius escaped to fight another day.

CLAUDIUS

10 BC–AD 54

CHRONOLOGY

10 BC Born in Gaul 1 August.
AD 37 Consul under his cousin Caligula.
41 Becomes emperor.
41–42 Annexes Mauretania.
43 Invades Britain; annexes Lycia.
44 Makes Judea a province.
46 Annexes Thrace.
47 Puts down revolt of the Iceni, under Boudicca's husband Prasutagus.
49 Annexes northern Palestine.
51 Establishes colonies in Germany.
52 Collapse of pro-Roman government in Armenia.
54 Dies 13 October.

▶ **AN UNHAPPY CHILDHOOD**

Born Tiberius Claudius Nero Germanicus on 1 August 10 BC in Lugdunum, modern Lyon, in Gaul, he was the son of the general Nero Claudius Drusus who died when Claudius was one year old. He was also nephew of the emperor Tiberius and grandson of both Mark Antony and Livia Drusilla, wife of the emperor Augustus. An ugly, sickly and clumsy child, he was left to his own devices. He spent his time reading and writing about history, producing some thirty books.

Much of Claudius's branch of the family was destroyed in the struggles for succession, but Claudius's luck changed when his cousin Gaius Caesar Germanicus – Caligula – became emperor in spring AD 37. On 1 July, Claudius became consul, taking public office for the first time at the age of 46. With the assassination of Caligula on 24 January 41, Claudius, the only remaining mature member of the dynasty, was proclaimed emperor by the Praetorian Guard. This was not popular with the Senate, but Claudius was maintained in power by the army, reigning as Tiberius Claudius Caesar Augustus Germanicus, though with no right to the name Caesar.

Preparations for the invasion of Britain began

CLAUDIUS WAS THE ROMAN emperor who extended Roman rule to North Africa, consolidated the empire in the east and made Britain a Roman colony.

Claudius ensured that no future emperor could rule without the support of the army

straight away, the first major expansion of the Roman empire since Augustus.

After the legions landed in Britain in AD 43, Claudius secured his position with the army by turning up for the crossing of the Thames and the capture of Colchester which, as Camulodunum, became the capital of his new province. Claudius established a colony of veterans there and sought to co-opt the rest of the country as a series of client kingdoms. He also attempted to suppress the Druids who, as in Gaul, were seen as a potent anti-Roman force. A master politician, Claudius named his son Britannicus to reinforce the idea that he was a great military commander who had added new conquests to the Roman Empire.

In AD 38 Claudius had married Valeria Messalina who continually cuckolded him. In AD 48, there were rumours that she had performed a wedding ceremony with the consul-designate Gaius Silius. This was a political threat to Claudius, who reacted by having Messalina and Silius executed. He then married his niece Agrippina. She had a son from a previous marriage, Domitius, who Claudius adopted. He was then known as Nero Claudius Drusus Germanicus Caesar or just Nero.

▶ NEW PROVINCES

Under Claudius, the kingdoms of Mauretania, Lycia in Asia Minor, Thrace and Noricum (central Austria and parts of Bavaria) were converted into provinces. But stable client kingdoms, such as Bosporus and Cilicia, were left alone. Herod Agrippa I, who had been awarded Galilee by Caligula, was rewarded for his loyalty with Judaea and Samaria, but when he extended Jerusalem's walls and invited other eastern kings to a conference at Tiberias, Claudius grew suspicious. Herod died suddenly in 44 and his former kingdom came back under Roman rule.

During Claudius's reign, he favoured his adopted son Nero over his natural son Britannicus. Agrippina was also ambitious for her son. When Nero was sixteen, Claudius became ill. It is thought that he had been poisoned, probably by Agrippina. He lingered a while and had to be poisoned a second time, dying on 13 October 54. At noon that day, the youthful Nero was acclaimed emperor. Already well known to the army and the public, he faced no serious challenges to his succession. Britannicus was poisoned the following year and Nero married Claudius's daughter Octavia.

CAREER HIGHLIGHTS

- *Although, by tradition, it is said that Claudius was found trembling behind a curtain after the murder of Caligula, only to find himself reluctantly proclaimed emperor, there are indications that he was behind the assassination. An astute politician, he forced many of those who opposed him in the Senate to commit suicide.*
- *By taking the name Caesar, when he had no legal right to it, Claudius began the process of changing it from being a family name to being a title, a title eventually to develop into*

  the appellation Kaiser and Czar. Claudius also established the pre-eminence of the army. No future emperor could rule without its support.
- *Claudius himself took part in the invasion of Britain, arriving in the war zone with his entourage in the late summer of AD 43. After a parade at Camulodunum, modern Colchester, he returned to Rome in triumph in AD 44, his military credentials now firmly established.*

TRAJAN

AD 53–117

Trajan's Column in Rome, commemorating the Emperor's conquest of Dacia.

CHRONOLOGY

53 Born 15 September Italica, Baetica (Spain)
70 Appointed consul.
89 Takes command of legion in Spain.
97 Adopted by Emperor Nerva; made governor of Upper Germany.
98 Becomes emperor.
101–106 Conquers Dacia.
105–106 Annexes the Nabataean kingdom in Arabia.
113/114 Reinstates the pro-Roman king of Armenia.
115 Annexes upper Mesopotamia.
117 Escapes death in earthquake in Antioch; dies 8/9 August in Selinus, modern Turkey.

▸ **THE FAVOUR OF DOMITIAN**

Born Marcus Ulpius Traianus in AD 53 in Spanish Baetica, he was the son of the Roman governor there. In the 70s, he served in Syria where his father had been moved as governor. In 89 he took command of a legion in Spain and put down the uprising of Antonius Saturninus along the River Rhine. This won him the favour of the Roman Emperor Domitian, who appointed him consul in 91.

Domitian was assassinated in 96 and replaced by Nerva, who adopted Trajan as his successor in 97. He was governor of Upper Germany until Nerva died in 98. Then he became emperor, taking the name Caesar Divi Nervae Filius Nerva Traianus Optimus Augustus. But he stayed on in Germany to settle disputes on the frontier, establishing two new provinces with large military garrisons there.

When he returned to Rome, he undertook major building work. But in 101, however, he resumed the invasion of Dacia (modern Romania) that Domitian had been forced to abandon by its king Decebalus. In 102, close to defeat, Decebalus prostrated himself before Trajan and was allow to continue as a client

TRAJAN WAS THE ROMAN EMPEROR who extended the empire to the east through Dacia, Armencia, Arabia and Mesopotamia.

Be luckier than Augustus and better than Trajan!

CORONATION GREETING TO NEW ROMAN EMPERORS FOLLOWING TRAJAN

king. But once Trajan had withdrawn, Decebalus started making raids across the Danube, challenging Roman authority again. Trajan returned, capturing the Dacian capital of Sarmizegethusa (modern Varhély) in 106 and Decebalus committed suicide rather than be captured. Trajan celebrated his triumph with gladiatorial games that lasted 123 days. He created a new province of Dacia north of the Danube, providing a defensive zone against nomads moving in from the steppes. The local people were subjected and Roman settlers took over the land.

▶ THE SECOND PARTHIAN WAR

Trajan devoted himself to domestic materials and building works for the next seven years. Then in 113, he began preparations for a second major war against the Parthians in Persia, Rome's traditional enemy in the east. In preparation, he had already annexed the Nabataean kingdom in Arabia. In 110, the Parthians deposed the pro-Roman king of Armenia. In 114, Trajan reinstated him, marching on into

Mesopotamia, taking Babylon and the Parthian capital of Ctesiphon.

Although these territories had been won easily enough, they were difficult to hold. There were uprisings. The Jews in Palestine and the Diaspora were particularly troublesome. Revolts were brutally suppressed. But gradually Trajan relinquished Roman rule over these newly-established provinces as he retreated westward. Leaving Hadrian in command in the east, Trajan, now a sick man, journeyed slowly back towards Italy. On 9 August 117 he died in Selinus (Cilicia in modern-day Turkey), naming Hadrian his successor on his death bed. One of Hadrian's first acts as emperor was to give up all of Trajan's conquests in the east.

Trajan's ashes were returned to Rome and burned in the base of his column. He was not seen as a god but as Jupiter's viceregent on earth and gradually his reputation diminished. By the late fourth century, new Roman emperors were hailed with the entreaty *felicior Augusto, melior Traiano*, 'be luckier than **Augustus** and better than Trajan'.

·TRAJAN'S ACHIEVEMENTS·

- *The vast wealth of Dacian gold and salt mines came to Rome as war booty, enabling Trajan to support an extensive building programme. In the capital, Apollodorus designed and built the huge forum. Already under construction was a sculpted column, precisely 100 Roman feet high, with twenty-three spiral bands filled with 2,500 figures, which depicted, like a scroll being unwound, the history of both Dacian wars.*
- *Trajan was responsible for building the first bridge across the Danube River which was*

built to supply his legions in Dacia. It was half a mile long and its 170ft spans were not exceeded for over a thousand years. When the Emperor Aurelian withdrew from Dacia he pulled down the bridge, but it is still commemorated on Trajan's column.
- *When Trajan reached the Persian Gulf, he is said to have wept, lamenting that he was too old to follow in Alexander the Great's footsteps and extend his empire into India. But in 116 he took the title Parthicus, in celebration of his victory in Persia.*

CONSTANTINE I

C. AD 272–337

C ONSTANTINE WAS THE FIRST
Roman emperor to convert to
Christianity. He also moved the capital
of the empire from Rome eastwards to
the ancient Greek city of Byzantium, which he
renamed Constantinople (modern Istanbul). He
seized the imperium by force of arms and laid
the foundations of Europe's post-classical culture

▶ A CHRISTIAN EMPEROR

Born Flavius Valerius Constantius on 27 February
271, 272 or 273 at Naissus in the province of
Moesia Superior (present-day Nish in Serbia) he

was the son of the army officer Flavius Valerius
Constantius and his concubine Helena. Later
responsible for Constantine's conversion, she
became St Helena. On 1 March 293, his father
became Caesar, or deputy emperor, as Constantius
I Chlorus. Constantine was brought up in the
eastern imperial court and, as a youth, fought in
Egypt. On 1 May 305, Constantius succeed
Augustus Maximian as emperor in the west. His
deputy was Flavius Valerius Severus, but
Constantius requested that his son Constantine be
allowed to join him from the east to fight the
Picts. Constantine had to make his way through
the territories held by the hostile Severus to meet
his father at Gesoriacum (modern Boulogne).
Together they crossed the channel. On 25 July
306, Constantius died at Eburacum (modern York)
with his son at his side, whom the Roman soldiers
in Britain immediately proclaimed emperor.

Constantine returned to the Continent and
established his capital in Trier in modern-day
Germany. Meanwhile Maximian's son – and
Constantine's brother-in-law – Marcus Aurelius
Maxentius took over in Rome. In 312
Constantine invaded Italy and beat Maxentius at
Milvian Bridge north of Rome. He became the
undisputed emperor in the west, with Licinius
now ruling in the east. In 324, Constantine

'By this sign will you conquer'

WORDS ACCOMPANYING CONSTANTINE'S MYSTICAL VISION OF THE CROSS

defeated Licinius at Adrianople and Chrysopolis (Edirne and Üsküdine in modern Turkey) to become emperor in both the east and west.

After killing Licinius, who was Constantine's brother-in-law, and his son, who was Constantine's nephew, Constantine also executed his own son Crispus and his wife Faustas, suspecting an incestuous relationship between them.

▸ CONSTANTINE'S NEW CAPITAL

On 8 November 324, less than two months after his defeat of Licinius at Chrysopolis, Constantine laid out the boundaries of his new city capital. The new walls were completed in 328 and the city was formally dedicated on 11 May 330. Constantinople resembled Rome, with the pagan shrines replaced with Christian churches. He

began the construction of the Hagia Sophia (Holy Wisdom) and Hagia Eirene (Holy Peace), and founded the Church of the Holy Apostles. Constantine did not convert, however, until 337. Soon after Easter, he began to feel ill and travelled to Drepanum, renamed Helenopolis (now Trapani, Sicily) in honour of his mother, to pray at the tomb of the martyr Lucian, his mother's favourite saint. He then went to Nicomedia (modern Izmit in Turkey), where he was baptized. A few weeks later, dressed in the white robes of a Christian neophyte, he died on the feast of Pentecost. His body was returned to Constantinople and placed in the Church of the Holy Apostles, as he had instructed, flanked by memorials to the Apostles themselves, six on each side.

IN THE SIGN OF THE CROSS

- *In 306 Maxentius pushed aside Severus to become emperor and his father Maximian defeated and killed Severus in 307. Soon after, father and son fell out, and Maximian fled to Constantine in Gaul, leaving Maxentius in control of Italy, Spain, and Africa. Then in 308 Lucius Domitius Alexander rebelled in Africa and proclaimed himself emperor. In 310 Constantine took Spain and, the following year, Africa was retaken by Maxentius, who was killed by Constantine at the Battle of the Milvian Bridge in 312, making Constantine the sole emperor in the west.*

- *Constantine fought the Battle of the Milvian Bridge in the name of the Christian God. The night before the battle, it is said, Christ had appeared to him in a dream and told Constantine to place his sign on the shields of his soldiers. In another version Constantine had seen the sign in the sky with the legend 'by this sign will you conquer'.*

  Constantine did as he was told and the new battle standard became known as the labarum.

- *Both Constantine and Licinius wanted to be sole ruler of the empire but in 313 they met in Milan and sealed an agreement with Constantine's half-sister Constantia's marriage to Licinius. However, hostilities erupted in 316 and battles were fought at Cibalae in Pannonia, where Licinius suffered heavy losses, and at Ardiensis in Thrace, where neither side won a clear victory. Licinius was forced to cede all his European provinces except Thrace. War erupted again in 324. This time Constantine defeated Licinius decisively, twice. Constantia made Constantine swear a solemn oath to spare her husband's life, but after a few months he ordered Licinius's execution. He also had the couple's 9-year-old son killed, leaving Constantine the sole and undisputed master of the Roman world.*

ALARIC I

C. AD 370–410

CHRONOLOGY

395 Becomes king of the Visigoths.
395–396 Plunders Greece.
397 Becomes master of Illyricum.
401 Invades Italy.
402 Defeated by Stilicho.
408 Invades Italy again and besieges Rome.
410 Sacks Rome; dies of fever.

A LARIC was the king of the Visigoths who led the army that sacked Rome in 410, an event that marked the end of the Roman Empire in the west.

▶ AN UNAPPRECIATED SACRIFICE

Born around 370 to a noble Visigoth family on Peuce Island, now in Romania, he served as commander of the Gothic troops in the Roman army under Emperor Theodosius I. During the Battle of the River Frigidus, Alaric led a detachment of Theodosius's army under orders from Flavius Stilicho on a particularly dangerous mission down a hot, dry, waterless canyon with enemy soldiers well hidden on the cliffs above picking off his troops. After the battle, Alaric regarded this part of the battle plan as having been devised to expend most of the Gothic troops in the place of regular Roman army units. Though Alaric remained loyal, he felt that his sacrifice for the Roman empire on that day was not appreciated and that he deserved promotion. Nevertheless, a close friendship had formed between Alaric and Stilicho.

When Theodosius died in 395, his troops rebelled and Alaric proclaimed himself their king. He moved on Constantinople itself, but was diverted by Roman troops into Greece, where he sacked Piraeus – sparing Athens itself – and ravaged Corinth, Megara, Argos, and Sparta. To placate him, the Eastern emperor Flavius Arcadius made him military governor of Illyricum in 397. From there, he played the eastern and western branches of the Roman Empire against each other.

In 401 Alaric invaded northern Italy, but on 6 April 402 was defeated by Stilicho at Pollentia, modern-day Pollenza. After another defeat at the hands of the Romans in 403, he withdrew from Italy. However he was still a player in the complex political game between the eastern and

'I am leaving you with your lives'

western empires. This resulted in another invasion of Italy in 408. Although he was defeated again, the Senate in Rome was forced to pay a huge tribute in compensation.

In 408, Stilicho was executed, a victim of power politics. An anti-barbarian party took over in Rome which urged Roman soldiers to massacre the wives and children of the barbarians still serving in the Roman army. This caused a massive defection to Alaric's camp.

▶ ON THE MARCH IN ITALY

Now with a massively strengthened army, Alaric invaded Italy again and marched right up to the walls of Rome. He besieged the city until he was bought off by a huge ransom from the Senate. However, he fell out with the Emperor Honorius, so he besieged Rome again and installed his own emperor, Attalus. But when Attalus refused Alaric permission to send an army to Africa when the lands that provided Rome with grain were overrun, he besieged the city once more.

On 24 August 410, allies within the city opened the gates and the Visigoths sacked the city. The sack of Rome is seen as a key event in history. But while the Visigoths took their share of plunder, they treated the inhabitants humanely and destroyed only a few buildings.

From there Alaric marched to the south with the aim of recapturing the grain fields of North Africa. But storms destroyed his fleet. Alaric turned northwards again, but was struck by fever and died. His brother Ataulf was elected his successor. It is said that Alaric was buried with his treasures near Cosenza in the bed of the Busento River, which was temporarily diverted from its course. That the secret of his burial place might be kept, the slaves employed in the labour were killed.

Although he failed to establish a Gothic regime of his own, Alaric exhausted Roman strength in the west, allowing the German Vandals and Suebi to invade Gaul and Spain. His attack on Rome also caused the Romans to withdraw from Britain, leaving it vulnerable to the invasions of Saxons and Picts.

THE SACK OF ROME

- *When Alaric laid siege to Rome for the third time in 410, the city gates were opened, possibly by disgruntled slaves. The city was taken and Alaric led his army in a grand procession through the streets. The Goths wrecked private houses and public buildings in their hunt for plunder, but few buildings were burnt. Alaric gave orders that no injury should be done to the Christian churches, but other buildings were stripped and all the gold and silver was carried away from the public treasury. Some nuns were stripped naked publicly and raped, but by and large Alaric's troops treated the Romans humanely.*

- *In the midst of the pillage Alaric dressed himself in splendid robes and sat upon the emperor's throne with a golden crown upon his head. Thousands of Romans were compelled to kneel down on the ground before him and shout out his name. Then the theatres and circuses were reopened, and Roman athletes and gladiators had to give performances for their conquerors. After three days of pillage, Alaric and his army marched out of Rome, carrying with them the riches of the city.*

FLAVIUS AETIUS

C. AD 390–454

The Roman army under Aetius defeats Attila the Hun at the Battle of the Catalaunian Plain.

CHRONOLOGY c. 390 Born in Durostorum, Moesia Inferior (modern Bulgaria)
• 423–425 Supports usurper John in Italy • 432 Elected consul for first
time and becomes principal adviser to Emperor Valentinian III • 433 Begins fight against rebels in
Gaul • 435–437 Destroys Burgundian kingdom at Worms • 437–439 Halts Visigoths at Toulouse
• 451 Defeats Attila the Hun in Battle of the Catalaunian Plain • 454 Stabbed to death by Valentinian

---

FLAVIUS AETIUS is often referred to as
the 'last of the Romans'. He defeated
Attila the Hun and slowed the
inevitable destruction of the Roman
Empire in the west by the barbarian nations.

▶ **COMBINED TACTICS**

The son of a Scythian soldier and a Roman
noblewoman, Aetius spent his youth as a
hostage of the Visigoth leader **Alaric**. Later he
was sent to the court of the Huns, where he
learned the arts of war. At a young age, it was
said, he could hold his own with grown men.
The Huns taught him to fight from the back of a
horse. This, combined with his knowledge of
standard Roman infantry tactics made him a
deadly foe.

From 423 to 425 he supported the usurper

John in Italy, then became a favourite of the
new emperor, Valentinian III. He was sent to
police Gaul and won a number of victories over
the Franks and the Visigoths who had settled
there. In 432, he became consul and the principal adviser to Valentinian and favourite of
Valentinian's formidable mother Placidia who
controlled the western empire in her son's name.
This made Aetius the most influential figure in
the Western empire, and he was given the title of
Patrician in 433.

In 435, the Burgundians posed a threat to
Gaul's Rhine border. Aetius called on his boyhood friends, the Huns, to join forces with him.
Together, in 437, they annihilated the
Burgundian kingdom at Worms. After halting
the Visigoths at Toulouse in 439, Aetius returned
to Rome.

'The Emperor has cut off his right hand with his left'

▶ SOLE RULER

However, in 445, Attila became sole ruler of the Huns. He broke the alliance with Rome, seeking instead to conquer the empire. In 451, he crossed the borders into northern Gaul. While preparing his army, Aetius negotiated an alliance with the Visigoths and Franks, as their settlements in Gaul were also under threat from the Huns. Together, under Aetius's command, they defeated the Huns on the Catalaunian (or Mauriac) Plain near present-day Châlons.

Attila was not finished, however. He began his march into Italy in 452. Unable to call on his allies, Aetius withdrew, sacrificing the cities of northern Italy. His scorched earth policy left Attila at the head of an army that was soon disintegrating due to hunger and disease. The Romans then turned and faced the invaders and Attila was forced to retreat northwards, out of the empire.

Although Aetius had saved the empire for the time being, his reward was death. Valentinian grew tired of being overshadowed by his great general. In September 454, Aetius was holding discussions with Valentinian concerning the marriage of his son to one of the emperor's daughters – with the aim of making his son emperor in due course. In a fit of temper, Valentinian drew his dagger and stabbed Aetius. A shocked courtier who had witnessed this said, 'The Emperor has cut off his right hand with his left'. The death of Flavius Aetius sounded the death knell for the empire in the west. The following year two Huns named Optila and Thraustila, who had been of Aetius's retainers, stabbed the emperor as he dismounted in the Campus Martius for archery practice. As the stunned Valentinian turned to see who had struck him, they finished him off. The soldiers standing close by had been followers of Aetius and none of them lifted a hand to save the emperor. The Western empire finally collapsed twenty years later.

AETIUS AND THE BARBARIANS

- *In 437, Aetius and his Hun allies totally devastated the Burgundians in a battle near the German frontier. The slaughter of Burgundians by the Romans and the Huns was so savage that the famous German folk legend of the Ring of the Niebelung was born out of this disastrous battle. The legend went on to become the epic poem Der Nibelungenlied, written c. 1200, which became the basis of Richard Wagner's Ring of the Nibelung.*
- *The Roman army and their Visigothic and Frankish allies under Aetius met Attila the Hun at a battlefield on the Catalaunian Plain near Châlons, France in 451. In the desperate fighting that lasted all day, Theodoric the Visigoth king was killed. However, Aetius got the best of the battle*

and the Huns only escaped complete annihilation because night fell and they escaped in the dark. Attila himself prepared a pile of captured saddles and flammable booty. He intended to set it on fire and leap on to the flames if the Romans came near, preferring death to capture. However the loss of life was so great on both sides that the Romans could not follow up their victory and Attila escaped with the remnants of his army.

- *Attila still had enough of a force to invade Italy the following year. Aetius, now deprived of his barbarian allies, skilfully employed strategic withdrawal and evasion to exhaust the invaders. After a negotiated settlement, Attila was forced to withdraw. Aetius had saved the empire.*

ATTILA THE HUN

C. AD 406–453

ATTILA THE HUN was the greatest of the barbarian leaders to attack the Roman Empire, invading Greece and Italy. His relentless onslaught on the now Christianized Empire earned him the Latin name *Flagellum Dei* – 'Scourge of God'.

Born to a family of nomadic Asiatic Huns around 406, Attila served under his uncle Ruga, whose attacks on the eastern empire had been so successful that the Romans paid him a huge tribute. In 434, Ruga died and Attila and his brother Bleda inherited a realm stretching from the Alps to the Baltic and the Caspian Sea.

▸ ATTILA'S ARMY

Bleda and Attila ruled jointly, with Attila taking command of the army. It was an army like no other at the time, consisting solely of mounted troops carrying 5-foot bows. They had no baggage train, as each man carried his own provisions on sturdy ponies, giving them the speed of movement to overwhelm larger forces. Sparing with the lives of his own men, Attila would move them up towards the enemy under cover. The first rank would then launch a flight of arrows high, forcing the enemy to raise their shields. A second rank would then fire low, directly at them. They would finish off any survivors with curved swords, maces and pickaxes.

Each 50,000-strong Hun tribe would supply a *tumén* of 10,000 warriors, led by a *khan*. Each *tumén* comprised ten squadrons of ten companies, each with ten units of ten horsemen. Attila would lead ten *khan* and their *tumén* into battle – 100,000 men in all.

'Where I have passed, the grass will not grow again'

Until 439, Attila seems to have spent his time subduing other barbarian peoples to the north. But then the eastern emperor failed to pay his tribute and Attila attacked, razing Singidunum (Belgrade) and other Balkan cities. A truce allowed the Romans to regroup, but in 443 Attila went on to destroy Naissus, modern Nis in Serbia, and Serdica, now Sofia in Bulgaria. He headed on towards Constantinople, taking Philippopolis and defeating the Romans in the east. Emperor Theodosius II was forced to pay the arrears of 6,000 pounds of gold, plus a tribute of 2,100 pounds a year from then on.

▸ ATTACKS IN THE WEST

Attila devastated the Balkans again in 447. Avoiding Constantinople, he drove southwards into Greece. He was stopped at Thermopylae, but the new treaty concluded in 449 was even more favourable to the Huns.

Attila then turned his attention to the weaker Western empire. Honoria, the sister of the Emperor Valentinian, had sent him a ring. She had been having an affair with her steward, who had been executed, and pregnant, she had begged the King of the Huns to rescue her. He took the ring as a marriage proposal and asked for half the Western empire as her dowry.

In the spring of 451, Attila forged an alliance with the Franks and Vandals and unleashed an attack on the heart of western Europe. In April he took Metz with an army of between 300,000 and 700,000. Rheims, Mainz, Strasbourg, Cologne, Worms and Trier were destroyed. It was said that Paris was saved because St. Genvieve was in the city.

Finally, Attila was stopped at Orleans. He was besieging the city when a Roman army under Flavius **Aetius**, supported by forces under the Visigothic king Theodoric I, arrived. In the bloody Battle of Catalaunian, Theodoric was killed, but Flavius dealt Attila his one and only defeat. Instead of retreating, Attila gathered his forces and invaded Italy, turning back at the gates of Rome, it is said, because he was so impressed by the holiness of Pope Leo I, who came out of the city to parley.

The Huns collected their booty and turned north. The 47-year-old Attila died on the way. He had taken a new wife, named Ildico, and after a day of heavy drinking, he withdrew to his marriage bed with his young bride. The next morning, he was dead, drowned in the blood from a nosebleed. After Attila's death, Germanic tribes revolted and his sons fell out among themselves. Within twenty years, the Huns ceased to be a military power. Without the wide Asiatic plains to graze their horses, they had to fight on foot, like other European armies.

A TRAIL OF DESTRUCTION

- *Attila's attack on Naissus (Nis, Serbia) in 441 so devastated the place that, when Roman ambassadors passed through to meet with Attila eight years later, the stench of death was still so great that no one could enter the city. They had to camp outside the city on the river, where they found the river banks covered with human bone.*
- *One chronicler of the Greek campaign of 447 reported, 'There was so much killing and bloodletting that no one could number the dead. The Huns pillaged the churches and monasteries, and slew the monks and virgins... They so devastated Thrace that it will never rise again.'*
- *When Attila invaded Italy in 452, he sacked Aquilean, Milan, Padua, Verona, Brescia and Bergamo. Survivors fled to the defensible islands and lagoons of the Adriatic and founded Venice.*

BELISARIUS

C. AD 505–565

CHRONOLOGY

c. AD **505** born in Illyria.
529 Joins imperial guard.
530 Victory over Persia at Dara.
532 Suppresses insurrection in Constantinople.
533–534 Attacks Vandals in North Africa and captures their king.
535 Ordered to recover Italy from the Ostrogoths.
536 Takes Naples and Rome.
537–538 Holds out against Gothic siege of Rome.
540 Takes Milan and Ravenna; accepts Goths' surrender.
542 Fights Persians again.
544 Returns to fight in Italy.
548 Recalled by Justinian.
559 Defends Constantinople against the Huns.
565 Dies in March

BELISARIUS WAS commander-in-chief of the Byzantine forces during the reign of Emperor Justinian I. He protected the Eastern empire from the Persians, reconquered Italy and re-established, briefly, the Western empire, and he saved Constantinople from both internal and external enemies.

▶ IMPERIAL GUARD COMMANDER

Born in the Balkan province of Illyria, Belisarius joined the imperial guard and rose to become its commander at the age of 25. He distinguished himself in Justinian's campaign against the Persians, 529–531. Showing himself skilled in both long-range skirmishing and pitched battles, he defended the Byzantine empire against Persian thrusts into Syria and Asia Minor. He won the Battle of Dara in 530, crushing a Persian army greatly outnumbering his own. Although he lost at Sura (Callinicum) in 531, Justinian negotiated a peace settlement.

In 532, Justinian was nearly toppled by the Nike Insurrection. Constantinople's militia, led by the rival teams of charioteers – the Blues and the Greens – rose up and tried to replace him. Belisarius bottled them up in the hippodrome and massacred 30,000 of them. He also married Antonina, a friend of Justinian's empress, Theodora.

Justinian chose Belisarius to lead a small force against the Vandals in 533. Within months he had overwhelmed them, captured Carthage and returned to Constantinople in triumph.

With a commander of such genius at his disposal, Justinian embarked on a more ambitious

With just 8,000 men, Belisarius held Rome against a force of over 50,000 Goths

plan – the re-conquest of Italy which was held by the Ostrogoths. With just 8,000 men, Belisarius took Sicily and Naples, and marched on Rome. The feeble, Romanized, Ostrogoth leader Theodatus fled, but his own people turned on him and killed him on the road to Ravenna. The warrior Witigis replaced him and returned to besiege Rome. Though vastly outnumbered, Belisarius resisted for a year. Finally, the Ostrogoths withdrew to Ravenna. Belisarius pursued them. They offered to surrender and make him emperor in the West. Belisarius refused and eventually captured their king, but Justinian became afraid that his general might seize his throne and recalled him.

▶ TAKING ROME

However, Byzantinium was once again under threat from the east. In 542, Belisarius repulsed the Persians, but Justinian accused him of disloyalty and stripped him of command. Only the influence of Antonina and Theodora saved him. In 544, he returned to fight the Persians and was then sent back to Italy, which his successors there had failed to hold. Although starved of men and money, he managed to take Rome a second time, before being recalled once again following the death of Theodora.

He was allowed to go into retirement, but was recalled to service in 559 to repulse the Bulgars at the gates of Constantinople itself. This did nothing to quiet the jealousy of Justinian, who had him jailed for conspiracy in 562. Belisarius was freed the following year and lived in retirement until his death in 565.

Ultimately, the Byzantines did not have the resources to hold Italy, apart from small enclaves in the south. The rest of Italy was taken by the Franks who had taken advantage of the weakened Ostrogoths to attack from the north.

DEFENDING ROME

- Belisarius was given just 15,000 men for his expedition to North Africa, where he would face a much larger force. However, the Vandal cavalry fought with the sword and lance, whereas Belisarius's men were trained as mounted archers, giving them the advantage. He defeated the Vandals in two battles and returned to Constantinople with the Gothic king, Gelimer, as his prisoner.
- With just 8,000 men, Belisarius held Rome against a Gothic force of over 50,000. As he scarcely had enough men to man the walls, there was no way he could guard all the gates so he had several walled up. He fortified the Milvian Bridge, but the Hun mercenaries left to defend it defected. Belisarius went on a reconnaissance and the deserters recognized him. The Goths attacked, but Belisarius and his men slaughtered 1,000. Returning to the city in the

dark, his men did not recognize him and refused to open the gates. So Belisarius turned and charged the pursuing Goths. After hours of close combat, he emerged uninjured. The Romans prevented siege towers being brought up to the walls by shooting the oxen pulling them. The defenders held Hadrian's tomb by breaking up the statues and dropping them on the attackers. Belisarius then sent troops to attack the Goths from the rear, killing 30,000.

- The Goths tried to starve Belisarius out. He agreed to a truce, during which reinforcements slipped into city. Belisarius sent out 2,000 horsemen to sweep through Tuscany. Meanwhile the Goths had already plundered the farms in the surrounding countryside and found themselves, rather than the Romans, starving. After a year and nine days, they withdrew.

ALFRED THE GREAT

AD 849–899

▸ THE SCHOLAR-KING

Born at Wantage, Berkshire, in 849, Alfred was the fifth son of Aethelwulf, king of the West Saxons. With little prospect of becoming king, Alfred became a scholar, visiting Rome in 853 and 855.

As each of Alfred's elder brothers succeeded to the kingship, Viking raids from Denmark grew worse. Beginning in the 790s, the Vikings had plundered the coasts and inland waterways of England. Permanent Danish settlements were established, and in 867, the Vikings seized York and established their own kingdom in the southern Northumbria. They overran the Anglo-Saxon kingdoms of East Anglia and Mercia. Moving on to Reading in 870, the Danish army launched its invasion of Wessex. They were met on the Berkshire Plains by a Saxon force under the combined leadership of Alfred's brother King Aethelred I and Alfred himself, and defeated. In 871, however, the Danes defeated a Saxon army at Basingstoke, and later in the same year a new Danish army landed in England. Wessex, the last independent English kingdom, seemed to stand on the brink of destruction. At the height of the crisis, King Aethelred died, leaving Alfred, his heir and successor, in sole charge of the Saxon army. With the kingdom in chaos, Alfred was

A S KING OF Wessex, Alfred the Great stopped England from falling to the Danes. Alone among the kings and queens of England he is dignified with the title 'the Great' partly as a result of his winning a victory against seemingly hopeless odds.

'Alfred's name will live as long as mankind shall respect the past' INSCRIPTION ON ALFRED'S STATUE, WINCHESTER

forced to buy off the Danish invaders, a situation that maintained peace for five years.

▶ VICTORY FROM DEFEAT

However, the Danes began encroaching on Wessex again in 876. In a surprise attack in January 878, they seized Chippenham in Wiltshire. The West Saxons fled or submitted. Alfred withdrew to the Somerset marshes, establishing a fortified base at Athelney. From there he began guerrilla actions against the Danes, winning a decisive victory in the Battle of Edington in May 878

But Alfred realized that he could not drive the Danes out of the rest of England, so he concluded peace with the Treaty of Wedmore. King Guthrum was converted to Christianity with Alfred as sponsor and the Danes settled in East Anglia as farmers. England was divided, with the land to the north and east of the Roman Watling Street under the control of the Danes, an area known as 'Danelaw'. But the partition gave Alfred control of areas of West Mercia and he took Kent in 885. Alfred then married one of his daughters, Aethelflaed, to the ealdorman of Mercia. He himself was already married to the Mercian noblewoman Eahlswith. Another daughter, Aelfthryth, married the Count of Flanders, Flanders being a strong naval power when the Vikings were settling eastern England.

In 886, he went on the offensive again and took London. All the English not under Danish control now accepted him as king. In 892, Alfred resisted another serious onslaught from the Continent, and by 896, the Danes had given up on their invasion. Alfred died on 25, 26 or 28 October 899 died and was buried in Newminster Abbey.

ALFRED'S LEGACY

- At around the time he fled to the Somerset marshes, Alfred is supposed to have stopped at a peasant woman's hut. She asked him to watch some cakes cooking on the fire. Lost in thought and at his lowest ebb, he let them burn and she chided him, not realizing he was the king. From then on, things began to look up.

- In 893, Bishop Asser wrote Alfred's biography. Describing the Battle of Edington in 878, he said, 'Alfred attacked the whole pagan army fighting ferociously in dense order, and by divine will eventually won the victory, made great slaughter among them, and pursued them to their fortress [Chippenham]... After fourteen days the pagans were brought to the extreme depths of despair by hunger, cold and fear, and they sought peace.' This unexpected victory proved to be the turning point in Wessex's battle for survival.

- The possession of London also made possible the re-conquest of the Danish territories in his son Edward the Elder's reign. Alfred may have been preparing for this, but continued attacks from the Continent meant he could make no further advance himself. Instead he concentrated on defensive measures. Old forts were strengthened; new ones built and manned. He reorganized his army and built a navy to repulse the seaborne invaders. He also maintained friendly relations with Mercia and Wales, who supplied troops for his army in 893.

- Alfred also built the English nation by encouraging learning. He translated a number of important Latin texts into English, attracted foreign artists to his court and began the Anglo-Saxon Chronicles – the greatest source of information on Saxon England.

ATHELSTAN

C. AD 895–939

CHRONOLOGY

c.895 Born.
924 Ascends to the throne 17 July.
925 Crowned at Kingston-Upon-Thames.
934 Lays waste to Scotland.
937 Victorious at the Battle of Brunanburh.
939 Dies 27 October at Gloucester.

as a noblewoman or a shepherd's daughter and Athelstan was raised by Edward's sister, Aethelflaed, at her court at Gloucester in Mercia and not at the Wessex capital Winchester. He was the favourite of his grandfather **Alfred the Great**.

▶ FIRST KING OF ALL ENGLAND

Athelstan was the most powerful of all Saxon kings and the first to rule over the whole of England. In the process he fought the Scots and other claimants to the throne.

When Edward died in 924, the Mercians immediately proclaimed Athelstan their king while the West Saxons were still deliberating, perhaps considering offering the crown of Wessex to a legitimate heir.

Once on the throne Athelstan was recognized as king by Sitric Caech of York, the Norse king who had refused to acknowledge Edward's sovereignty. This was perhaps because Athelstan's power base in Mercia made him more of a threat to Northumbria. Sitric married Athelstan's sister Eadgyth on 30 January 926, but by March 927 he was dead. Sitric's brother, Guthfrith, king of Dublin, then tried to claim the throne. But in July 927 Athelstan met the kings of Scotland and Strathclyde at Eamont Bridge and made them swear they would not support Guthfrith. Athelstan defeated Guthfrith and sent him back to Ireland, then took the throne of York, the first Saxon king to do so: previous kings in Northumbria had been Angles and Vikings.

During 926 Athelstan had summoned the

BORN THE ELDEST SON of Edward the Elder, king of Wessex and Mercia, Athelstan may not have been legitimate. His mother is variously described

'King of the English, elevated by the Almighty... to the Throne of the whole Kingdom of Britain'

Welsh princes to a meeting at Hereford. To stop Welsh attacks against Mercia, he fixed the border between England and Wales – the disputed southern stretch was to run along the Wye – and he exacted tribute from them.

Athelstan then went to Devon where the Cornish were in revolt. He expelled the Cornish from Exeter, forcing them back across the Tamar, which became the border between Cornwall and England. He refortified Exeter and held the Cornish king hostage against further trouble.

The peace between the English and the Scots lasted for seven years. During that time Athelstan built up his defences. He befriended the king of Norway, Harald Fairhair, who sent his seven-year-old son, Haakon, to be educated in the English court. Haakon later deposed his brother, Erik Bloodaxe, creating problems for Athelstan's successors.

▶ EUROPEAN ALLIANCES

Athelstan also made alliances with the major powers in Europe. His sister Edgiva married Charles III of France, and another sister, Edhilda, married the influential Hugh, Count of Paris.

Yet another sister Eadgyth married Otto, Duke of Saxony, who went on to become the German emperor. A half-sister probably married Gorm the Old, the first king of united Denmark, and his aunt Elfreda married Count Baldwin of Flanders.

But peace with the Scots was not to last. In 934 the Scottish King Constantine married his daughter to Olaf Guthfrithson of Dublin, which Athelstan saw as a breach of the Eamont treaty. He raised an army and marched north, devastating Scotland. But after the death of Guthfrith in 937, Constantine and Olaf joined forces, taking York and attacking Mercia. Athelstan met them at Brunanburh, perhaps near Nottingham, and won the most decisive of all Saxon victories, reigning in peace for a further two years.

Athelstan died unmarried and childless aged 44, and was succeeded by his half-brother Edmund. He is buried at Malmesbury Abbey, Wiltshire.

FIRST KING OF ENGLAND

- According to the Anglo-Saxon Chronicle, in 924 Athelstan was chosen king in Mercia, and consecrated at Kingston. He gave his sister [Edith] to Otho, son of the king of the Old-Saxons... 'This year King Athelstan and Sihtric king of the Northumbrians came together at Tamworth, the sixth day before the calends of February, and Athelstan gave away his sister [name unknown] to him.'
- In 926: 'This year appeared fiery lights in the northern part of the firmament; and Sihtric departed; and King Athelstan took to the kingdom of Northumbria, and governed all the kings that were in this island – First, Howel, King of West-Wales; and Constantine, King of the Scots; and Owen, King of Monmouth; and Aldred, the son of Eadulf, of Bamburgh. And with covenants and oaths they ratified their agreement in the place called Emmet, on the fourth day before the ides of July; and renounced all idolatry, and afterwards returned in peace.'
- In 937: 'This year King Athelstan and Edmund his brother led a force to Brunanburh, and there fought against Anlaf; and, Christ helping, had the victory: and they there slew five kings and seven earls.'

CNUT I

C. AD 994–1035

CHRONOLOGY

c. AD 994 Born.
1013 Joins father's invasion of England.
1016 Becomes King of England.
1019 Becomes King of Denmark.
1027 Secures recognition by the kings of
Scotland; visits Rome.
1028 Becomes King of Norway.
1035 Dies 12 November, at Shaftesbury,
Dorset.

Bluetooth and his great-grandfather was King
Gorm who had united Denmark. In the year 1000,
the Saxon King Aethelred II – also known as
Aethelred the Unready (meaning 'ill-advised') –
began plundering the Isle of Man and parts of the
Danelaw in an attempt to drive the Vikings out. In
1002 he formed an alliance with Richard, Duke
of Normandy, by marrying his sister Emma, and
ordered the massacre of all Danes in England.
Swein Forkbeard's sister and his brother-in-law,
Pallig, were among those killed and Swein came
to England, raiding the south and east in 1003
and 1004, to avenge their deaths. But a famine
forced him back to Denmark in 1005.

▸ INVADING ENGLAND

The raids continued, however, with Swein
extracting huge amounts of silver 'Danegeld'.
Then in 1013 the young Cnut accompanied his
father on a full-scale invasion. Taking the
Danelaw first, he swept through the rest of the
country. Aethelred fled to Normandy and the
Anglo-Saxon Chronicle recorded that '...all the
nation regarded him [Swein] as full king'.

When Swein died the following year,
Aethelred returned and expelled the Danish army,
which was now under the command of Cnut.
Cnut returned in 1015 and on the death of
Aethelred in 1016 was elected king at
Southampton. However, London picked
Aethelred's son Edmund Ironside as its king

CNUT I, ALSO KNOWN as Cnut the
Great, was a Viking warrior and went
on to become the ruler of an empire
which, at its height, included England,
Denmark, Norway and part of Sweden.

Born the son of the king of Denmark, Swein I
Forkbeard, he was the grandson of Harold

'Let all men know how empty and worthless is the power of kings.'

instead, but Cnut beat Edmund at the Battle of Ashington on 18 March and the kingdom was divided. The Treaty of Olney gave the Danelaw and the Midlands to Cnut, while Edmund retained the south. But Edmund died on 30 November and Cnut became the first Viking king of the whole of England. In 1017 he married Aethelred's widow, Emma, to prevent any challenge from her two sons by her first marriage, who remained in Normandy – with unforeseen consequences.

▶ KING OF DENMARK

Cnut's brother, Harald, King of Denmark, died in 1018 and Cnut returned home to take over his realm. Two years later, Cnut renewed the Danish claim to Norway. Using bribery to foment unrest, he drove out the Norwegian king Olaf II Haraldson and left his English mistress Aelfgifu and their son to run the country. Scotland also submitted to Cnut. To consolidate political unity in England, he removed the fortifications and defensive walls and ditches that had separated the Danelaw from the rest of the country and he went to Rome to secure recognition from the pope.

As ruler of the Viking homelands, he was able to protect England against attacks, maintaining twenty years of peace during which trade flourished. He was the first English king to protect the English against external threats as well as internal strife. He showed respect for the old English laws with their safeguards for individual rights. And he promoted himself as an 'English' king, making amends for the wrongdoings of his Viking forebears, building churches and generously endowing others.

Cnut died in 1035, aged about forty. He was buried in Winchester, the capital of the Saxon kingdom of Wessex and home to his court. However, under his sons, his Anglo-Scandinavian empire had began to break up. Aelfgifu's second son, Harald, became king of England but died in 1040. Cnut's legitimate son Harthacnut, who became king of Denmark in 1035, succeeded and ruled England until 1042. The Anglo-Saxon Chronicle said of him 'He did nothing worthy of a king as long as he ruled.' None of Cnut's children produced heirs, so one of his wife Emma's sons by Aethelred, Edward 'the Confessor', returned from Normandy to take the English throne in 1042.

TURNING BACK THE TIDE

- Cnut had learned that his obsequious courtiers claimed he was 'so great, he could command the tides of the sea to go back'. But Cnut was a religious man and knew his limitations. He had his throne carried to the seashore and sat on it as the tide came in, commanding the waves to advance no further. His idea was to show that, though kings might appear great in the minds of men, they were impotent in the face of God. However, his gesture seems to have misfired. Down the ages he has been remembered,

ironically, as the king who thought he could turn back the tide.
- Although Cnut was an avowedly Christian king and was a favourite of the Pope, when he withdrew from England in 1014, he put his hostages ashore at Sandwich badly mutilated. He was also behind a number of political murders. And, while having two children, Harthacnut and Gunhild by his wife Emma, Cnut had two more, Harald and Swein, by his English mistress, Aelfgifu.

HAROLD II

C. AD 1020–1066

CHRONOLOGY

c. AD 1020 Born
1044 Becomes Earl of East Anglia.
1051 Banished with his father.
1052 Invades England.
1053 Becomes Earl of Wessex and Kent.
1063 Subjugates Wales.
1066 Crowned King of England 6 January;
killed 14 October.

HAROLD II IS LARGELY remembered for his defeat by William the Conqueror at the Battle of Hastings, dying with an arrow in his eye. What is forgotten is that he very nearly won. He had successfully invaded England himself fourteen years earlier and, just three weeks before the Battle of Hastings, he had defeated a powerful Viking force at Stamford Bridge.

▶ EXILE

Harold was the son of Godwin, the Earl of Wessex and Kent, who was the most powerful man in England during the reign of Edward the Confessor. His father had the king make his young son Earl of East Anglia. But in 1051 Godwin refused to carry out Edward's order to attack the town of Dover, in retribution for the townspeople's perceived maltreatment of some visiting Frenchmen. Godwin was forced into exile, but returned the following year with a large army led by Harold. Faced with civil war, Edward reinstated the family's lands and titles. Godwin also forced the king to dismiss many of the Normans in his service.

Godwin died in 1053, apparently choking to death at King Edward's dinner table. Harold succeeded to his father's titles as Earl of Wessex and Kent and took his place as Edward's right-hand man. He also secured titles for his three brothers, Leofwine, Gyrth and Tostig.

Tostig was made Earl of Northumbria. Together Harold and Tostig subjugated Wales. But in 1065,

the people of Northumbria rebelled against the cruel rule of Tostig. To safeguard his own position, Harold bowed to the rebels' demands and relieved Tostig of his earldom. Tostig sailed for Normandy, now Harold's bitter enemy.

▶ A QUESTION OF SUCCESSION

On his deathbed, King Edward the Confessor had named Harold as his successor, although he had previously promised the crown to his cousin William, Duke of Normandy, during his twenty-five-year exile there. William's claim was strengthened when Harold, shipwrecked on the coast of Normandy, allegedly promised to support William's claim – admittedly under some duress. Even so, his supposed oath was used to secure Papal support for an invasion when Harold assumed power after Edward's death on 5 January 1066. When he was crowned the following day, Harold faced not just the rival claim of William, but also that of the King of Norway, Harald III Hardrada, supported by Harold's renegade brother Tostig.

Harold prepared his army for William's expected invasion. But his fleet had to be used to ward off Tostig's raids on the coast. Fortunately, unfavourable winds kept William in France. Running short of supplies, Harold dismissed his fleet in early September, hoping the weather would prevent any further threat that year. Meanwhile Tostig and Hardrada had joined forces and invaded England. Harold marched

'I offer him six feet of English earth, or rather more, as he is taller than most men'

north and defeated the invaders at Stamford Bridge, near York, on 25 September. Both Tostig and Hardrada were killed.

While Harold was away, the wind had changed, allowing William to cross the English Channel and land unopposed. Harold hurried south, arriving in London on 5 October. But his men were weary and his reinforcements untrained and ill-equipped.

He faced William near Hastings on 14 October 1066. The hard-fought battle lasted all day and seemed to be going Harold's way, when he was killed. His brothers Gyrth and Leofwine were also killed in the battle, as was Harold's personal retinue of soldiers, his housecarls, making further resistance useless. William quickly reached London, and was crowned king of England in Westminster Abbey on Christmas Day.

THE BATTLE OF HASTINGS

- *After taking York, Tostig and Hardrada camped at Stamford Bridge on the River Derwent, where they were taken completely by surprise. No one expected Harold's hastily mustered 2,000-man army to march the 200 miles from London to York in just five days. The Norwegians were divided by the River Derwent. Those on the north side had to fight with their backs to the river. Many were forced into it and drowned. One axe-wielding Viking managed to hold the bridge for some time, but he was despatched by an Englishman in a small boat who speared him from below. Once across the river, Harold offered Tostig the chance to change sides. Unable to extricate his men from the Norwegian position amid fierce fighting, Tostig asked what terms Harold would offer Hardrada. Harold replied, 'Six feet of English earth, or more, as he is taller than other men.' On that note, the peace overtures foundered and both Tostig and Hardrada were slaughtered in the battle. Reinforcements called in from the Norwegian fleet were also massacred.*
- *When William rode out of his Hastings stronghold at 6am on 14 October 1066 he found Harold's army already formed up twelve ranks deep along a high ridge. The English flanks were protected by streams and*

hollows; the rear by a steep slope. At the bottom of the ridge, the ground was marshy. William sent his troops through a narrow strip of firm ground, forming them up at the foot of the ridge. At 9.30am, Norman archers moved forward and fired. Their arrows met a wall of English shields. The archers, now exposed, suffered huge losses. Next the Norman infantry went in, to be cut down by English two-handed battle axes. An uphill cavalry charge faltered, but when the cavalry pulled back, undisciplined English recruits chased after them. The Norman line began to give. A rumour that William was dead spread panic, but William lifted his helmet to show he was alive and they held. Occasional feints lured more Englishmen down the hill to their deaths. But this tactic was also costly in Norman lives. By evening, William knew he had to win that day or surrender. The next day, Harold would have reinforcements. He ordered an all-out assault. This time the archers fired high in the sky, thinning the English ranks. The shield wall had to be shortened, allowing the Normans to attack from the flanks. But it took a further two hours for them to scythe their way through to where Harold, the last English king, had fallen.

CHARLES MARTEL

C. AD 688–741

CHRONOLOGY

c. AD 688 Born.
714 Seizes power in Austrasia.
716 Defeats the Neustrians at Amblève.
717 Victory at Vincy.
718 Lays waste to Saxony.
719 Victory at Soissons.
720–730 Re-asserts authority over southern Germany.
732 Halts Muslims at Poitiers.
737–738 Campaigns through southeast France.
741 Dies 21 October at Quierzy.

C HARLES MARTEL re-established the Frankish domains in Gaul, defended Christian western Europe from the expanding Muslim empire and paved the way for Charlemagne.

Born about 688, he was the illegitimate son of Pepin II, the king of the Franks who died in

714. His heir was his 6-year-old grandson Theodoald. Pepin's widow Plectrude had the 26-year-old Charles thrown into prison, established herself at Cologne and assumed the guardianship of her grandson. But in 715 the western province of Neustria rebelled, starting a revolt of all the subjugated states. Duke Etudes of Aquitaine seized the chance to extend his territory. Meanwhile the Saxons had crossed the Rhine and the Arabs had crossed the Pyrenees.

Charles escaped from prison but, as head of the national party of Austrasia, eastern province, was defeated by Ratbod, duke of the Frisians, near Cologne in 716. He made an alliance with the Neustrians and forced Plectrude to acknowledge him as their king. But Charles surprised the Neustrians at Amblève in 716, beat them a second time at Vincy near Cambrai on 21 March, 717 and pursued them as far as Paris.

Turning back on Cologne, he forced Plectrude to step down and give him his father's inheritance. To maintain the semblance of legitimacy, he made the Merovingian Clotaire IV the puppet king of Austrasia (the Merovingians were the royal house), while ruling himself as 'Mayor of the Palace'.

Charles Martel – 'the Hammer' – retained Europe for Christianity

▸ DEVASTATION OF SAXONY

Charles then punished the Saxons for invading Austrasia, devastating their country as far as the banks of the Weser in 718. When Ratbod died in 719, Charles seized Western Friesland, formerly held by Pepin. The Neustrians joined forces with Aquitaine, but Charles hacked their army to pieces at Soissons. With the death of King Clotaire IV, Charles put the Neustrian king Chilperic on the throne, reconciling the two great fractions of the Frankish Empire. In return Neustria and Aquitaine recognized the authority of Charles. And when Chilperic died in 721, Charles appointed another Merovingian, Thierry IV, who was still a minor.

A second expedition against the Saxons in 720 re-established the Frankish monarchy as it had been under Pepin. For the next six years Charles devoted himself to asserting Frankish authority over the Germanic tribes. In 725 and 728 Charles went into Bavaria to quell moves towards independence, taking as his mistress the Princess Suanehilde. In 730 he marched against Lantfrid, Duke of the Alemanna, who he subjected, bringing southern Germany back under Frankish control.

▸ A CHRISTIAN WARRIOR

Meanwhile the Muslims from Spain had been threatening southern Gaul. In 725 they had reached Burgundy. Although Duke Eudes had been able to repulse them in 721, he was now forced to negotiate with them, giving his daughter in marriage to Othmar, one of their chiefs. This angered Charles, who defeated the Duke in 731. However, the death of Othmar that year left Aquitaine defenceless.

In 732 Abd-er-Rahman, Governor of Spain, crossed the Pyrenees at the head of an immense army, overwhelmed Eudes, and advanced to the Loire. In October, 732, Charles met Abd-er-Rahman outside Poitiers and defeated him in the Battle of Tours.

In 733–734 Charles suppressed the rebellion instigated by the Frisian duke, Bobo, who was slain in battle, and subdued Friesland once more. In 735, after the death of Eudes, Charles entered Aquitaine, quelled a revolt and made it a fiefdom. He then banished the Muslims from Arles and Avignon, defeated their army on the River Berre near Narbonne, and in 739 checked an uprising in Provence.

Charles' power during his final years was so great that he did not appoint a successor to King Thierry IV who died in 737, assuming full authority himself without legal right. He died at Quierzy on the Oise on 21 October 741.

THE HAMMER

- In October 732, Charles defeated Abd-er-Rahman and slew him at the Battle of Tours. The battlefield has not been located, but it is thought that Charles destroyed the Muslim advance with his cavalry near Poitiers. This was the last attempt by the Muslim empire to invade Frankish territory and Charles Martel has been given the credit for retaining Europe for Christianity. It was this battle, it is said, that gave Charles his

- name, Martel – French for 'the Hammer' – because of the merciless way he attacked the enemy.
- Charles Martel never assumed the title of king. But when he died, he divided the Frankish lands between his sons Pepin the Short and Carloman. However, Pepin's son was Charlemagne, who managed to re-unite the empire that Charles Martel had built and extend it.

CHARLEMAGNE

AD 742–814

CHRONOLOGY

AD **742** Born 2 April at Aachen.

768 Becomes joint ruler of Frankish domains with his elder brother.

771 Becomes sole ruler on death of this brother.

774 Invades Lombardy.

775–777 Subdues Saxony.

778 Besieges Saragossa.

788 Takes Bavaria; campaigns in Hungary and Austria.

800 Acclaimed emperor in Rome.

804 Finally quells all resistance in Saxony.

814 Dies 28 January at Aachen.

CHARLEMAGNE WAS KING of the Franks. In military campaigns that lasted for over four decades he extended his rule over most of western and central Europe and had himself recognized as Holy Roman Emperor.

▸ A BOYHOOD AT WAR

Born 2 April 742 at Aachen in present-day Germany, he was the son of Pepin the Short, who struggled to maintain the Frankish empire re-united under his father **Charles Martel**. The young Charlemagne accompanied his father on military expeditions into Aquitaine and Lombardy. When Pepin died he left his kingdom to his two sons, Carloman and his younger brother Charlemagne. But when Carloman died in 771, Charlemagne ignored the rights of Carloman's sons and re-united the kingdom.

Carloman's widow fled to the Lombard court of King Desiderus. Even though Desiderus was Charlemagne's father-in-law, he supported the claim of Carloman's sons over Charlemagne's. So Charlemagne invaded Lombardy.

Next he attacked the pagan Saxons. In 777 at a diet held in Paderborn, he met with Arabs from northern Spain who were in rebellion against the

Charlemagne's fusion of cultures marks the beginning of modern European civilization

emir of Cordoba. In 778, to aid the rebels, he laid siege to Saragossa that summer. Unable to take the city, he was forced to withdraw across the Pyrenees, fighting the Basques on the way.

Charlemagne then returned to his campaign against the Saxons. In 788 he deposed his cousin Duke Tassilo III of Bavaria and annexed his country. After subduing the other Germanic tribes, he moved into Hungary, Austria and Bosnia.

▶ CHARLEMAGNE'S ARMY

His army consisted mainly of foot soldiers armed with spears and axes and protected by shields and leather vests. However, he also had cavalry armed with long swords – the precursors of medieval knights – who charged the enemy before the infantry went in. There was little in the way of manoeuvring once the fighting started and Charlemagne depended for his victories on superior intelligence, through a network of scouts and spies, and the greater number and skill of his men. They were not full-time soldiers, but rather farmers and townsmen who were called to arms in the spring for a campaign that would last until autumn. They were not paid and had to bring their own arms and supplies, though these were supplemented by herds of cows Charlemange drove behind his army. Their reward was booty.

In April 800 Pope Leo III was attacked in Rome and fled to Charlemagne's court for protection. That November, Charlemagne marched back into Rome and restored him to the papal see. In return, Leo crowned Charlemagne Holy Roman Emperor. This was not entirely welcome. Charlemagne had been in St Peter's to have his son consecrated as king, when the pope put a crown on Charlemagne's head, proclaiming him 'Augustus and emperor'. Charlemagne then needed recognition from the eastern empire to legitimize his claim. He offered marriage to the Empress Irene, ruler of Constantinople, but his attempt to reunite the eastern and western empires failed when Irene was deposed in 802. In 812, the Byzantine emperor Michael I recognized Charlemagne's title, though the eastern emperors continued to maintain that they were the true heirs of the Roman Caesars.

After that Charlemagne ceased to expand his domain, secured his borders and began a programme of law-making and education, in which Latin was taught and books and manuscripts copied. Charlemagne died of pleurisy on 28 January 814. His embalmed body was seated in his tomb at Aachen. Although Charlemagne's new empire only survived for thirty years after his death, his fusion of German, Roman and Christian cultures marks the beginning of modern European civilization.

CONVERTING THE SAXONS

- *As well as expanding his own territory, Charlemagne took Christianity to the pagans of central Europe. The most obdurate were the Saxons. Between 772 and their final subjugation in 804, Charlemagne conducted 18 campaigns against the Saxons. He conducted mass baptisms in 775–777 where Saxons were given the choice of converting to Christianity or death. In 782, he slaughtered some 4,500 in a mass execution. In all, more*

than a quarter of the population of Saxony and Westphalia were killed.
- *On Christmas Day 800, when Charlemagne knelt to pray in St. Peter's Basilica in Rome, Pope Leo III crowned him emperor of the newly restored Holy Roman Empire. The Byzantine empire braced itself for his attack. Instead Charlemagne entered into negotiations and, in 812, the emperor Michael I recognized him as emperor in the West.*

EL CID

C. AD 1043–1099

Born Rodrigo Diaz de Vivar at Vivar near Burgos in the Spanish kingdom of Castile, he grew up in the household of Prince Sancho, the eldest son of King Ferdinand I. On Ferdinand's death, his kingdom was divided among his five children. Sancho II was given Castile and his brother become Alfonso VI of Leon.

▶ STANDARD BEARER TO THE KING

On his accession in 1065 Sancho gave El Cid the highest position at court – standard bearer or head of royal armies. Together they attacked the Moorish kingdom of Saragossa, making its king al-Muqtadir a tributary of the Castilian crown. But Sancho had greater ambitions. He believed that Ferdinand's kingdom should be re-united and El Cid led a successful campaign against Alfonso. But in 1072 Sancho was assassinated and Alfonso became king of the united kingdoms of Castile and Leon.

E L CID, from the Spanish Arabic *as-sid* meaning 'The Lord', was also known in Spain as El Campeador – 'The Champion'. He was a Castilian military leader who fought in the wars between Christians and Muslims in mediaeval Spain. He is now a Spanish national hero and, having never lost a battle, is seen as an embodiment of chivalry and virtue.

El Cid Campeador: 'the Lord who wins battles'

After forcing Alfonso to swear that he had taken no part in the murder of his brother, El Cid continued in the royal service, marrying Alfonso's niece Jimena in 1074. However, El Cid was always treated with suspicion as the Castilians, who had not reconciled themselves to being ruled by Alfonso, saw him as their natural leader. He lost his position as standard bearer to Count García Ordóñez and, when he was sent as ambassador to the Moorish king of Seville, he was accused of keeping money and treasures that were due to King Alfonso.

He fought for Seville against Granada, defeating a superior Granadine force under Ordóñez at Cabra and capturing Ordóñez himself. Then in 1081, he led a raid on Moorish Toledo, which was under Alfonso's protection, severing relations with the king completely.

Disinherited and exiled, he became a mercenary, working for the new king of Saragossa, al-Mu'tamin, who was proud to have his kingdom defended by such a famous Christian warrior. In 1082, he beat the armies of the Moorish king of Lérida and his Christian allies, and in 1084, he defeated the armies of King Sancho Ramírez of Aragon. For these victories, he was richly rewarded.

In 1086, a confederation of Berber tribes called the Almoravids invaded Spain from North Africa. Alfonso was crushed by them at Sagrajas on 23 October 1086 and recalled El Cid from exile. Their reconciliation was short-lived, however, and El Cid set about making himself master of Valencia.

▶ **TAKING CONTROL IN VALENCIA**

First he defeated the forces of Barcelona who were encroaching on the area at Tébar in May 1090. Then in November 1092, he lay siege to Valencia, taking it in 1094, and gave the kingdom to Alfonso, on the proviso that he remained Lord of Valencia. El Cid struggled to maintain the Christian presence in the largely Muslim town by Christianizing the city's chief mosque in 1096.

In 1099, the city was attacked by a huge force of Almoravids. El Cid encouraged his men to fight without fear and won a magnificent victory. But his son Diego Rodríguez was killed in fighting at Toledo. After that, El Cid was no longer merciful with his Muslim prisoners.

He ruled Valencia until his death there on 10 July 1099 at the age of 56. His widow Jimena continued to rule, but in 1102 she was forced to abandon Valencia to the Almoravids, when Alfonso VI withdrew his support. The city was burnt and El Cid's body taken back to Castile and reburied in the monastery of San Pedro de Cardeña near Burgos. Valencia remained in Muslim hands until 1238.

SONG OF EL CID

- By 1092, El Cid had taken the countryside surrounding the wealthy Moorish city of Valencia and its ruler al-Qadir was his tributary. But in October 1092, al-Qadir was killed in an Almoravid-backed coup. El Cid lay siege to the city with a force of 7,000 men. The Almoravids tried to break the siege in December 1093, but failed. El Cid marched into the city as its conqueror in May 1094.
- El Cid was commemorated in a twelfth-century biography and Spain's oldest known epic poem El cantar de mío Cid – The Song of the Cid. Some 3,700 lines have survived. In it, his service to the Moors is hardly mentioned. The poem has served as the inspiration for many subsequent works.

SALADIN

1137/38–1193

1137/38 Born in Tikrit, Mesopotamia.
1169 Commands Syrian troops in Egypt.
1171 Seizes power in Egypt.
1174 Seizes control of Syria and seeks to unite Syria, Mesopotamia, Palestine, and Egypt.
1187 Defeats crusader army at Hattin and takes Jerusalem.
1191 Defeated by Richard I at Arsuf, but denies him Jerusalem.
1193 Dies in Damascus 4 March.

SALADIN WAS RENOWNED for his chivalry and culture, even among his enemies. He united the Muslim world, defeated the Christian army of occupation left by the Second Crusade, held Jerusalem against the Third Crusade and founded the Ayyubid dynasty in Egypt.

▶ RIGHTEOUSNESS OF THE FAITH

Born in Tikrit, Mesopotamia (now Iraq) in 1137 or 1138, the son of a Kurdish governor, his full name was Salah al-Din Yusuf ibn Ayyub, which means 'Righteousness of the Faith, Joseph, Son of Job'. After studying theology at Damascus, he joined the staff of his uncle Asad ad-Din Shirkuh, a military commander under the Turko-Syrian emir Nureddin, who was striving to expel the crusaders from the Middle East. When his uncle died, Saladin succeeded him and, after ordering the assassination of the vizier, seized power in Egypt. He abolished the Shi'ite caliphate and returned Egypt to Sunni Islam.

When Nureddin died in 1174, Saladin took Syria and went on a twelve-year campaign to unite all the Muslim territories of Syria, Mesopotamia, Palestine and Egypt. By 1186, the crusader states in Palestine were surrounded and Saladin declared a *jihad* or holy war to expel them. To this end, he founded mosques and colleges, and commissioned religious works.

In response to the threat, the crusader leader Guy de Lusignan mustered the garrisons from all the crusader castles into one large army. They pursued Saladin who lured the hapless crusaders into the desert. On 4 July 1187, when they were parched and exhausted, he turned on them at Hattin in Galilee, annihilating the crusader army and capturing de Lusignan and the splinters of the 'true cross' he was carrying with him.

'I would rather be famed for skill and prudence than for mere audacity'

▶ CONQUERING THE CRUSADERS

With the crusader castles now unmanned, Tiberias, Acre, Toron, Beirut, Sidon, Nazareth, Caesarea, Nabulus, Jaffa and Ascalon quickly fell to Saladin – though he failed to take Tyre – and on 2 October 1187, after eighty-eight years of crusader occupation, Saladin entered Jerusalem. Unlike the bloodbath that had occurred when the crusaders took the city, the Muslim re-conquest was marked by the civilized behaviour of Saladin and his troops. He even freed Guy de Lusignan after he gave his word that he would not continue fighting.

But Guy de Lusignan did not live up to his promise and began a two-year siege of Acre. The re-conquest of Jerusalem prompted the Third Crusade. When Richard I arrived in Palestine in 1189, he quickly took Acre and marched on Jerusalem, beating Saladin at the Battle of Arsuf. However, Saladin then instituted a scorched earth policy that made it impossible for Richard to take Jerusalem.

After a year's skirmishing, he came to an agreement with Richard to leave the crusaders with a narrow strip of territory along the coast and allowed Christians to visit the holy places in Jerusalem and the rest of Palestine. When the Bishop of Salisbury visited the Holy Land, he had a long talk with Saladin, who wanted to know what Christians thought of the two leaders.

'My king stands unrivalled among all men for deeds of might,' said the bishop, 'but your fame is also high and were you but converted to the true faith, there would not be such princes as you and he in the whole world.'

In response, Saladin praised Richard's courage, but added, 'For my part, I would rather be famed for skill and prudence than for mere audacity.'

Saladin withdrew to his capital at Damascus, where he contracted yellow fever and died on 4 March 1193, aged 55. He was buried in a vast tomb next to the great mosque in Damascus. Once he was dead his empire was divided up between his family. By 1229 Jerusalem was back in Christian hands and the Ayyubid dynasty crumbled in 1250.

THE CAPTURE OF JERUSALEM

- *In July 1187, 15,000 crusaders under Guy de Lusignan were camped at Sepphoris, at the south end of the Sea of Galilee. Hearing that Saladin had attacked Tiberias to the north, they went to relieve the besieged city. But Saladin blocked the road with an army of 18,000, forcing the crusaders out on to an arid plain and harassing them with mounted archers. They camped on a plateau above Hattin. During the night Saladin moved his men up, surrounding the Christians and cutting them off from their water supply. At dawn the thirsty Christians made a dash for a nearby lake but Saladin drove them back against two large hills called the Horns of Hattin. The knights made useless charges,*

- *leaving the foot soldiers exposed. Most were slaughtered, but Saladin spared the lives of Guy and most of the Christian lords.*
- *Saladin probably did not realize the reaction his taking of Jerusalem in 1187 would have in Europe. Two Christian kings arrived in the Holy Land to mount the Third Crusade. Saladin also underestimated Richard I's tactical ability, giving him an easy victory at Arsuf. However, his strategic sense was superior. By laying the country waste, he denied the crusaders the food and water they needed to marched on Jerusalem. They were forced to retreat without taking the city and Richard I returned to England leaving Jerusalem in Muslim hands.*

RICHARD I

1157–1199

RENOWNED AS A GREAT KING of England, Richard spent little time there and lived his life as a French warlord constantly campaigning, rather than as a regal administrator. His prowess on the battle-field earned him the sobriquet *Coeur de Lion* – 'Lion-Heart' or 'Lion-Hearted'.

▸ A REBELLIOUS SON

Born on 8 September 1157 in Oxford, the son of Henry II and Eleanor of Aquitaine, he was brought up in France. He became Duke of Aquitaine at the age of eleven, and Duke of Poiters at fifteen. With his brothers, he rebelled against his father. The rebellion failed though his father had to invade Aquitaine twice before Richard would submit. His mother was impris-oned. Richard was pardoned, but continued to fight to hold on to his possessions and suppress

rebellions. At one point, when Henry wanted him to give Aquitaine to his younger brother, the future King John, known as 'Lackland', or *Jean Sans Terre*, he even joined forces with Philip II, king of France, who probably became Richard's homosexual lover. Together they chased Henry from Le Mans to Saumur. With his older brother now dead, they forced Henry to acknowledge Richard as his heir and harried him to his death on 6 July 1189.

Richard then succeeded his father as Duke of Normandy. Two months later, he was crowned king of England though he showed little interest in the country, spending only six months in England in the remaining ten years of his life. As soon as he had raised an army, he headed for the Holy Land on crusade, leaving England in the hands of his mother Eleanor of Aquitaine, who held it against the intriguing of his brother John. His aim was to take Jerusalem from Saladin who had captured it two years before.

▸ THE CRUSADER KING

He planned to winter in Sicily on the way but, finding the Sicilians inhospitable, took Messina by force, making his nephew heir to the Sicilian throne by marrying him to the king's daughter. He also invaded Cyprus on his way to Palestine,

Despite being England's best-known king, Richard I spent only six months in the country

where he landed with his ally Philip II of France on 8 June 1191, and joined the siege of Acre (now Akko in Israel) which had been going on for two years. Within six weeks, Richard had defeated the Muslim defenders, taken the city and put 2,700 prisoners to the sword.

Richard welded an international bunch of crusaders into a force. He marched them down the coast, so they could be supplied by his ships. On the way, they were harassed by Saladin's mounted archers, but Richard stopped his men breaking formation to mount an attack. And at Arsuf on 7 September, he beat Saladin in a decisive battle.

But as Saladin retreated towards Jerusalem, he left scorched earth behind him. Away from the coast and his ships, Richard could not supply his men and he was forced to give up his ambition of taking Jerusalem. For the next year, skirmishing continued, then in September 1192 Saladin agreed to a three-year truce, which left Acre and a thin coastal strip in crusaders' hands and gave Christians the right to visit the holy places in Jerusalem.

Richard headed home, but his ship was wrecked near Venice. He travelled overland in disguise but was captured near Vienna in December 1192 by a personal enemy, Duke Leopold of Austria. The English people then had to raise an enormous ransom of 150,000 marks, organized by Eleanor of Aquitaine. Richard also had to surrender his kingdom, though it was returned to him as a fief. Meanwhile his brother John tried to seize the throne with the aid of Philip II. Richard was released in February 1194 and returned to England where he was crowned a second time. John was banished, though later reconciled with his brother. Within a month Richard was back in Normandy, leaving England in the hands of Hubert Walter, his chief minister and archbishop of Canterbury. In France Richard fought a prolonged campaign against Philip II. In 1192, while besieging the castle of the Archbishop of Limoges at Châlus, he was hit in the shoulder by a crossbow arrow. Gangrene set in and he died on 6 April 1199, aged 42.

ON CRUSADE

- Between 1175 and 1185, Richard's reputation grew because of the ruthlessness with which he put down revolts in his French possessions. And in 1179 he took what was thought to be the impregnable castle of Taillebourg in Saintonge.
- Richard marched his crusader army down the coast of Palestine in battle order with three divisions of three columns, defended from Saladin's horse-borne attacks by crossbowmen. On 7 September 1991 at Arsuf, Saladin attacked in force. Richard kept the crusaders on the defensive for most of the day, repelling attack after attack. Then when the Muslim forces were tiring, the Master of the Knights Hospitallers, commanding the rearguard, suddenly charged. Richard then ordered the whole crusader force to surge forward, taking the Muslim army by surprise. The rout was complete and Richard's force was so disciplined he stopped them chasing the fleeing Muslim soldiers, who tried to lure the crusaders into the desert. Seven thousand of Saladin's men were killed against a loss of 700 crusaders.
- For five years, Richard fought Philip II of France to hold on to the English possessions in France, which were lost when his brother John succeeded him. As well as fighting across Anjou, Maine, Touraine, Aquitaine and Gascony, he built major fortifications including the great fort at Château-Gaillard on an island in the River Seine.

GENGHIS KHAN

C.1162–1227

FOUNDER OF AN EMPIRE that
stretched from Korea in the east to
Poland in the west, Vietnam in the south
to the Arctic Ocean in the north,
Genghis Khan is remembered for his Mongol
hordes. But he did not win his empire by force
of numbers and barbarity alone, but by his
meticulously organized campaigns.

▶ IN EXILE

The year of his birth is sometimes given as 1155

or 1167, but 1162 is the date favoured in
Mongolia. According to legend, he was born
with a clot of blood in his hands. The son of the
Mongol leader Yesügei, he was named Temüjin
after a Tartar chieftain defeated by his father the
year he was born.

When Temüjin was nine, his father was poisoned and he was forced into exile with his
mother. They survived a harsh winter, then
Temüjin was captured and held prisoner with a
heavy wooden collar around his neck. He used

Genghis consolidated his rule by slaughtering en masse anyone who stood against him

this to knock out his guard and escaped while his captors were feasting.

When Temüjin's wife was stolen, he appealed to Toghril, leader of a neighbouring tribe, to help recapture her. Together they reunited Temüjin's scattered people and in 1194, Temüjin was named 'Genghis Khan' – variously translated as 'universal', 'rightful' or 'precious' lord.

The Chin dynasty in Peking asked the Mongols for help to fend off raids by the Turkic Tartars. Together with Toghril, Genghis attacked, taking over western Mongolia. Subsequently he fell out with Toghril, but emerged victorious from the resulting civil war.

▶ CONSOLIDATING POWER

During these early campaigns Genghis had built an impressive army. Like Attila the Hun 700 years earlier, he organized his men in ten squadrons, each of ten companies, comprising ten units of ten horsemen. Their leaders were family and trusted family clan members, and discipline was rigid. His fast, mobile units comprised mounted bowmen, light cavalry and heavy cavalry who wore leather armour and wielded lances and sabres.

As the Chin dynasty had appealed to him for help, Genghis reasoned that they must be weak. So he attacked China, breaching the Great Wall in 1208 and taking Peking in 1215. Then he turned west. A former Mongol enemy named

Kuchlug had made himself ruler of the Muslim Turkic peoples there. A Mongol army of 20,000 swept through the area and Genghis oversaw the execution of Kuchlug in 1218, adding his lands to his growing empire. The Korean peninsula also fell that year.

He aimed to open trade relations with the Khwarizmian kingdom to the west, but when his emissaries were killed he sacked the trading centers of Bukhara and Samarkand and invaded what is now Iran, Iraq and Turkestan. He then occupied Pakistan and northern India, and invaded Russia in 1222.

He consolidated his rule over the Muslims of Central Asia by respecting their faith and exempting their religious leaders from taxation, and by having the populations of cities that stood against him slaughtered en masse. Returning to Mongolia in 1224, he had to travel south again in 1226, when the kingdom of Hsi-Hsia rebelled, and defeated the rebels in the Battle of the Yellow River. Now over 60, he died still campaigning the following summer. His body was returned to Mongolia for a secret burial. His son Ogedei succeeded him and when the rebellious city of Ning-hsia fell to him, he put the entire population to the sword as his father had ordered.

Genghis Khan's sons and grandsons managed to hold on to much of his vast empire for the next 150 years.

CAREER HIGHLIGHTS

- *When Genghis Khan invaded northern China in 1206, he found that his horsemen were ineffective against the large cities there – the Mongols were a nomadic people and there were no cities in Mongolia at the time. So he employed Chinese engineers to help him with siege warfare. After that he continued to employ foreign engineers and craftsmen in the Mongol army.*

- *When the Tangut kingdom of Hsi–Hsia rebelled, Genghis Khan took a year to prepare his response. He waited for winter to attack, so that his army could cross the frozen waterways there. In the Battle of the Yellow River (1226), he lured the Tanguts out onto the ice, cut down their cavalry with archers and slaughtered the survivors with his armoured horsemen.*

ALEXANDER III OF SCOTLAND

1241–1286

CHRONOLOGY 1241 Born 4 September • 1249 Crowned king of Scotland • 1255 Seized by pro-English faction • 1262 Comes of age and takes over government • 1263 Repels invasion by Norwegian king • 1286 Takes possession of Hebrides and the Isle of Man • 1286 Dies 18 March

ALEXANDER III OF SCOTLAND repelled the last Viking attempted invasion of Scotland, consolidated it as one nation against the encroachment of the English and ruled over a golden age of stability and prosperity.

Born 4 September 1241 at Roxburgh, Alexander III was the son of Marie de Coucy of France and Alexander II who established a clearly defined border with England, leading to an unprecedented period of peace between the two

countries. He came to the throne at the age of seven. At 10 he was married to Margaret, the 11-year-old daughter of Henry III of England, who appointed himself 'Principal Counsellor to the Illustrious King of Scotland' – part of his plot to take control in Scotland. In 1255 Henry installed the hand-picked Grand Council of Lords to govern Scotland. This lost Scotland its autonomy, but had the advantage of maintaining peace with England.

Alexander III successfully repelled the last Viking invasion of Scotland

▶ PEACE WITH ENGLAND

Alexander began to rule in his own right in 1262. As there was no longer a threat from the south, Alexander aimed to settle his northern and western borders. He asked King Haakon of Norway to sell him the Western Isles as his father had done in 1249. When Haakon again refused, the Earl of Ross, one of Alexander's nobles, launched an attack on Skye.

Haakon's response was swift. In July 1243 150 longships arrived sailed from Norway with Haakon at their head. They stopped off at Kirkwall on Orkney in the hope of raising more men. But a solar eclipse over Orkney was regarded as a bad omen.

The Viking invasion fleet was joined by Magnus, King of Man, in the Sound of Skye. Together they took the Mull of Kintyre and the Island of Bute. By late August the longships had rounded Arran. Meanwhile Alexander waited at Ayr. The two armies were now within twenty miles of each other.

Alexander sent monks to parley under a flag of truce. They carried Scotland's peace terms and were instructed to keep the talk going as long as possible. Each day that passed, more Scotsmen rallied to Alexander's flag, while Haakon was expecting no reinforcements. Alexander was also safe on land, while Haakon's forces were at sea and the autumn was closing in.

The diplomacy dragged on until late September, then Haakon moved in for the kill, and the Norsemen surged up the Firth of Clyde. The Scots readied themselves for a fierce battle, but on 1 October a storm struck, scattering Haakon's fleet.

▶ LORD OF THE ISLES

Over the next two days there was some desultory skirmishing between the two armies, but the Norwegians soon saw that the Battle of Largs was lost. They retired in good order and sailed for Lamlash Bay on Arran, where they reassembled for the voyage home. Haakon did not make it. He died in December while taking shelter at Orkney. His son Magnus V, ceded the Hebrides and the Isle of Man to Alexander. The island chieftains took little notice of the change of sovereignty. But still the Western Isles were now nominally Scottish.

In 1275 Alexander's queen died, followed by his two sons. Alexander remarried, hoping his new bride, the French princess Yolande, would give him a new heir. Six months after his wedding Alexander left a meeting with his high council at Edinburgh Castle to return to Yolande. The weather closed in, and Alexander became lost. His horse returned riderless. The next day the king's body was found at the foot of a cliff at Kinghorn. His infant granddaughter 'the Maid of Norway' succeeded him. With no mature male heir to take the throne, however, bloody conflict with England was soon to break out.

A NATION AT PEACE

- *The Battle of Largs (1263) was almost a non-event as battles go, little more than a few skirmishes. But Alexander had won the battle before it had begun. Realizing that his army was safe on land, while Haakon's was vulnerable at sea, he stalled, waiting for the autumn weather to turn in his favour. Storms scattered the invader.*

- *During the reign of Alexander III, behind secure borders, the Scots began to think of themselves as one nation. There were no serious rebellions and the Scottish nobles built castles to rule their own areas, and everyone benefited from the prosperity that peace brought.*

EDWARD I

AD 1239–1307

E DWARD I, also known as Edward Longshanks, is generally thought of as the greatest warrior king of medieval England. He subdued the Welsh, fought

in the crusades and won a long-running campaign against the Scots.

▶ WAR WITH LLYWELYN

Born 17 June 1239 in Westminster, the eldest son of Henry III, he was made Earl of Chester at the age of 15 and given land in Wales, Ireland and France. The following year, he went to war against Llywelyn ap Gruffudd, prince of Gwynedd, with the support of his father. Edward then turned against Henry III and joined his uncle Simon de Montfort, who was seeking to limit the powers of the crown. However, in May 1260 he was reconciled with his father. At the Battle of Lewes on 14 May 1264, he led a charge that routed part of de Montfort's army, but he took off in pursuit. De Montfort's main force then attacked, capturing both Henry and Edward. After a year's captivity, Edward escaped, defeated Montfort and freed the king. Enfeebled by his incarceration, Henry allowed Edward to take control of government.

Edward's campaigns against William Wallace earned him the sobriquet 'Hammer of the Scots'

Eager for combat, Edward joined the crusade of King Louis IX of France. But Louis died on the way. Edward achieved no great victories, but enhanced his reputation as a fearless warrior. He learned of his father's death in 1272 on the way home, but dawdled in France, returning to England to be crowned in August 1274.

Edward reorganized the army, relying on paid professional soldiers, rather than those supplied by the barons. In 1277, he led an army of 6,000 men into Wales, cutting paths through the forests, building roads to aid his advance and ordering the building of a castle wherever he camped. Ships from the Cinque ports cut off the Welsh from their grain supplies from Anglesey. The Welsh leader Llywelyn was killed in 1282 and his brother, David, was the first man to be hanged, drawn and quartered in 1283. Subsequent rebellions by the Welsh in 1287 and 1294 were ruthlessly crushed.

▶ WARS IN SCOTLAND

In 1290, Scotland found itself without a clear successor to the crown and called on Edward to arbitrate. He found for John de Balliol in the hope of extending English power over Scotland. But Balliol turned against Edward and formed an alliance with France. Edward invaded, stormed Berwick, defeated the Scots at Dunbar, deposed Balliol and named himself King of Scotland, taking the Stone of Scone, the traditional coronation seat of Scottish kings, with him to Westminster.

Then in 1297, the Scots revolted under the leadership of William Wallace. After a prolonged campaign, Wallace was defeated, captured and, in 1305, subjected to the same gruesome death as David, his Welsh counterpart.

The Scots revolted again in 1306, this time under Robert the Bruce. Edward died at Burgh by Sands, near Carlisle, on the way to confront him. His rather less able son Edward II took over and was defeated at Bannockburn in June 1314, famously the Scots' last victory over the English. Edward I's body was returned to London and buried in Westminster Abbey.

EDWARD'S BATTLES

- *After being taken prisoner at the Battle of Lewes (1264), Edward escaped from captivity at Hereford in May 1265, took charge of the royalist forces and kept de Montfort behind the River Severn. De Montfort's son was advancing with a large relieving army. Edward put his army between them. Outnumbered two to one, he made a forced march and attacked the son's army at dawn at Kenilworth on 1 August, taking the enemy completely by surprise. He then turned on de Montfort's smaller force. By skillful manoeuvring, he trapped de Montfort in a loop in the River Avon at Evesham, slew him and rescued Henry.*
- *Edward deployed Welsh archers armed with longbows against the Scottish spearmen, giving him victory at the Battle of Falkirk on 22 July 1298. His continuing campaign against William Wallace over the next five years earned him the sobriquet 'Hammer of the Scots'.*

EDWARD III

1312–1377

| CHRONOLOGY | 1312 Born in Windsor 13 November • 1327 Crowned king 29 January; fights the Scots • 1330 Executes Roger Mortimer • 1333 |

Fights the Scots again • 1340 Assumes the title of king of France • 1346 Lands in Normandy; beats French at Crécy 26 August • 1347 Takes Calais • 1355 Attacks in France and Scotland • 1356 Victory at Poiters; Scotland surrenders • 1377 Dies 21 June in Sheen, Surrey

EDWARD III LED ENGLAND into the Hundred Years' War with France. He is largely remembered for his victory at the Battle of Crécy in 1346 where the English longbow came into its own.

▸ **THE BOY KING**

Born in Windsor, Berkshire, in 1312, the eldest son of Edward II and Isabella of France, Edward

was made Duke of Aquitaine in 1325. In 1326, his mother and her lover Roger Mortimer invaded from France, overpowering the king who was forced to resign and was later murdered in gruesome fashion. At the age of 15, Edward III was crowned king, but for the next four years his mother and Mortimer ruled in his name.

Under their aegis, Edward took part in a failed campaign against the Scots in 1327. As a result,

The battle of Crécy is seen by many commentators as the beginning of the end of chivalry

he was forced to sign the Treaty of Northampton, recognizing Scotland as an independent realm. Soon after, he began to assert his own independence. In 1330, he had Mortimer arrested and executed, ending the political influence of Isabella. He then reversed his policy on Scotland and, briefly, put his own man on the throne.

▶ THE HUNDRED YEARS' WAR

Edward had a claim on the throne of France and made attempts to invade in 1339 and 1340. In 1346, he tried again, landing near Cherbourg in July with his eldest son, **Prince Edward, the Black Prince.** They advanced rapidly through Normandy, taking Caen. Hearing that Philip VI was massing an army near Paris, he moved north to allow a clear line of retreat into Flanders. But after crossing the Somme, he turned to face the French at the village of Crécy in Ponthieu, where he won a famous victory on 26 August 1346, giving him control of northwest France. He then lay siege to and captured Calais, but lack of funds forced him to call a truce in September 1347.

Edward returned to England in triumph in October, celebrating his victory with a series of tournaments. The following year he rejected an offer to become Holy Roman Emperor. He continued fighting small-scale actions in Scotland and France, while Edward, the Black Prince, employed his father's defensive tactics to win the Battle of Poitiers in 1356.

In 1359, Edward besieged Rheims, where he planned to be crowned king of France. However, the stout resistance of its inhabitants forced Edward to withdraw and seek another truce. The crown of France continued to elude him.

As Edward grew older, the fighting was left to his sons Edward, the Black Prince, and John of Gaunt. But as the tide of French national sentiment rose, they lost the English possessions in France one by one. When the Black Prince died in 1376, Edward believed that the death of his son was a punishment for usurping his own father's throne. He died in Sheen, Surrey, the following year and is buried in Westminster Abbey.

THE BATTLE OF CRÉCY

- *In a battle with the Scots at Halidon Hill in 1333, Edward perfected the defensive tactics that would bring him victory in France. He dismounted his men-at-arms and flanked them with archers. When the Scots attacked the heavily armed men in the center, they were cut down by the English longbows. Then when the English counter-charged, the Scots fled.*

- *Before the Battle of Crécy, Edward took up carefully prepared positions. His left flank was protected by a forest and an earthworks he ordered his troops to dig. His right was protected by the river and more pits and earthworks were dug in front of his line to* *break any French attack. Edward himself withdrew to a windmill on the ridge behind his main force, where he had an overview of the battlefield. Again his men-at-arms were ordered to dismount, but this time contingents of archers were dispersed among them, while behind the line he kept a mounted reserve, ready for the counter-attack. Philip VI of France fell into the trap. Outnumbering the English by three to one, his army attacked Edward's positions on a broad front. They were cut down by English arrows and, despite repeated attacks, were unable to dislodge the English from their well-prepared positions.*

EDWARD THE BLACK PRINCE

1330–1376

EDWARD the third's eldest sonn:
e, and figure; he that wonn ,
in the feild : and did aduaunce,
ough the trembling hart of Fraunce.
oousand at Poiters, gaue fight,
nsand slew and put to flight ,
dnd took prisoner their King
Bow-men, with y gray goose winge
tetyes , weare euer trid ;
and draw conquest to theire side :
ouerran a part of Spaine :
aftard, calmd King Pedros raigne:
n theire come wee yet perceaue;
aglish arrow: a full sheaf
vict orious battaile shew .
ange out of the trusty bow .
hewers of arrows that day spent .
shrill vict orie as they went .
s fights, the black Prince wonn.
ck not his complection
thless memory bee erected;
Archery, toe much neglected .

ted to all the worthy
trew louers of
Archery *

Tho: Cecill
sculp:

Hee died
the 40 of his
age who 1376
buried at
Canterb.

POITIERS

CHRONOLOGY	1330 Born 15 June in Woodstock, Oxfordshire • 1333 Created Earl of Chester • 1343 Created Prince of Wales • 1346 Fights at Battle of

Crécy • 1356 Beats French at Battle of Poitiers • 1362 Created Prince of Aquitaine • 1367 Wins Battle of Nájera • 1371 Returns to England ill • 1376 Dies at Westminster 8 June

ONE OF THE OUTSTANDING commanders of the Hundred Years' War, Edward was apparently named the Black Prince by the French, perhaps because he was said to wear black armour. The nickname was not recorded in England until the 16th century.

▶ WINNING HIS SPURS

Born the eldest son of **Edward III**, he was created Duke of Cornwall at the age of seven and was the first duke to be created in England. He became Prince of Wales in 1343. In 1346 he joined his father's campaigns in France. At the age of 16, he won a reputation for valour at the

'Courage, I serve'

Battle of Crécy, where an English army of 10,000 defeated 60,000 Frenchmen.

▸ CAPTURING THE KING

In 1355 he led his own expedition into Aquitaine, and on 19 September 1356 he defeated and captured John II of France at the Battle of Poitiers. As well as paying a ransom of 3,000,000 gold crowns, John was forced to cede Aquitaine to England. Edward became its ruler in 1362 and, with his wife Joan of Kent, maintained a lavish court at Bordeaux.

In 1367 he went to the support of Peter the Cruel of Castile and temporarily restored him to his throne by the victory of Nájera on 3 April. As a reward, Peter is said to have given him a ruby that now adorns the British imperial state crown. However, the campaign ruined his health. The high cost of the war forced Edward to levy taxes in Aquitaine. In 1368 his nobles protested to Charles V of France on behalf of Aquitaine.

In the resulting war, much of Aquitaine turned against him. The Black Prince fought on with mercenaries whom he could not afford to pay. They failed to quell the revolt, but under his direction they captured and burnt the city of Limoges in 1370, massacring its citizens.

By 1372 Edward's failing health forced him to leave his holdings in France, charging his brother John of Gaunt with the impossible task of holding them. The aging Edward III had relaxed his hold on the government and the Black Prince, aware that he would not live to succeed his father, tried to strengthen the hand of the clerical party against John of Gaunt so that the accession of his son (later Richard II) would be assured. To that end he supported, and possibly directed, the proceedings of the so-called Good Parliament of 1376, which, among other things, impeached two followers of John of Gaunt and removed Alice Perrers, the king's mistress, from court. The Black Prince died shortly afterwards.

THE BATTLE OF POITIERS

- *At the Battle of Crécy in 1346, Edward III, who was directing the battle from a hill, put his son in the front line. When the Black Prince sent a message asking for reinforcements, his father ignored it, determined that his son win his spurs without help from other knights. He won his spurs and the Prince of Wales's feathers – three white ostrich plumes taken from the helmet of the King of Bohemia, a French ally, on the battlefield. And he coined the motto that goes with the job: originally homout; ich dene – 'courage; I serve'. The Black Prince was declared the hero of Crécy.*
- *In 1355 the Black Prince invaded France with an army of 60,000 men. He captured rich towns and gathered a great deal of booty, but lost so many men by sickness that he had only about 10,000 men left when he*

met the French force of 45,000 at Poitiers. Early on the morning of 14 September 1356, the battle began. For hours the English withstood the onslaught of the French. Again the English longbowmen played a vital role, firing up to twelve arrows a minute – twice as many as the French bowmen. Then a body of English horsemen charged furiously on one part of the French line, while the Black Prince attacked another part. This sudden movement caused confusion among the French. Many of them fled. Thousands of prisoners were taken, including the King of France. At the victory parade in Poitiers, the king was allowed to ride on a beautiful white horse, while the Black Prince rode on a pony beside him. He was then sent to London, where he was held for ransom.

TAMERLANE

1336–1405

▸ TIMUR THE LAME

Born in Kesh, near Samarkand in 1336 to a minor military family, he was named Timur. However, he was injured by an arrow-wound while stealing sheep that left him partially paralysed down his left-hand side and was consequently known as Timur Lenk or Timurlenk in Turkish, which translates as 'Timur the Lame', 'Tamerlane' or 'Tamburlaine'. He rose to become prime minister of his local region Transoxania (modern Uzbekistan) under the Chagatai governor Ilyas Khoja in 1361. But he rebelled to join his brother-in-law Amir Husayn. Together they defeated Ilyas Khoja in 1364 and completed their conquest of Tranoxania by 1366.

In 1370, he turned against Husayn and killed him. Making himself ruler in Samarkand, he claimed sovereignty over the Mongols, declaring himself a direct descendent of Genghis Khan. Over the next ten years, he occupied Turkestan and sent troops into Russia in support of

A MUSLIM of Turkic origins, Tamerlane set out to restore the Mongol empire of **Genghis Khan**. In a lifetime's warfare, he conquered a vast area, but is chiefly remembered for his barbarity.

'As there is but one God in heaven, there ought to be but one ruler on the earth'

Tokhamysh, the Mongol Khan of the Crimea. They occupied Moscow and crushed the Lithuanians.

Tamerlane's army exceeded 100,000 horsemen, armed with bows and swords. They were organized along the lines of the armies of Genghis Khan and **Attila the Hun**, with each man carrying all he needed on his own pack horses. They were highly motivated and fiercely loyal to Tamerlane, who possessed a talent for tactics.

▶ THE CONQUEST OF ASIA

In 1383, Tamerlane turned his attention to Persia, completing his conquest in 1385. Over the next eight years, he completed his conquest of Iraq and Central Asia. During that time, he came into conflict with Tokhamysh and his Golden Horde. In 1391, he defeated Tokhamysh on the Russian steppes, defeating him again on the River Kur and occupying Moscow in 1395.

Meanwhile, Persia had revolted. Tamerlane returned and put down the uprising with unbridled savagery, massacring entire cities and building pyramids of the inhabitants' skulls. Then he moved into India and laid waste to Delhi: it took over a century for the city to recover.

While he was in India, the Mameluk sultan of Egypt and the Ottoman sultan Bayazid I had encroached on his territory. In 1399 he set out to punish them. In 1401 he defeated the Mameluk army in Syria, and slaughtered the inhabitants of Damacus. In Baghdad, 20,000 were massacred and the city's monuments levelled. The following year he defeated the Ottoman army near Ankara and extended his empire to the Mediterranean, taking Smyrna (modern Izmir) from the kings of Rhodes.

Tamerlane returned to Samarkand. Even though he was then 68, in December 1404 he set off again to conqueror China. In February 1405 he fell ill and died in Otrar, near Chimkent (modern Shymkent in Kazakstan). His body was embalmed and taken back to Samarkand where it now lies in the great tomb of Gur-e Amir.

Although his empire was divided among his sons and grandsons when he died, his younger son Shah Rokh ruthlessly reunited it by slaughtering all rivals. Tamerlane's empire remained influential into the sixteenth century, and his descendants became the Great Mughals of India.

A PENCHANT FOR SLAUGHTER

- *On 24 September 1398, Tamerlane crossed the Indus on the pretext that the Muslim rulers of Delhi were treating their Hindu subjects with unnecessary tolerance. After the Battle of Panipat on 17 December 1398, he ordered the slaughter of 100,000 captured Indian soldiers. He then massacred the inhabitants of Delhi, stripped the city and destroyed everything his men could not carry. He even took ninety captured elephants to carry stones to build a new mosque at Samarkand.*

- *While Tamerlane was in India, the Ottoman sultan Bayazid I annexed Anatolia. Tamerlane struck back in August 1400 and the two armies eventually met at Çubukovasi, near Ankara, on 20 July 1402. Bayazid's Turkmen vassals promptly deserted to Tamerlane and the Ottomans were overwhelmed. Bayazid was captured and died a prisoner in 1403.*

HENRY V

1387–1422

CHRONOLOGY

1387 Born 16 September at Monmouth.

1399 Created Prince of Wales.

1403–1408 Fights Welsh rebels.

1413 Becomes king of England 21 March.

1414 Suppresses Lollard rising.

1415 Makes war with France; captures Harfleur in September; 25 October wins Battle of Agincourt.

1416 Wins Battle of the Seine.

1420 Becomes regent of France and heir to French throne.

1422 Dies 31 August at Bois de Vincennes, France.

HENRY V RESUMED ENGLAND'S traditionally aggressive policy towards France and victory at the Battle of Agincourt in 1415 made England the pre-eminent kingdom in Europe.

The eldest son of Henry IV and Mary de Bohun, Henry was born at Monmouth in Wales on or around 16 September 1387. When his father was exiled in 1398, he was taken in by his cousin Richard II. Educated by the powerful Henry Beaufort, bishop of Winchester, he was the first king who could read and write English. In 1399, his father returned, deposed Richard and took the crown. Henry, as heir to the throne, was created Prince of Wales.

▸ VICTORY IN WALES

Already an accomplished soldier at the age of 14, he won successive victories over the Welsh usurper Owen Glendower. At 16, he commanded his father's forces at the Battle of Shrewsbury, consolidating his power. However, Shakespeare has given him the reputation of being a feckless and dissolute youth, who reformed when he came to the throne. There may be some truth in this, as such tales can be traced back to within twenty years of his death.

'We few, we happy few, we band of brothers'

WILLIAM SHAKESPEARE, HENRY V ACT IV SCENE III

When he became king on 21 March 1413, he quickly put down the Lollard rising, led by Sir John Oldcastle, and thwarted a plot to assassinate him by nobles still loyal to Richard II – part of the ongoing War of the Roses. Henry distracted English attention from domestic concerns by renewing the Hundred Years' War against France. He demanded the return of Aquitaine and other lands ceded by the Treaty of Calais in 1360. In 1415, he proposed to marry Catherine of Valois, daughter of Charles VI of France, demanding the old Plantagenet lands of Normandy and Anjou as his dowry. Charles refused and Henry declared war, now pursing a claim to the French throne.

▶ THE ENGLISH IN NORMANDY

Landing 11,000 men in Normandy in August 1415, he captured Harfleur the following month. But, by then, he had lost nearly half his troops, largely due to disease. They headed for Calais, in the hope that they could make it back to England. But their retreat was blocked by some 20,000 to 30,000 men under Charles d'Albret,

constable of France. On 25 October 1415, Henry won a decisive victory over them at Agincourt. At the Battle of the Seine in August 1416, Henry gained mastery over the English Channel. By 1419 he had captured Normandy, Picardy and much of the Capetian stronghold of the Ile-de-France.

Charles VI was forced to sign the Treaty of Troyes in May 1420. Under it, Henry married Catherine on 2 June. Henry became both Charles' son-in-law and regent, and Charles passed over his own son to name Henry heir to the French crown. The hard life of a soldier had aged Henry prematurely, but he nevertheless went back to campaigning. During the sieges of Melun and Meaux, his health collapsed. He died of dysentery at the château of Vincennes on 31 August 1422.

Had he lived just two months longer, he would have been king of both England and France. His only son, the future Henry VI, was born while he was away campaigning and he never saw the child.

THE BATTLE OF AGINCOURT

- *At Agincourt (1415), the French unwisely picked a battlefield with a narrow 1,000-yard front between two woods, making it difficult for their knights to manoeuvre. Henry dismounted his 900 men-at-arms. They were protected by formations of 5,000 archers, who were drawn up behind lines of sharpened stakes. The English archers provoked the French to attack. Their cavalry charge was broken by the stakes. The French knights in their heavy armour then attacked on foot across muddy ground. At first, the*

English gave ground. But the French arrived in such numbers that there was no room to raise an arm to strike a blow. Henry then sent in his archers, armed with swords and axes. They hacked down thousands of Frenchmen, capturing thousands more. But these too were despatched when another French attack threatened. The French lost 4,500 men at arms and 1,500 knights – the cream of the French nobility, including the constable of France himself. The English lost just 450.

GUSTAVUS II OF SWEDEN

1594–1632

CHRONOLOGY 1594 Born in Stockholm 9 December • 1611 Commands Swedish forces in East Gotland; becomes king of Sweden 30 October • 1613 Concludes peace with Denmark • 1617 Concludes peace with Russia • 1619 Captures ports of Polish Livonia • 1629 Agrees to truce with Poland • 1630 Joins Thirty Years' War • 1631 Defeats imperial forces under Graf von Tilly at Battle of Breitenfeld • 1632 Defeats Tilly again at the Battle of the River Lech; dies at Battle of Lützen, Saxony, 6 November

GUSTAVUS II, also known as Gustavus Adolphus, king of Sweden, led the strongest European army of the seventeenth century through a series of victories against Denmark, Russia, Poland and Germany. His revolutionary development of the arts of organizing an army led him to be called the 'Father of Modern Warfare'.

▶ A MILITARY UPBRINGING

Born in Stockholm on 9 December 1594, the son of Charles IX of Sweden, he was groomed to be a military leader from an early age. At the age of sixteen, he was commanding the Swedish forces in East Gotland, winning a number of battles against the Danish invaders. When Charles IX died in 1611, the Swedish parliament was so impressed with his military achievements that they waived the age requirement so he could take the throne.

The new king was immediately faced with wars with Denmark, Russia and Poland. Leaving

Gustavus was perhaps the first commander to integrate artillery with his infantry and cavalry

domestic affairs in the hands of his able chancellor Axel Oxenstierna, he invaded Denmark while the Danish army was on Swedish soil. Though this bold move failed militarily, it brought about peace with Sweden's nearest and most threatening opponent.

Between 1613 and 1617, he fought a victorious campaign against Russia, acquiring territory for Sweden and cutting off the Muscovites' access to the Baltic. Gustavus then started a long series of wars against Poland. In 1619, he took the Polish ports of Livonia, on the eastern coast of the Baltic. After a two-year truce, he swept along the southern coast of the Baltic, agreeing to a six-year truce with the exhausted Poles in 1629. By this time, Gustavus was known as the 'Lion of the North'.

▶ FIGHTING THE EMPIRE

In 1630, he joined the Thirty Years' War, not just to support the Protestant cause, but also to halt the encroachment of the Holy Roman Empire. After negotiating an alliance with France, he landed 16,000 men on the coast of Pomerania, took the port of Stettin and pushed the imperial forces back from the coast. He won a brilliant victory against Graf von Tilly at the Battle of Breitenfeld in September 1631. Gustavus and Tilly met again at the River Lech the following year. On 16 April, Gustavus crossed the river under a heavy smokescreen and defeated the imperial army, leaving Tilly mortally wounded. He was replaced by Albrecht von Wallenstein, who repulsed the Swedes when they attacked his fortified positions at Alte Veste on 3 September 1632.

Despite heavy losses, Gustavus attacked Wallenstein's entrenched positions at Lützen, near Leipzig on 16 November 1632. This time the Swedes were victorious but Gustavus, cut off from his men, was shot and killed just a few weeks before his thirty-eighth birthday.

Gustavus had built an unbeatable army by conscripting every young man in Sweden for twenty years. They were highly disciplined and taught to fight as a single unit with drills and field manoeuvres. Gustavus came up with the idea of dividing his musketeers into three ranks which fired volleys in turn while the others reloaded. He also integrated artillery support into his infantry and cavalry units. The organizational reforms and tactics he introduced were copied for more than a century afterwards.

ROUTING TILLY

- *At the Battle of Breitenfeld (1631), the imperial army, under Graf von Tilly, routed the Saxons on Gustavus's left and attempted to turn his flank. In the heat of battle, Swedish troops were moved across to create a new front, the first time this had been done in modern warfare. Gustavus's right withstood seven hours of cavalry charges, then Gustavus himself led a counterattack around Tilly's left, capturing his guns. The imperial infantry squares were cut down. Seriously wounded, Tilly escaped, leaving 12,000 dead.*

Gustavus took Leipzig the following day.
- *At the Battle of Lützen (1632), the Swedish attack was delayed by foggy weather. Leading from the front, Gustavus made a cavalry charge directly into the enemy strength. Isolated in the fog with an escort of only three men, Gustavus was cut down. But his army were so well trained that they did not retreat or surrender at the news of the death of their leader. They rallied and attacked, earning Gustavus one final, posthumous victory.*

OLIVER CROMWELL

1599–1658

1599 Born 25 April in Huntingdon.
1628 Elected MP for Huntingdon.
1642 Civil war breaks out; seizes Cambridge castle.
1643 Defeats Royalists at Grantham, Burleigh House, Gainsborough and Winceby.
1644 Victorious at Marston Moor.
1645 Helps reform army; victorious at Naseby.
1648 Defeats Scots at Battle of Preston.
1649 Execution of Charles I.
1649–1650 Campaigns in Ireland.
1650 Defeats Charles II at Dunbar and Worcester.
1653 Becomes Lord Protector of England.
1654 Ends First Anglo-Dutch War.
1655 Takes Jamaica from the Spanish.
1658 Dies 3 September.
1661 Disinterred and hanged.

Army, which was instrumental in maintaining Britain as a military power for centuries after his death.

Born in Huntingdon on 25 April 1599, he was a gentleman farmer before entering parliament in 1628. A religious convert in his twenties, he became a Puritan, eager to rid the church and politics of any vestiges of Roman Catholicism.

▶ OLIVER'S ARMY

When the Civil War broke out between Charles I – a Catholic sympathizer – and parliament, Cromwell seized Cambridge Castle. Although he was in his 40s and had no military experience, he raised a troop of cavalry, taking only 'godly men of good character', believing that only religious zeal could defeat the king's more experienced troops. He drilled his men thoroughly. Armed with two flintlock pistols and a 3-foot double-edged sword, they advanced – not at a gallop, but at a fast trot, so that they could

OLIVER CROMWELL WAS A Parliamentary general during the English Civil War, and was largely responsible for achieving victory over the royalists. Afterwards, he subdued Wales, Ireland and Scotland. He also helped create the New Model

'Put your faith in God and keep your powder dry'

manoeuvre or be recalled and reform to take advantage of the enemy's weaknesses. Once within range, they fired their pistols, then drew their swords for the charge.

These tactics were enormously successful, winning him a series of victories against the royalists in eastern England in 1643 at Grantham, Burleigh House, Gainsborough and Winceby. In 1644, Cromwell's cavalry won the parliamentary forces a decisive victory at Marston Moor. Afterwards, officers who had earned their commissions by being MPs stood down under the 'Self Denying Ordinance' and the New Model Army was formed with officers who had shown their worth in the field.

▶ DEFENDING THE REVOLUTION

On 14 June 1645, the New Model Army crushed the Royalists at Naseby. However, when a second Civil War broke out in 1648, Cromwell put down a rebellion in Wales and defeated an invading army of the king's Scottish supporters at Preston on 16 August.

In 1649, Cromwell was one of the 135 com-missioners to sign the king's death warrant. He then pacified Ireland and defeated the forces of Charles II at Dunbar and Worcester.

Offered the throne as king, Cromwell became Lord Protector instead, which gave him the powers of a military dictator without the accountability of a king. Eager to export the Puritan revolution to the Catholic Spanish empire in the Americas, he sent an expedition against Hispaniola. Failing to take it, they took Jamaica instead. He also brought the First Anglo-Dutch War, which had begun in 1652, to a successful conclusion in 1654.

He died of malaria in London on 3 May 1658 and was buried secretly in Westminster Abbey thirteen days before his state funeral. His son Richard succeeded him, but lacked his authority. After Charles II was restored to the throne in 1661, his body was dug up, hanged as a regicide at Tyburn and buried at the foot of the gallows. His head was stuck on a pole on top of Westminster Hall, where it remained throughout the reign of Charles II.

A RUTHLESS PACIFICATION

- At the Battle of Marston Moor (1644), Oliver Cromwell's cavalry scattered the royalist horse under Prince Rupert. He then reformed his troops and went to the aid of parliamentary leader Sir Thomas Fairfax on the right, enveloping the center of the royalist army. Some 3,000 to 4,000 were killed, many prisoners and cannon were captured, and Cromwell emerged as leading parliamentary soldier.

- The ruthless nature of Cromwell's pacification of Ireland was partially a response to the earlier massacre of English settlers. At Drogheda near Dublin he massacred the garrison in September 1649, though he had been just as ruthless at Basing Hall in England in 1645. He wrote that it would 'tend to prevent the effusion of blood for the future'. Even though the massacre shocked some commentators at the time and has been a source of enmity ever since, sacking cities that refused to surrender was well within the rules of war of the time, and discouraged further resistance.

- Cromwell rarely attacked unless he had numerical superiority. But at Dunbar in 1650, his 12,000 faced nearly twice that number. Using a rainstorm to disguise his movements, he attacked and defeated Charles II's Scottish army. He destroyed the remnants of it at Worcester the following year, and brought all of Britain back under one government.

SIR THOMAS FAIRFAX

1612–1671

CHRONOLOGY

1612 Born at Denton, Yorkshire, 17 January.
1629–1631 Fights the Spanish in Holland.
1639 Joins Bishops' Wars against the Scots.
1640 Knighted.
1642 English Civil War breaks out: Fairfax is appointed commander-in-chief of the Parliamentary army.
1643 Takes Leeds and Wakefield; defeated at Adwalton Moor; victorious at Winceby.
1644 Victorious at Nantwich and Marston Moor; wounded at Helmsley Castle.
1645 Creates New Model Army; victorious at Naseby and Langport.
1647 Crushes royalists again in Maidstone and Colchester.
1648 Refuses to condemn the king.
1650 Resigns as commander-in-chief.
1658 Restores parliamentary rule after death of Cromwell.
1660 Invites Charles II to return.
1661 Retires from public life.
1671 Dies at Nun Appleton, Yorkshire, 12 November.

S IR THOMAS WAS THE commander-in-chief of the parliamentarian army during the English Civil Wars, the founder of the New Model Army and the strategist responsible for Parliament's victory.

Born in Denton near Ilkley, Yorkshire, on 17 January 1612, he was the son of Ferdinando, 2nd Baron Fairfax, and attended Cambridge in 1626. In 1629, Fairfax joined Sir Horace Vere's army, fighting for the Dutch in their attempt to gain independence from Spain, and married Vere's daughter Anne when he returned to England in 1631. In 1639 he marched with King Charles I against the Scots in the First Bishops' War. Although the war ended before any fighting took place, Fairfax was knighted for his services in January 1640.

▸ **FOR PARLIAMENT**

With the beginning of the English Civil War in 1642, most of the Yorkshire gentry sided with the king. But Sir Thomas and his father declared for parliament. Leading the local cavalry, they took Leeds in January 1643 and occupied Wakefield in May, but were defeated by the Marquis of Newcastle at Adwalton Moor in June 1643, which left the royalists in control of most of Yorkshire. Fortified in Hull, the Fairfaxes kept Newcastle's army occupied in the north with lightning raids and prevented a royalist advance into East Anglia.

Fairfax left his father in command at Hull and crossed the Humber to join Oliver **Cromwell** at the Battle of Winceby in Lincolnshire in October

'He hath more wit than to be here'

ANNE FAIRFAX, DURING THE TRIAL OF KING CHARLES I, JANUARY 1649

1643. Fairfax won another victory over the royalists at Nantwich in January 1644, opening North Wales to the parliamentarians. Together with Cromwell, he won a decisive victory at Marston Moor in July 1644, but was wounded during the siege of Helmsley Castle, Yorkshire, in September. And in 1645, he was appointed commander of the New Model Army.

He won the deciding battle of the First Civil War at Naseby in June 1645, then marched into the royalist-held West country, and finished off the royalist army at Langport in July, taking Bristol in September 1645. The last remnants of the king's army were crushed at Torrington in February 1646, surrendering at Truro on 13 March 1646. In June 1646, the royalist headquarters of Oxford also surrendered to Fairfax.

▸ THE SECOND CIVIL WAR

During the Second Civil War, Fairfax crushed the royalist uprising in Kent, then starved the Essex royalists into Colchester. Although he ordered the execution of the royalist commanders Sir Charles Lucas and Sir George Lisle on the grounds that they had broken their parole and committed treason by taking up arms against parliament, he refused to attend the king's trial. When his name was called, his wife Anne famously cried out, 'He hath more wit than to be here.'

Fairfax remained in England during Cromwell's Irish campaign of 1649. He resigned as Lord General of the Army in 1650, refusing to invade Scotland against Charles II's forces. Command of the New Model Army then passed to Oliver Cromwell.

In 1657, Fairfax's daughter Mary married the Duke of Buckingham, who was in secret communication with Charles II. When Buckingham was sent to the Tower in 1658, Fairfax interceded for him, provoking a bitter quarrel with Cromwell who was now Lord Protector.

Fairfax joined forces with General George Monck to restore parliamentary authority after Cromwell's death and was a member of the parliament which invited Charles II to return in 1660. Incensed by the desecration of Cromwell's remains he retired from public life in 1661 and lived quietly in Yorkshire until his death on 12 November 1671.

THE NEW MODEL ARMY

- In 1645, Fairfax was appointed Lord General of the New Model Army as he was one of the few parliamentarian commanders not required to relinquish his rank by the 'Self-Denying Ordinance'. The New Model Army brought all the parliamentary forces together under one command and was the first large professional army in English history. Their red coats were to serve as a symbol of the British army for generations to come.
- At Naseby, Northamptonshire, on 14 June 1645, Fairfax deployed his men behind the brow of a hill, hiding his numbers. The royalists made a successful cavalry charge on the parliamentary left, while the royalist infantry pushed back the center. But the royalist cavalry galloped past the parliamentarian rear, where they were checked by the defenders' fire. On the right Cromwell charged, routing the rest of the royalist horse, then turned on the royalist infantry. Fairfax's dragoons attacked the royalist right. With no horse to defend them, the king's infantry were killed or captured. Some 500 officers were taken, along with the artillery and the baggage train. Charles fled, allowing Fairfax to retake Leicester.

PRINCE RUPERT

1619–1682

CHRONOLOGY 1619 Born 17 December in Prague • 1620 Family flees to Dutch Republic • 1636 Visits Charles I in England • 1637 Fights against imperial forces in Thirty Years' War • 1638 Captured and held for three years • 1642 Travels to England; Civil War starts; fights at Battle of Edgehill • 1643 Victorious at Battle of Chalgrove Field; takes Bristol; defeated at Marston Moor • 1644 Appointed commander-in-chief of king's army • 1645 Beaten at Battle of Naseby; surrenders Bristol • 1646 Banished from England • 1648 Heads royalist fleet harassing English shipping • 1651–1653 Becomes pirate in Caribbean • 1653 Joins Charles II in France • 1660 Returns in England following the Restoration • 1665–1667 Fights in Second Anglo-Dutch War • 1670 Appointed first governor of Hudson's Bay Company • 1672–1674 Fights in Third Anglo-Dutch War • 1682 Dies 29 November in London

P RINCE RUPERT WAS THE LEADING royalist general during the English Civil Wars, winning several notable victories in the early stages.

'Rupert of the Rhine', as he was known, was the son of Frederick, king of Bohemia, and Elizabeth Stuart, sister of Charles I. Born in Prague, Bohemia (now the Czech Republic) on 29 November 1619, the following year his family

was driven out of Bohemia into the Dutch Republic.

In 1636, he visited his uncle Charles I in England, then saw action fighting with the Dutch against the imperial forces in the Thirty Years' War. In 1638 he was captured and held prisoner in Austria for three years. After he was released, he returned to England, shortly before the outbreak of the English Civil Wars in August 1642.

A scientist and an artist, Prince Rupert is best remembered as a dashing cavalier

▸ EARLY VICTORIES

He commanded the royalist cavalry at the first engagement of the war, the Battle of Edgehill, after training his men in the 'Swedish' tactics of **Gustavus** Adolphus. The following year, he won a more decisive victory at the Battle of Chalgrove Field. In 1644, he raised the siege of York. At Marston Moor, however, he met his match in Oliver **Cromwell**, who had learnt the art of cavalry tactics by observing Prince Rupert at Edgehill.

He escaped south with 6,000 men and was given command of the king's forces, but his authority was undermined by the king's counsellors and he was denied a free hand with strategy. After taking Leicester in May, he was forced into battle at Naseby in June. His battle plan was sound, but he lost control of his cavalry and lost the day. He surrendered Bristol in September and, after the surrender of the king in July 1646, he was banished from England by Parliament.

▸ ALL AT SEA

He took charge of the royalist fleet in 1648 and began harassing the trade of the fledgling English Republic. When he was forced from the Mediterranean, he took to piracy, without notable success; he joined Charles II in exile in France with just one ship and one prize.

When Charles was restored to the throne in 1660, Rupert was given command of the navy, where he met with more success in the Second and Third Anglo-Dutch Wars (1665–1667 and 1672–1674). He also became the first governor of the Hudson's Bay Company.

A cultured man, he was a member of the Royal Society. A scientist and an artist, he is credited with introducing the art of mezzotint printing to England, although he will always be remembered as a dashing cavalier. He died in London on 29 November 1682.

THE BATTLE OF EDGEHILL

- *When 14,000 royalists met 14,000 parliamentarians at Edgehill on 23 October 1642, Prince Rupert had drawn up a battle plan, and charged at the Parliamentary cavalry opposite. Seeing this, Sir Faithful Fortescue tore off his orange sash and joined the royalists. The remaining cavalry fled, riding through their infantry, and four infantry regiments broke and ran. Rupert's men made off after them leaving the royalist army with no cavalry, while the Parliamentarian still had a reserve. The royalist foot-soldiers attacked, but were harassed from the rear by the Parliamentary cavalry. The king's standard was lost, but when Rupert's cavalry returned to the battlefield, the battle was stalemated and the engagement broken off. That night, a royalist crept into the Parliamentary camp and stole back the king's standard. Rupert*

recommended that the king march directly on London, while the Parliamentary forces were in disarray. This bold strategy might have won the Civil War for the king, there and then.

- *After attempting to steal the Parliamentary army's pay wagon, Prince Rupert was heading back to the king's headquarters at Oxford when eight troops of Parliamentary horse caught up with him and he turned to meet them at a cornfield at Chalgrove 18 June 1643. The Parliamentarian dragoons were hiding behind a hedge to fire on the royalists. With typical brio, Rupert led a charge through the hedge while another regiment went round it. The roundheads were routed leaving many dead. The royalists lost only 12 men and the way to Bristol was now open.*

WILLIAM OF ORANGE

1650–1702

1650 Born 14 November in The Hague • 1672 Appointed stadtholder; fights invasion of French and English at sea • 1677 Marries Mary, daughter of James II of England • 1678 Concludes peace • 1686 Forms anti-French League of Augsburg • 1688 Lands at Brixham unopposed • 1689 Takes throne jointly with Mary; declares war on France • 1690 Victorious at the Battle of the Boyne • 1692 Glen Coe massacre 1702 Dies 19 March, London

A S STADTHOLDER, or viceroy, in The Netherlands, William successfully defended his country against invasion. He was then invited to become king of England, famously crushing opposition in Ireland at the Battle of the Boyne.

▸ BROUGHT UP TO RULE

William was born in The Hague on 14 November 1650, eight days after the death of his father William II, Prince of Orange and stadtholder of five of the United Provinces of the Netherlands. His mother Mary Stuart, daughter of Charles I of England, died when he was ten.

Although he was excluded from office by his father's adversary Johan de Witt, he was brought up to rule. However, when the French invaded in 1672, William and a few raw troops managed to halt their advance by flooding the polders. Then panic broke out. Johan de Witt was murdered and William made stadtholder.

Charles II of England threatened to join the attack on Holland. But while his navy held off the English in the Third Anglo-Dutch War, William built an army and recaptured the fortress at Naarden in September 1673. He then joined forces with the Holy Roman Emperor Leopold I and took Bonn. Fearing encirclement, the French

'There is one certain means I can be sure never to see my country's ruin: I will die in the last ditch.'

pulled out of the United Provinces. England made peace in 1674; the French in 1678.

As the son of Mary Stuart, William already stood fourth in line to the throne of England. In 1677, he married his cousin Mary, daughter of Charles II's brother, who came to the throne as James II in 1685. A declared Roman Catholic, and a bigot of some note, James had already enraged his Protestant subjects with his dictatorial ways, and they appealed to William for help. The birth of James's son in 1688 raised fears of a Catholic succession and William was invited to intervene. He landed at Brixham on 5 November 1688 with an army. James fled and William and Mary took the throne jointly in February the following year.

▸ THE BATTLE OF THE BOYNE

England was happy to have a Protestant monarch back on the throne, but there was dissent in Ireland and Scotland. James landed in Ireland and took command of 50,000 Catholics. The Protestants fled and James besieged Londonderry. When he failed to take the city he withdrew to Dublin, where he set up a Catholic parliament and robbed the Protestants. William arrived in Ireland in June 1690 and on 1 July 1690 defeated James at the Battle of the Boyne. James again fled, though his men fought on for another year.

Armed resistance collapsed in Scotland, but when the MacDonald clan were slow in swearing an oath of allegiance to William, they were massacred in Glen Coe.

William continued campaigning on the Continent, but the British showed little appetite for war. Mary died of smallpox in 1694 and William died in 1702 after his horse stumbled over a molehill in Richmond Park. Jacobites traditionally toast the 'little gentleman in a black velvet suit' – the mole.

THE GLORIOUS REVOLUTION

- On 3 November 1688 William arrived in the Straits of Dover with some 600 ships, flying a flag bearing the motto: 'The liberties of England and the Protestant religion I will maintain.' On 5 November 1688 he landed at Brixham, Devon, and entered Exeter four days later. James's army was at Salisbury. William struck out after it, but James withdrew and tried to negotiate. When his terms were refused, he fled. William ordered free elections in January 1689. The new parliament drew up a Declaration of Rights and, on 13 February, asked William and Mary to accept the Crown. This ousting of James and William's invasion, through the lack of bloodshed, became known as the Glorious Revolution.
- Landing at Carrickfergus on 14 June 1690, William marched south to engage the Jacobite army, which retreated before him. By 30 June he reached the top of a hill overlooking the River Boyne at Oldbridge where the river could be forded. The terrain, William decided, was suitable for a short and conclusive battle. James had 30,000 men including French infantry and Irish cavalry. William had 36,000 men of various nationalities. A shot from an Irish sniper grazed William's shoulder. The armies began to move at 4 am on 1 July. William's right crossed the river a few miles upstream and turned the left flank of the Irish army. The French moved to counter this, leaving the ford near Oldbridge defended by untrained Irish infantry. Once battle was joined they were easily defeated. William was in the thick of the battle, inspiring his men, while James held back. Fearing encirclement he fled from the battle field and the country. His army withdrew in good order and fought on for another year. The Battle of the Boyne is celebrated by Protestants in Northern Ireland to this day.

JOHN CHURCHILL, DUKE OF MARLBOROUGH

1650–1722

Spanish Succession turned Britain from being an insignificant off-shore island into a great power.

Born John Churchill, the son of an impoverished royalist family in Devon in 1650, he began his career as a page to James, the Duke of York, at the age of 17, gaining his position through his sister who was James's mistress. He in turn became the lover of Lady Castlemaine, the mistress of Charles II.

▸ EARL OF MARLBOROUGH

His contacts at court gained him a commission in the foot guards. Over the next two years he saw action in North Africa, served in the Anglo-French fleet defeated by the Dutch at Solebay on 28 May 1672 and fought beside many French officers whom he would later face as enemies.

In 1674, he married Sarah Jennings the lady-in-waiting and lover of James' daughter Anne,

O NE OF THE GREATEST GENERALS England ever produced. Marlborough's succession of victories on the Continent during the War of the

'Marlborough has good claim to being Britain's greatest soldier' PROFESSOR RICHARD HOLMES

a future queen. When Charles II died, James acceded to the throne and Churchill put down the rebellion of the Duke of Monmouth, Charles II's illegitimate son and Protestant pretender to the throne. But when Protestant England turned against the Catholic James, Churchill switched his allegiance to the new king, **William of Orange**, who rewarded him with the earldom of Marlborough.

He served in Flanders and Ireland between 1689 and 1691, but then in 1692 was imprisoned in the Tower of London, suspected of plotting the return of James II. But when William died and Anne came to the throne, Marlborough became captain-general of the Anglo-Dutch forces fighting the French in the War of the Spanish Succession.

▶ WAR OF THE SPANISH SUCCESSION

After invading the Spanish Netherlands (modern Belgium) in June 1702, he defeated the French at Blenheim and knocked their ally Bavaria out of the war. After defeating the French again at Ramillies in 1706, he captured Antwerp and Dunkirk. Two years later, Marlborough was surprised by an even more powerful French force under Marshall Vendôme at Oudenaarde. Until then he had fought set piece battles, but he quickly turned from defence to offence, securing another victory.

He then attempted to invade France. His Dutch allies pulled out, but he managed to take Lille on 11 December 1708. While the French tried to make peace, Marlborough besieged Mons. Then on 11 September 1709, he fought the French under Marshall Villars at Malplaquet. Marlborough launched a fierce assault against the French center, which only held with the commitment of their reserves. With the French reserves now committed, Marlborough sent in his own and the French line broke. But this time the French casualties numbered just 12,000 against the allies 21,000.

Two years later, the Tories came to power and argued that, because of these massive casualties, Britain should commit itself to sea power, rather than fight on land. Marlborough was dismissed and went into exile, accused of misappropriating public funds. He was restored to favour when George I came to the throne in 1714, but he lived in retirement until his death in 1722.

THE BATTLE OF BLENHEIM

- *In 1704, Marlborough marched his army 250 miles into Germany to Blenheim in Bavaria where he surprised the main French force on 13 August. He inflicted 34,000 casualties on the enemy at a cost of 12,000 of his own – a quarter of his army. This shattered the French army's reputation of invincibility. The Austrian prince Eugene of Savoy made him a prince of the Holy Roman Empire and Queen Anne gave him £10,000 and ordered Blenheim Palace to be built for him in Oxfordshire.*
- *At Ramillies on 23 May 1706, Marlborough made a feint to the right, then smashed through the center. Although the Dutch bore the worst of the fighting, Marlborough himself barely escaped with his life. But eventually the French fled with losses five or six times those of the allies.*
- *At Oudenaarde on 11 July 1708, Marlborough was forced into battle before his Austrian allies could reinforce him. However, he quickly took advantage of confusion among the French commanders, and enveloped the French army, inflicting 18,000 casualties at the cost of only 7,000.*

CHARLES XII OF SWEDEN

1682–1718

CHARLES XII OF SWEDEN spent his entire adult life fighting the Great Northern War of 1700 to 1721. His leadership on the battlefield and his modernization of the army made Sweden a considerable military force in the early eighteenth century.

▶ ABSOLUTE MONARCH

Born the eldest son of Charles XI in Stockholm on 17 June 1682, he lost his mother when he was eleven. He was just fifteen in 1697 when his father died, leaving him absolute monarch of Sweden. His father's training had fitted him well for the job. He was an excellent horseman, but inclined to take risks. He was also well trained in the military arts and his father had left him a well-trained army.

In April 1700, a coalition between Denmark, Saxony, Poland and Russia formed. Charles

The lasting result of the Northern War was the end of Sweden as a great power

ordered an attack on Zealand in August and forced Denmark out of the war. He then took personal command of the army and beat the Russians at Narva. Next he attacked Poland. Victories at Poltosk in 1703 and Fronstadt in 1706 allowed him to depose Augustus II, king of Poland and elector of Saxony, and put his own king on the throne. Then he marched into Saxony.

Meanwhile, Peter the Great had found time to rebuild his army, and had been taking back Sweden's provinces in the eastern Baltic piecemeal. Charles launched attacks from his Polish bases in 1707 but, in 1708, made the mistake of invading Russia. He scored an initial success with a victory at the Battle of Holowczyn on 4 July 1708. The Russians then retreated, instigating a scorched earth policy. Charles then tried to link up with the Cossacks to the south, but Peter beat the Cossacks in October 1708. He also destroyed the Swedish supply train at Lesnaya on 9 October. Charles retreated into the Ukraine for the winter, losing 20,000 men in the process.

▸ INTO DISASTER

The following spring he was faced with the choice of withdrawing to Poland or engaging a more powerful Russian force. He attacked the fortified Russian camp at Poltava on 28 June, even though he had been shot through the foot before the battle. After eighteen hours fighting, the Swedes were utterly defeated: only Charles

and 1,500 men escaped the slaughter. The bulk of his men surrendered three days later, while Charles and a small escort fled south to Turkish-held territory.

At Charles's urging, the Turks declared war on Russia – four times – but the support they were expecting from Sweden never turned up. Eventually the Turks got sick of their uninvited guest and besieged him in his camp at Bender in Moldavia, with the aim of handing him over to Augustus, who was now restored in Poland.

In 1714, he escaped and rode in disguise through Hungary and Germany back to Swedish Pomerania. There he began a rearguard action, while trying to hatch alliances with France and the Jacobites, who were rebelling in Britain once again, this time against George I, elector of Hanover.

Returning home to Sweden for the first time in ten years, he began rebuilding his army. He planned to begin a new offensive with an invasion of Danish Norway. In the autumn of 1718, his 60,000-man army began besieging Fredrikshald – now Halden. During the siege he was fatally shot in the head, sparking rumours that he was shot by one of his own men.

He was succeeded by his sister Eleonora, who began peace talks. The resulting Treaty of Nystad of 1721 guaranteed Sweden's autonomy, but stripped it of its Baltic possessions, leaving Russia the major power in the region.

FIGHTING THE NORTHERN WAR

- At the age of 18, Charles landed in Livonia in October 1700 and besieged the Russians at Narva. On 20 November, he advanced his force of just 10,000 in a blizzard, taking Peter the Great and his army of 70,000 completely by surprise. Defeating them, he forced the Russians out of the Swedish trans-Baltic provinces.

- In just three years, Charles had taken Poland and Saxony, defeating their armies and occupying their capitals. His seemingly invincible army had also swept his other enemies out of the Baltic region. Russia wanted to make peace: instead Charles attacked.

JOHN CAMPBELL, DUKE OF ARGYLL

1678–1743

CHRONOLOGY

1678 Born 10 October in Petersham, Surrey.

1694 Given command of a regiment of foot.

1702 Distinguishes himself at the siege of Kaiserswerth.

1703 Succeeds his father as Duke of Argyll.

1705 Promotes union with England in Scottish parliament.

1706 Joins Marlborough's second campaign in War of Spanish Succession.

1708 Victorious Battle of Oudenarde.

1709 Distinguishes himself at Battle of Malplaquet.

1711 Acts as commander-in-chief in Spain.

1715 Serves as commander-in-chief during the Jacobite rebellion.

1740 Dismissed from office.

1743 Dies 4 October in Petersham.

JOHN CAMPBELL DISTINGUISHED himself on the battlefield during the War of the Spanish Succession and as commander-in-chief during the Jacobite rebellion of 1715.

Born on 10 October 1678 in Petersham, Surrey, he was the son of the first Duke of Argyll. In 1694, his father introduced him at the court of King William, who gave him command of a regiment of foot. In 1702, during the **Duke of Marlborough's** first campaign in the War of the Spanish Succession, he distinguished himself at the siege of Kaiserswerth, near Düsseldorf.

▸ **POLITICAL INFLUENCE**

The following year, he succeeded his father as Duke of Argyll and became a privy councillor. In 1705, nominated Lord High Commissioner to the Scottish parliament, he gave an opening speech commending the Protestant succession and union

'I cannot have a worse opinion of anybody than of the Duke of Argyll' JOHN CHURCHILL, DUKE OF MARLBOROUGH

with England. This earned him a peerage and he became Earl of Greenwich and Baron of Chatham.

He became a brigadier-general under Marlborough in 1706, and fought with distinction in the Battle of Ramillies, commanded in the trenches in Ostende until their surrender and took Menin. At Oudenarde on 11 July 1708, the battalions under his command were the first to engage the enemy, and held their ground against superior numbers, a key factor in the successful outcome of the battle.

Campbell also took part in the siege of Lille in the same year, which ended with the surrender of the city on 8 December, and took Ghent on 3 January 1709. Promoted lieutenant-general, he took Tournay on 10 July and distinguished himself again at the Battle of Malplaquet on 11 September, despite a falling-out with the Duke of Marlborough.

Installed as a knight of the garter in 1710, he took command of the English forces in Spain the following year, but could do little except hold his own until the Peace of Utrecht ended the war. Then he was appointed commander-in-chief in Scotland and governor of Edinburgh castle.

By now he was calling for the dissolution of the Union, a turnaround satirized by his old friend Jonathan Swift, with whom he now fell out. However, it fell to Campbell to crush the Jacobite rebellion of 1715, which followed the succession of George I.

▶ THE JACOBITE UPRISING

That summer, the Earl of Mar raised the Jacobite clans and the northeast for James Stuart, the Old Pretender. He advanced to Perth, then marched south to force a passage at Stirling. At the Battle of Sheriffmuir on 13 November 1709, Campbell managed to halt his advance with a much smaller force. Hopes of a southern rising faded and James arrived from the Continent too late to help. Campbell was made Duke of Greenwich in honour of this action.

Campbell remained in Scottish politics, defending the interests of Scotland against the English, until he was forced from office in 1740, after a speech attacking the government. Nevertheless, when he died on 4 October 1743, a marble memorial was erected in his name in Westminster Abbey.

A DIFFERENCE OF OPINION

- At the Battle of Malplaquet on 11 September 1709, Campbell played a critical role by dislodging the enemy from the nearby Sart woods. During the engagement several musket balls passed through his coat, hat and periwig. This won him the admiration of his troops, whose perils and hardships he shared. But it seems to have begun a feud with Marlborough, who he regarded as a rival. He opposed Marlborough's request to be made captain-general for life and accused him of prolonging the war, causing Marlborough to write, 'I cannot have a worse opinion of anybody than of the Duke of Argyll.'
- At the Battle of Sheriffmuir on the grey morning of 13 November 1709, Argyll's 4,000 men faced an army of 12,000 insurgents. His left fled, but the center and right repulsed the Highlanders' first onslaught, then his cavalry chased them from the field. Their leader, the Earl of Mar was one of those who fled. So while the battle was technically a draw, the Jacobite force was divided. Argyll took the field and Mar sued for peace.

CHARLES STUART, THE YOUNG PRETENDER

1720–1788

CHRONOLOGY

1720 Born 31 December in Rome.
1744 Joins abortive French invasion of England.
1745 Arrives in Scotland and raises Highland revolt; takes Edinburgh; victorious at Battle of Prestonpans; advances into England.
1746 Defeated at Culloden; flees to France.
1766 On death of his father, styles himself Charles III.
1788 Dies 31 January in Rome.

C HARLES STUART WAS PRETENDER to the throne of England and Scotland. He led the 1745 uprising in Scotland and invaded England.

Born in Rome on 31 December 1720, Charles Stuart was the eldest son of James Stuart – the Old Pretender – and grandson of the James II deposed by **William of Orange** in the Glorious Revolution. Charles's father had made several attempts to become king of Britain.

▶ AN ABORTIVE INVASION

As a Catholic nation, France backed the Stuart claim to the English throne and in 1743, during the War of the Austrian Succession, hostilities broke out between England and France. France tried to invade England and Charles Stuart joined the invasion fleet, but it was destroyed by a storm in 1744.

But the French King Louis XV did not give up. He told James Stuart that if he invaded England he would supply him with arms and ammunition. By then James was fifty-seven, and felt he was too old to become involved in another military campaign. But at twenty-five, Charles Stuart was keen to have a go and landed on the west coast of Scotland with a handful of men in July 1745.

In the Scottish Highlands, disaffected clansmen rallied to Charles Stuart, who had been nicknamed Bonnie Prince Charlie. With an army of over 2,000 Catholics, he marched on Edinburgh, where his first move was to capture Holyrood, the ancient palace of Scottish kings. The English army arrived soon afterwards but Charles won an easy victory at nearby Prestonpans, and with 5,000 men, he marched into England, reaching Derby by December.

Charles had hoped that English Catholics would rally to his flag, but he found that the crowds in the towns he passed through showed great hostility. This mattered little to Charles as

'For King James and no Union with England'

Louis XV had promised that 12,000 French soldiers would invade England and come to his aid. But Louis XV did not keep his promise. Charles was still keen to march on London at the head of his victorious army, but his officers got cold feet at the prospect of facing the 30,000 English troops that were now massing. They argued that without the support of the French or the populace they would certainly be beaten. Reluctantly, Charles returned to Scotland.

▶ **DEFEAT AND FLIGHT**

Another English army, this time led by the **Duke of Cumberland**, followed Charles back into Scotland. Completely outnumbered, Charles's army were chased into the Scottish Highlands, where he won a minor victory at Falkirk in January 1746. Then in April 1746, Charles Stuart decided to turn and fight a decisive battle with the English army. They met at Culloden Moor on 16 April. Cumberland's army devastated the Jacobites and Charles fled the field.

For the next five months, he was pursued through the Highlands with a reward of £30,000 on his head, but Charles still had many loyal supporters who were willing to hide him.

He took refuge in the Hebrides, where he met Flora Macdonald who was visiting some friends. She let him join her party disguised as Betty Burke, an Irish spinning maid, and got permission from the English to sail to Skye. At Skye, Flora and Charles parted when he escaped by ship to France.

When the English learned of her role in his escape, she was imprisoned in the Tower of London but was pardoned the following year.

Charles Stuart settled in Avignon. But when James Stuart died in 1766, Pope Clement XIII, keen to improve relations with Britain, refused to recognize Charles Stuart as king. Styling himself Charles III, he roamed the Continent, alienating any remaining support with his drunken, debauched behaviour. Charles Stuart married Princess Louise of Stolberg in 1772, but produced no heirs. When he died in 1788 the Stuart claim to the throne came to an end.

THE BATTLE OF PRESTONPANS

- *Hanoverian General Cope landed at Dunbar on 17 September 1745 with 2,500 men. He decided to make a stand at Prestonpans in a defensive position which was thought to be ideal, with two stone walls on their right, a bog on their left, the sea behind and a deep moat-like ditch in front. Along with his well-armed men, he had artillery. The Jacobites had none. But when the battle started, the artillery only seemed to enrage the Highlanders and Cope's defensive position proved to be merely a trap. The Jacobites attacked just after dawn. In the fifteen minutes the battle lasted, Cope lost between 300 and 500 killed. Some 1,400 were taken prisoner, of which 900 were wounded. Between 175 and 200 escaped with Cope at*

their head. Only about 40 Jacobites were killed and 75 wounded. They had also taken enough money and weapons for their invasion of England.

- *The Battle of Falkirk of 17 January 1746 took place in foul weather. Some 8,000 Hanoverians found themselves facing an equal number of Jacobites with the wind and lashing rain in their faces. The artillery was mired in the mud and the cavalry had to charge up hill. They broke off after twenty minutes. In that time, 420 Hanoverians had been killed, many more wounded and taken prisoners. The Jacobites lost 50, with between 60 and 80 wounded. But a large English force was now on its way and Charles fled northwards.*

WILLIAM AUGUSTUS, DUKE OF CUMBERLAND

1721–1765

CHRONOLOGY — 1721 Born William Augustus on 15 April in London • 1726 Created Duke of Cumberland • 1745 Becomes commander of the allied forces in the War of Austrian Succession; defeated at the Battle of Fontenoy; Jacobite rising begins • 1746 Defeats Charles Stuart at Culloden • 1747 Defeated at Battle of Lauffeld and Battle of Hastenbeck • 1765 Dies 31 October in London

THE DUKE OF CUMBERLAND defeated Charles Stuart, the Young Pretender, at the Battle of Culloden and brutally suppressed the 1745 Jacobite uprising, earning himself the nickname 'Butcher Cumberland'.

Born William Augustus, the third son of George II, in London on 15 April 1721, he was created the Duke of Cumberland in 1726. He became a soldier and commanded the British, Hanoverian, Austrian and Dutch forces at the Battle of Fontenoy on 11 May 1745, where they were resoundingly defeated by the French under Marshal Maurice de Saxe. Later that year he was

'No quarter'

recalled to England to oppose the invasion of the Jacobite forces under Charles Edward **Stuart**, grandson of the deposed King James II. Stuart had already routed a superior force at Prestonpans with the blood-curdling 'Highland charge' which the Scots had been using since Bannockburn.

▶ **BUTCHERY AT CULLODEN**

By the time Cumberland caught up with Charles Stuart at Culloden in April 1746, he had developed a new strategy to counter the highland charge. His men stood their ground and cut down the Highlanders with disciplined volleys and grapeshot. Some 1,000 Scotsmen were killed.

After the battle when asked for orders, Cumberland wrote 'No quarter' on the back of a playing card. It was the nine of diamonds – still known as the 'curse of Scotland' north of the border. As a result of this action he was given the epithet 'Butcher': a flower was also named after him to commemorate his success against the Scots at Culloden. In England it is known as the Sweet William but in Scotland it is known as the Stinking Billy.

▶ **THE KING'S REVENGE**

After their victory the English were determined to make sure the Highland clans did not rebel again and George II gave instructions that the Scots should be punished for supporting Charles. The Duke of Cumberland remained in Scotland for three months, rounding up some 3,500 men and executing about 120. The land of those he executed was given to Scotsmen who had remained loyal. Meanwhile Cumberland's soldiers killed anyone they thought retained Jacobite sympathies. The English army also destroyed the Highlanders' homes and took away their cattle. As a result some 40,000 Highlanders emigrated to America. Laws were also passed that made it illegal for Highlanders to carry weapons, wear tartan or play the bagpipes.

The Duke of Cumberland returned to the Continent to lose the Battle of Langfeld to Saxe in July 1747. During the Seven Years' War (1756–63) that followed, he was beaten by the French again at the Battle of Hastenbeck in Hanover in July 1757. Under the resulting peace treaty, the Convention of Klosterzeven, which Cumberland signed in September 1757, he promised to evacuate Hanover, George II's father's birthplace and treasured possession. George sacked Cumberland and tore up the agreement.

Cumberland became ill in the summer of 1765 and died from a brain clot on 31 October.

MASSACRE AT CULLODEN

- At Culloden, the Duke of Cumberland put the infantry in three ranks. The front rank were ordered not to fire until the Highlanders were only twelve yards away. While the front rank reloaded, the second rank fired their guns. By the time the third rank had fired their guns, the first rank were ready to fire again. This system had first been used by Gustavus II a hundred years before. But Cumberland's infantry now used firelocks which were faster to reload than the old matchlocks. The new guns were also fitted with bayonets, so that even if some of the enemy were able to reach the English front lines they were able to defend themselves against the broadswords of the Highlanders. At Culloden, for once the English did not run away when the Highlanders charged. Their disciplined volleys brought the Highlanders down before they reached the English lines. Unable to get close enough to use their broadswords, some Highlanders even resorted to throwing stones.

LORD HORATIO NELSON

1758–1805

His heroic status was enhanced by his ability
to inspire and gain the respect of his men, not
least due to his insistence on honouring their
role in his victories. But Nelson was also a complex man, combining a buccaneer's spirit with an
almost fanatical sense of his duty to his
country and to his King.

This overriding element of Nelson's character
is demonstrated in one of his most famous utter-
ances, at the hoisting of the signal flag at
Trafalgar, when he flew the signal: 'England
expects every man will do his duty'.
Nelson was born in Burnham Thorpe, in Norfolk,
on 29 September 1758. His father combined
farming with being the local rector. But the
young Horatio was not interested in working the
land. Instead, he enlisted in the Royal Navy,
aged just twelve, a common age for 'young
gentlemen' to join the Navy at the time. With
the help of his uncle, Captain Maurice Suckling,
he developed experience of several ships and
studied navigation.

Nelson's career rise was swift, serving on
board the vessel *Carcass* at the age of fifteen,
on expedition to the Arctic Sea. At eighteen he

HORATIO NELSON IS WIDELY
regarded as Britain's greatest ever
naval commander. It was his victory
over the French and Spanish at
Trafalgar in 1805, when the Royal Navy defeated both enemy fleets, that established a naval
supremacy for the British that would last
throughout the following century.

'No captain can do very wrong if he places his ship alongside that of the enemy.'

became a lieutenant and before his twenty-first birthday was given command of the frigate *Hinchinbrook*. Much of Nelson's early career was spent in the seas off Canada and around the West Indies. In 1794, Nelson took command of the 28-gun *Boreas*, and was assigned to enforce the Navigation Act in the vicinity of Antigua. This followed the American Revolution and Nelson was commanded to enforce a trading ban between the now-foreign American traders and British colonies in the Caribbean Sea.

During this period he met Fanny Nesbit, a doctor's widow and later married her, on 11 March 1787, at the end of his tour of duty in the Caribbean. He was put on the Navy's retired list until war broke out with France in 1793.

▶ WAR WITH FRANCE

Nelson spent the following seven years fighting the French. He was first assigned to the Mediterranean, where he was based in the Kingdom of Naples.

In 1794 he was shot in the face during an operation at Calvi on Corsica, and lost the sight of his right eye. His remaining eye suffered from the extra burden and he was slowly going blind in the years leading up to his death.

He became a Rear Admiral in 1797 and following intense fighting in the Canary Islands he lost his right arm. After the Battle of the Nile, Nelson went to Naples to recuperate. It was here that he met Lady Emma Hamilton, wife of the British ambassador, who would become his consort until his death.

▶ THE 'NELSON BRIDGE'

During the Battle of the Nile in 1797, Nelson's *Captain* became so much mauled as to be incapable of further service. Rather than surrender the ship, Nelson laid the *Captain* aboard the starboard quarter of the *San Nicolas* and led a boarding party on to the ship. Meanwhile, the *San Josef* had entangled itself aloft with the *San Nicolas* which was now on fire. Seven of the boarding party were killed and several wounded, provoking Nelson into determined action. More men were ordered aboard the *San Nicolas* and, to the cry of 'Westminster Abbey or glorious victory!' charged on to the *San Josef* using the *San Nicolas* as a stepping stone. Nelson took both ships, and this move was afterwards called 'Nelson's Patent Bridge for boarding First rates'. Successive naval victories saw Nelson promoted to commander-in-chief of the British fleet in 1803. On board his flagship HMS *Victory*, a first-rate ship of the line of 104 guns, he blockaded the French fleet, commanded by Villeneuve, for two years, before finally confronting and destroying it – despite its having joined with the Spanish – off Cape Trafalgar, on the Spanish coast, on 21 October 1805. During the battle he was shot by a French sniper, and died shortly afterwards, although not before he had heard the news of the British victory.

NELSON'S LEGACY

Nelson's great legacy was undoubtedly his role in securing supremacy for the British on the high seas. His defeat of the French and Spanish fleets allowed British trade to flourish around the world, laying the foundations for Britain's emergence as an economic superpower.

Nelson will also be remembered as a popular hero of the eighteenth and nineteenth centuries. He was regarded as a model of duty and devotion to one's country and it is difficult to overstate the huge popular reverence in which he was held. The news of his death at Trafalgar produced an outpouring of grief perhaps unequalled by anything else in British history, and his funeral at St Paul's Cathedral in London was a vast state occasion.

SIR JOHN MOORE

1761–1809

CHRONOLOGY 1761 Born 13 November in Glasgow • 1776 Commissioned in the 51st Foot • 1794–1795 Fights in Corsica; commands brigade • 1798 Serves in West Indies and Ireland • 1799 Wounded at Battle of Alkmaar, Holland • 1800 Wounded at Alexandria; commands division • 1808 Serves in Spain; leads the retreat to Corunna • 1809 Defeats French at Corunna; dies in battle 16 January

S IR JOHN MOORE led the famous retreat to Corunna, where he defeated the French. Although he died within a year of the start of the Peninsular War,

the **Duke of Wellington** said of him, 'We would not have won, I think, without him.'

Born in Glasgow on 13 November 1761, the son of a doctor, he became the stepson of the

'We would not have won, I think, without him'

DUKE OF WELLINGTON ON SIR JOHN MOORE, 1809

Duke of Argyll. Commissioned in the 51st Foot in 1776, he saw service in the American Revolutionary War from 1779 to 1783. He served as a Member of Parliament from 1784 to 1790. Taking command of the 51st Foot in 1790, he saw action against the fledgling French Republic three years later. From 1794 to 1795 he fought in Corsica, where he had temporary command of a brigade. He then went to the West Indies and saw action in the Irish rebellion of 1798.

Wounded at the Battle of Alkmaar in 1799 during the Anglo-Russian invasion of Holland, he was then sent to Egypt to command a division under Sir Ralph Abercromby. Wounded again at Alexandria the following year, he returned to England in 1803 and was knighted in 1804.

▶ NEW TACTICS

When Napoleon gathered his forces on the French coast ready to invade England, Moore was sent to Kent to command a brigade. At Shorecliffe, he drilled his men in skirmishing tactics, taught them the use of cover and encouraged individual initiative. His disciplinary system, which depended on example and encouragement rather than the lash, became the basis for training in the British army and he is now recognized as the patron saint of the Royal Green Jackets and the other light infantry regiments.

▶ RETREAT INTO VICTORY

In 1808, he was sent to support the Swedes and narrowly escaped being imprisoned by the mad Swedish king. He was then given his first independent command as head of the British expeditionary forces in the Iberian Peninsular. The French having been expelled from Portugal in October 1808, Moore moved into northern Spain with 27,000 men to support the Spanish forces, only to discover they had already been beaten. Rather than withdraw into Portugal, he moved north from Salamanca to attack Marshal Nicolas Soult's French corps which was 100 miles from Madrid and unaware of Moore's presence. Learning that Napoleon had cut off his line of retreat, he withdrew to Corunna, where the Royal Navy could evacuate his men. But outside Corunna, he turned and defeated Soult. Dying of his wounds after the French had been repulsed, he said, 'I hope my country will do me justice.'

Few other than Wellington, who succeeded him as commander in the Iberian Peninsular, recognized his contribution. Wellington made good use of his 'Shorncliffe boys' throughout the rest of war. He also adopted Moore's much criticized defensive style in battle, which led to the defeat of Napoleon in the Peninsular and at Waterloo.

THE RETREAT FROM CORUNNA

- In campaigns in the West Indies and Ireland, Moore developed new infantry tactics with which his name has become associated. He deployed light infantry in loose skirmishing order ahead of close formations of line infantry.
- On 22 December 1808, Moore learnt that Marshall Soult and Napoleon himself were advancing on him. He led his men on a forced march of 250 miles in winter over the snow-clad mountains of northwest Spain

towards Corunna, deploying his light troops to cover his retreat. His army was ragged and exhausted when he reached Corunna, but he turned and took Soult on, defeating him in a defensive battle. Moore was widely criticized for his retreat, but he turned it into a strategic victory which postponed the French conquest of Spain for a year. This kept the flames of Spanish resistance burning in the darkest period of the Peninsular War, and saw that Napoleon never returned to Spain.

ARTHUR WELLESLEY, DUKE OF WELLINGTON

1769–1852

CHRONOLOGY

1769 Born 1 May in Dublin.

1787 Commissioned in 73rd Foot.

1794 Rises to command of 33rd Foot.

1794–95 Sees first action in Flanders.

1799 Defeats Sultan of Mysore.

1803 Victorious at Assaye.

1808–14 Series of victories in Peninsular War.

1815 Defeats Napoleon at Battle of Waterloo.

1828–30 Prime Minister.

1852 Dies 14 September Walmer Castle in Kent.

EVEN BEFORE HE DEFEATED **Napoleon** at the Battle of Waterloo, the 'Iron Duke' was hailed as the 'conqueror of the conqueror of Europe' for his series of victories against the Napoleonic forces in the Peninsular War. He established himself as the foremost military leader of his time for his mastery of co-ordinated manoeuvres and his ability to exploit the terrain.

▶ DISSOLUTE BEGINNINGS

Born Arthur Wellesley on 1 May 1769 in Dublin, he was the fifth son of an impoverished Anglo-Irish peer. Educated at Eton and the French military academy in Angers, he made little impression on his tutors and at the age of sixteen he bought himself a commission in the 73rd Regiment of Foot. At twenty-five, he purchased

another rank, this time the command of the 33rd Foot. Until 1794, he saw no action, spending his time socializing and getting involved in politics. His unit was then sent on an ill-fated campaign against Revolutionary France in the Netherlands. He commanded the rear guard while the main force withdrew and witnessed first hand how the incompetence of his superiors led to a needless loss of life.

In 1796, he was posted to India, where he gave up gambling and heavy drinking, earning himself a reputation for self-discipline. His career received a boost when his eldest brother Richard became viceroy and in 1799 he defeated the Sultan of Mysore, who was allied to the French, at Seringapatam. Promoted major-general, his force of 7,000 defeated Mahrattas' army of 40,000 at Assaye. Napoleon was not impressed, later dismissing Wellington as a 'Sepoy general'.

In 1805, he returned to England to be knighted. In 1807, he led an expedition to Denmark, winning the conflict's only major battle at Kioge on 29 August. The following year he embarked for Portugal with 17,000 men to face Napoleon's forces there. There followed a series of victories: at Roliça and Vimiero in 1808, at Oporto and Talavera in 1809, at Bussaco in 1810, at Salamanca in 1812 and at Vitoria in 1813.

'Nothing except a battle lost can be half as melancholy as a battle won'

Wellington preferred to be on the defensive. While he was supplied by the Royal Navy, he would leave scorched earth behind him to starve and exhaust the enemy. He would withdraw to heavily fortified defensive positions where the terrain would protect his troops from artillery fire, while skirmishers would break up enemy assaults or direct them on to strongly defended positions. Superior fire power, and well-trained, highly-motivated troops then assured victory.

He also showed flair in the attack and used his army as a mobile force that could strike devastating blows against the French who overstretched themselves by trying to hold vast tracts of land against Spanish guerrillas. Although he dismissed his men as 'the scum of the earth', they admired him because he kept them well fed, was sparing with their lives and showed personal bravery on the battlefield. He turned the British army from a rabble led by amateurs into a professional fighting force.

▶ SAVING THE WORLD

Now a marquis and a field marshal, Wellington drove the French out of the Iberian Peninsula and defeated them once again at Toulouse in 1814. He was about to pursue the survivors when he heard of Napoleon's abdication. With Napoleon now in exile on Elba, the newly created duke attended the Congress of Vienna in 1815. But before the delegates could complete their peacemaking, news came that Napoleon had escaped and was marching on Paris again. The Russian Czar, Alexander I, turned to Wellington and said, 'It is for you to save the world again.'

With the assistance of the Prussian forces under Field Marshal Gebhard Leberecht von Blücher, Wellington defeated Napoleon at Waterloo. Returning to England, he entered parliament, joined the cabinet and rose to become prime minister from 1828 to 1830, although he was unpopular. After holding other senior political positions, he became commander-in-chief of the army in 1842. He retired from public life in 1846 and died at Walmer Castle in Kent on 14 September 1852 at the age of eighty-three. Given a state funeral, Wellington is buried in St Paul's Cathedral.

THE BATTLE OF WATERLOO

- *After Wellington's victory at Talavera in 1809, Napoleon sent another army under Marshal Michel Ney which was driven back when it met Wellington's forces lined out along the top of a steep ridge at Bussaco in 1810. Wellington then fell back into Portugal behind the celebrated fortifications of the Lines of Torres Vedras. For the next two years his victories, though numerous, were inconclusive. However in 1811–12 Napoleon directed his full force against Russia. His peninsular armies, which once numbered more than 200,000, were not reinforced and 30,000 men were withdrawn for the Grand Army's march eastwards. By 1814, Wellington was marching into France.*
- *At Waterloo (1815), Wellington, as usual,* *selected the most defensible terrain – the only high ground in the vicinity. His army was outnumbered by 72,000 to 68,000. However, Napoleon made a major blunder in delaying the attack from early morning to midday, to allow the field to dry. This gave time for the Prussians under Blücher to reach the battlefield. Although the British repelled four attacks, it is possible that the center would have given, if Napoleon had not been preoccupied holding his eastern flank against the Prussians. The flank secured, he sent the élite Imperial Guard against the British. But Wellington had had time to re-organize his forces. The Imperial Guard were cut down and an allied advance routed the French.*

NAPOLEON BONAPARTE

1769–1821

N APOLEON WAS A MAN of towering ambition. His personal courage and military genius brought him from obscurity to mastery of the Continent in just fourteen years. However, in his efforts to unite Europe, he managed to unite it against him.

Born Napoleone Buonaparte on 15 August 1769 to a family of minor Tuscan nobility in Corsica, shortly after it had been ceded by the Genoese to France, he went to the mainland to be educated in French military schools. In support of the French Revolution, his artillery unit was sent to Toulon which had been taken by the British. They were expelled in 1793. His heroism in this action brought him to national prominence and, when Corsica declared its independence, he took the French spelling of his name.

▸ EARLY PROMISE

Napoleon was in Paris in 1795, when a column of royalists marched on the National Convention. He dispersed them with the notorious 'whiff of grapeshot' – a single artillery volley – and saved the republic. As a reward, he was given command of the French army of Italy. His dynamism inspired his war-weary men to a series of victories over the Piedmontese and Austrians at Lodi, Castiglione, Arcola and Rivoli.

Although in command of Italy and Austria, Napoleon realized that France was too weak to mount a cross-Channel invasion of Britain.

Instead he invaded Egypt, with the aim of disrupting Britain's trade with India, and defeated the Mamelukes at the Battle of Pyramids in July 1798. However on 1 August, the French fleet was destroyed by **Nelson** in the Battle of the Nile. Napoleon then tried to invade Syria, but failed to take Acre. He abandoned his army and headed back to France. Although the French army in Italy was defeated in spring 1799, he was still popular and on 9 November he staged a coup, making himself first consul. After narrowly defeating the Austrians at the Battle of Marengo in 1800, he revised the French Constitution and declared himself 'consul for life'. He instituted a law known as the Napoleonic Code, crowning himself Emperor in 1804.

'Power is my mistress'

After a brief period of peace, Britain resumed its war against Napoleon, sinking his fleet in the Battle of Trafalgar in 1805. But Napoleon knew that the war had to be won on land. In a brilliant campaign to the east he swept through Germany and Poland. At the Treaty of Tilsit, he divided Europe with the Russian Czar Alexander II, instituting the Continental System which sought to ruin Britain by closing the Continent's ports to British shipping. However, in 1807 he put his brother on the throne of Spain and seized Portugal, Britain's ally, sparking the Peninsular War. This dragged on for six years and ended with Wellington driving the French out of Spain.

In the meantime, eager for an heir, Napoleon divorced his Creole wife Josephine, who was past child-bearing age, and married Marie Louise, the daughter of the Austrian emperor. Fearing France's closer ties with Austria, the Czar looked to Britain. In order to enforce the Continental System, Napoleon invaded Russia in June 1812. He defeated the Russian army at the Battle of Borodino in September, and marched into Moscow, only to find it deserted. With the winter drawing on, he had no alternative but to retreat. As he did so, the weather closed in, destroying his Grand Army.

▶ THE HUNDRED DAYS

Then all Europe united against Napoleon. He was defeated at the Battle of Leipzig in October 1813. With **Wellington** advancing over the Pyrenees, Napoleon was forced to abdicate in 1814 and was exiled to the Isle of Elba. On 1 March 1815, he escaped and returned to France. The French army was sent to capture him, but instead rallied to his side. They marched on Paris, but one hundred days later he was defeated by Wellington and Blücher at the Battle of Waterloo. Exiled to St Helena, he spent the rest of his life polishing his image for posterity. On 5 May 1821, aged fifty-one, he died. His body was returned to France in 1840, where it lies in a magnificent tomb in Les Invalides in Paris.

A LEGACY OF VICTORY

- *In August 1793, the Royal Navy seized the port of Toulon, which was then besieged by French Revolutionary forces. Although he had sustained a bayonet wound himself, Napoleon took command when his commander was put out of action. His concentrated fire on the British fleet drove them out of the harbor. He was hailed as a hero and promoted to brigadier-general.*
- *At the Battle of Lodi (1796), Napoleon personally led the bayonet charge across a bridge against the Austrian rearguard, earning himself the affectionate nickname 'the Little Corporal'.*
- *At the Battle of Marengo (1800), Napoleon's forces were outnumbered. Pushed back four miles, they seemed beaten. In the nick of time, reinforcements arrived, giving him victory.*
- *At the Battle of Austerlitz (1805), 68,000*

Napoleonic troops defeated 90,000 Austrians and Russians when Marshal Nicolas Soult broke through the center, splitting the two allied armies.
- *At the Battle of Borodino (1812), Napoleon refused to commit the 20,000-man Imperial Guard and 10,000 other fresh troops, leaving the Russian army strong enough to harass him on the retreat from Moscow that winter.*
- *According to the victorious Duke of Wellington, the Battle of Waterloo (1815) was 'the nearest run thing you ever saw in your life'. It seems likely that Napoleon would have won if he had not delayed his attack from early morning until noon to allow the field to dry sufficiently for his cavalry to charge. This gave the Prussian forces under Field Marshal Gebhard Leberecht von Blücher the time they needed to reach the battlefield.*

MICHEL NEY

1769–1815

MICHEL NEY WAS the ablest of Napoleon's commanders. His personal courage inspired those he led and Napoleon called him 'the bravest of the brave'.

Born the son of a cooper in Saarlouis, Alsace, on 10 January 1769, he ran away to enlist in the 5th Hussars at the age of nineteen. He saw

'The bravest of the brave'

NAPOLEON ON NEY

action in the Revolutionary Wars and rose rapidly through the ranks. As general of a division he played a significant role in the Army of the Rhine's victory at Hohenlinden in 1800.

▶ A FIERY TEMPER

Known to his men at *la rougeaud* ('the redhead') – not just for the colour of his hair, but for his temper – he led an invasion of Switzerland in 1802. And when Napoleon crowned himself emperor in 1804, Ney was one of the eighteen generals he made Marshals of the Empire.

Ney campaigned with Napoleon for the first time in 1805, winning his first victory at Elchingen on 14 October. He contributed to the defeat of the Prussians at Jena in 1806 and the Russians at Eylau and Friedland in 1807. In 1808, he went to fight in Spain and Portugal. Again he exhibited personal bravery there, but his temper saw him relieved of his command for insubordination in 1811.

He was recalled to Napoleon's command for the invasion of Russia. After the Battle of Borodino, Napoleon created him Prince de la Moskowa. Wounded at Smolensk, he led the rearguard during the retreat from Moscow.

He continued to fight for Napoleon during the campaign in Germany in 1813, where he was wounded twice more, as the allies forced them back into France. But when Paris fell in 1814, Ney acted as spokesman for the other marshals and insisted that Napoleon abdicate.

▶ SWITCHING SIDES

Ney pledged allegiance to Louis XVIII, the restored Bourbon monarch, and was allowed to keep his titles. He served as commander of VI Military district and governor of Besançon. When Napoleon returned to France from exile in Elba on 1 March 1815, Ney promised the king to bring Napoleon to Paris in a cage. But he found that the Bourbons were not popular in his military districts and when his soldiers cheered Napoleon, Ney changed sides and rejoined the Emperor.

At Quartre Bras on 15 June 1815, Ney failed to prevent Wellington from consolidating his forces. At Waterloo, his reckless and repeated charges on the British infantry squares destroyed the cavalry and contributed to Napoleon's defeat. During a last charge, he shouted, 'Come and see how a marshal of France can die!'

He survived the battle with a blackened face and a broken sword. Arrested, he was tried for treason and died by firing squad in the Luxembourg Gardens on 6 December 1815.

A BRAVE COMMANDER

- *At Elchingen on 14 October, Ney led his VI Corps against 9,000 Austrians trying to escape Napoleon's encirclement at Ulm. He personally led the charge across a key bridge, capturing it, and then assaulted the town itself. Some 32,000 Austrians surrendered. Two months later Napoleon defeated the Russo-Austrian armies at Austerlitz and Ney was created Duke of Elchingen.*

- *Ney started the retreat from Moscow with 10,000 men. He fought numerous delaying actions, exposing himself to artillery fire and Cossack attacks. By the time he reached the Kovono Bridge leading out of Russia on 13 December 1812, he had only a few hundred men left. Ney picked up a musket and fought in the front line like a common soldier. When everyone was across, Ney followed – the last French soldier to leave Russian soil.*

LORD HOWARD OF EFFINGHAM

1536–1624

Lord Howard's flagship, the *Ark Royal*, originally named the *Ark Raleigh*.

CHRONOLOGY 1536 Born • 1569 Helps suppress rebellion of Catholic lords • 1573 Becomes Lord Howard of Effingham • 1585 Becomes Lord High Admiral • 1588 Commands English fleet against Spanish Armada • 1596 Commands attack on Cadiz • 1597 Made Earl of Nottingham • 1599 Made Lord Lieutenant-General of England • 1601 Helps put down Essex's uprising • 1624 Dies 14 December near Croydon, Surrey.

LORD HOWARD OF EFFINGHAM was the lord high admiral commanding John Hawkins and Sir Francis **Drake** who saw off the Spanish Armada in 1588.

Born Charles Howard, he was the eldest son of William, the first baron of Effingham. He is said to have served at sea under his father during the reign of Queen Mary. When Elizabeth I – his cousin – came to the throne, he immediately took a prominent place in court, serving as ambassador to France in 1559.

In 1562, he represented Surrey in Parliament

and in 1569 he was General of the Horse under the Earl of Warwick, who put down the rebellion of the Catholic lords of the north. The following year he commanded a squadron of ships guarding the Queen of Spain when she sailed down the Channel from Flanders, though his mission may have had a more warlike purpose. He was knighted in 1572 and became Lord Howard of Effingham on his father's death in 1573.

▶ LORD HIGH ADMIRAL

In 1585, he became Lord High Admiral. The fol-

'lieutenant-general and commander-in-chief of the navy and army prepared against Spain'

lowing year he was a commissioner at the trial of Mary Queen of Scots and urged Elizabeth to sign her death warrant. In December 1587, he received a special commission as 'lieutenant-general and commander-in-chief of the navy and army prepared to the seas against Spain'. Effingham paid for much of the fleet himself and he raised his flag on Sir Walter Raleigh's 800-ton *Ark Royal*.

Effingham was responsible for the cautious tactics adopted when the Armada appeared in the Channel. He restrained Drake and Hawkins, keeping the English ships out of range of the Spanish galleons, harassing them from a distance. This prudence paid off: the Armada was destroyed as much by bad weather as English action.

He had little idea of the scale of the victory he had won at the time as many of his men had come down with typhus. He put them ashore at Margate and spent time personally finding them lodgings in barns and outhouses.

'It would grieve any man's heart to see them that have served so valiantly die so miserably,' he wrote. Eventually the Queen paid their expenses.

When news came in 1596 that the Spanish were preparing another invasion fleet, Effingham and the Queen's favourite, the Earl of Essex, took a fleet to destroy it and sacked Cadiz.

▶ **RIVALRY WITH ESSEX**

The following year Effingham was created Earl of Nottingham. This caused a jealous rift with Essex, who claimed credit for Cadiz. But the Queen was more concerned with a renewed Spanish threat and made Effingham Lord Lieutenant-General of England, in charge of all her land and sea forces.

When Essex rebelled, Effingham helped put down the uprising and served as a commissioner at his trial, making certain the Queen's favor . He was at her deathbed in 1603, when she named James VI of Scotland her successor.

Under James, he served on the commission considering the union of England and Scotland, and was commissioner at the trial of the Gunpowder Plotters. He died at the age of 88 at Haling House, near Croydon in Surrey.

EFFINGHAM AND THE ARMADA

- In preparation for the Armada, Effingham divided his fleet into three. He remained mid-Channel, while Drake, off the Breton Island of Ushant (Ouessant), and Hawkins, off the Scillies, guarded the entrance. At their various actions off Plymouth, St Alban's Head and St Catherine's, Effingham acted as leader, though Drake and Hawkins were give considerable freedom.

- Effingham was criticized for personally leading the attack on the San Lorenzo, stranded off Calais, rather than attacking the main force which was, by then, off Gravesend. But Raleigh praised him above his critics, pointing out that the Spaniards had an army aboard their ships, while Effingham had none. 'They had more than he had, and of

higher building and charging,' Raleigh wrote, 'so that had he entangled himself with those great and powerful vessels, he had greatly endangered this kingdom of England.'

- In 1596, Effingham and Essex took a fleet of seventeen ships and numerous transports to Cadiz, arriving on 20 June. The Spanish fleet fled. Some grounded on the mud and were set on fire by their own men. Two were taken and, later, bought into the Royal Navy. More would have been taken if Essex had not landed straight away, forcing Effingham to follow him. Together they sacked the town and demolished the fort. Sixty-six men were knighted as a result of this action.

SIR FRANCIS DRAKE

c.1540–1596

| CHRONOLOGY | c.1540 Born in Devonshire • 1595 Sails to the Caribbean • 1572 Obtains licence as privateer • 1577 Sets out on circumnavigation • |

1580 Returns to England with spices and plunder • **1587** Attacks Cadiz • **1588** Defeats Spanish Armada • **1596** Dies 28 January off Puerto Bello, Panama

SIR FRANCIS DRAKE was a pirate, privateer and naval captain who perfected new naval tactics and strategies that won him a great deal of plunder while keeping England safe from the predations of Spain.

Drake was born the son of a yeoman father, who fled to Kent with his family during the Catholic uprising in the West Country of 1549. At the age of thirteen, Drake was apprenticed to a coastal vessel plying the ports of the North Sea. When the captain died, he left the ship to Drake, by then already an exceptional sailor.

'Sir Francis Drake is a fearful man to the king of Spain' LORD BURGHLEY

▶ DRAKE THE PRIVATEER

At the age of twenty-three, he sold his ship and joined the fleet of the Plymouth merchant John Hawkins, a kinsman, on a pirating expedition to the Caribbean. Only Hawkins and Drake escaped from an abortive attack on the Spanish port of San Juan de Ulúa off the coast of Mexico. This made Drake's reputation. Already fired by a fierce anti-Catholicism, he now swore vengeance on the Spanish. In 1572, he obtained a privateer's licence – a letter of marque – from Elizabeth I. He took and plundered the city of Nombre de Dios on Panama. On a hill behind the town, he saw the Pacific for the first time.

Now wealthy, he returned to England to prepare a raid into the Pacific, which was then still barred to all by Spanish ships. Setting sail from England in 1577, he found his way through the Strait of Magellan in August the following year. After plundering the Pacific coast of South America, he tried to make his way home via the Northwest Passage, around Canada. When this proved impossible he set sail west, crossing the Pacific and the Indian Oceans, before returning to the Atlantic and England in 1580.

▶ 'SINGEING THE KING OF SPAIN'S BEARD'

In 1585, Elizabeth I put him in command of twenty-five ships which he used to plunder Spanish possessions in the Caribbean so successfully that he nearly bankrupted the king of Spain, Philip II. Philip had more reason to be fearful of Drake the following year when he attacked Cadiz, burning the shipping there – an action Drake called 'singeing the King of Spain's beard'. Although this delayed Philip's plans to invade England, the Armada set sail in 1588, only to be destroyed by Drake, Hawkins and Effingham.

Drake was appointed Lord Mayor of Plymouth in 1581, and proved to be an effective one. The sea, however, was in his blood, and he set sail on his last voyage in 1596, aiming, once again, to enrich himself at the expense of the Spanish in the Caribbean. But as fever spread through his fleet, Drake himself succumbed on 28 January. He was buried at sea off Puerto Bello (Portobello) in Panama.

DESTROYING THE ARMADA

- *Drake's three-year round-the-world voyage (1577–1580) in the Golden Hind made him the first captain to complete the circumnavigation. The Portuguese adventurer Ferdinand Magellan had died in the Philippines en route in 1521.*
- *In 1586, Elizabeth I asked Drake to thwart Philip II's plans to invade England. With a fleet of thirty ships, he sailed into the Spanish port of Cadiz, burned at least thirty-three ships at anchor there and destroyed thousands of tons of supplies destined for the Armada.*
- *When the Spanish fleet sailed into the English Channel in July 1588, Drake avoided*

being drawn into close-quarters conflict with the heavily armed Spanish galleons. Instead, he used the superior sailing qualities of the smaller English ships to stay out of range while harassing the Armada with long-range fire. When the Spanish tried to shelter from the bad weather off Calais, Drake used fire ships to drive them out to sea. Storms dispersed the Armada, wrecking numerous ships that tried to make it back to Spain around the north of Scotland. The defeat of the Armada marked the beginning of the end for Spanish sea power and made Drake a national hero.

JAMES WOLFE

1727–1759

CHRONOLOGY 1727 Born 2 January in Westerham, Kent • 1741 Commissioned in Royal Marines • 1743 Fights French at Dettingen • 1746 Fights Jacobites at Falkirk and Culloden • 1758 Captures Louisbourg on Cape Breton Island • 1759 Dies 13 September in Quebec

ALTHOUGH RACKED WITH tuberculosis, at the age of thirty-two, General James Wolfe led a daring assault which took Quebec from the French in 1759, making Canada British.

Born in Westerham, Kent, on 2 January 1727, the son of lieutenant-general Edward Wolfe, he was commissioned in the Royal Marines at the age of fourteen, but transferred almost immediately to the 12th Regiment of Foot to secure promotion, as was the custom of the time. At sixteen, he was the acting adjutant of his new regiment when they fought the French at Dettingen in 1743. Then in 1746 he was acting aide-de-camp to General Hawley at Falkirk and Culloden during the Jacobite Rebellion.

▸ INTO THE SEVEN YEARS' WAR

In 1750, he was promoted to lieutenant-colonel and given command of the 20th Foot. Although

'Mad is he? Then I hope he will bite some of my other generals' GEORGE II ON WOLFE

already ill with tuberculosis, Wolfe gained a reputation as a brilliant trainer of men. When the Seven Years' War broke out in 1757, Wolfe saw action in the failed raid on Rochefort on France's Atlantic coast.

In 1758, he led a daring amphibious assault against Cape Breton Island, Canada, capturing the fort of Louisbourg from the French. Wolfe returned to England in an attempt to restore his health, but the prime minister William Pitt the Elder, promoted him to major-general and sent him back to Canada to take Quebec.

In June 1759, Wolfe's force of 5,000 sailed up the St Lawrence River and moored at the island of Orleans, opposite the city. A French army under the Marquis de Montcalm was well entrenched in fortified positions along the high cliffs of Quebec's river frontage and refused to come out to fight. But Wolfe was ill and had no time to spare. After an abortive attack at Beauport east of the city, he took his men a mile up river and landed at a cove near Cape Diamond, which still bears Wolfe's name. From it a steep path led up the Heights of Abraham, which could be climbed with difficulty and appeared only to be lightly guarded at top.

▶ WOLFE ON THE FOLD

Wolfe was among the first to land, and climbed up the steep and narrow path, with room enough only for the men to pass in single file. The pass was also broken up by cross-ditches, and it was this very inaccessibility that had led the French to disregard the possiblity of an attack from this direction. The light infantry and Highlanders scrambled up the woody precipices, pulling themselves by the roots and branches. They surprised the guards posted on the summit who fled and by the break of day Wolfe found himself in possession of the Plains of Abraham.

Imagining that this force was only an advance guard, Montcalm came out to fight. In the ensuing battle, both Wolfe and Montcalm were killed. Quebec surrendered five days later, and the following year Montreal was taken, leaving the whole of Canada in British hands.

Many contemporaries asserted that Wolfe's courage in the assault on the Heights of Abraham verged on insanity. 'Mad is he?' asked George II. 'Then I hope he will bite some of my other generals.'

THE CAPTURE OF QUEBEC

- *In June 1758, Wolfe began his assault on Louisbourg, leading the landing through rough seas and under heavy fire at Kennington Cove. The 1,200 defenders there were pushed back to the fortress. Wolfe captured the Light House battery and reduced the island's main battery to rubble. With its batteries silenced, the fortress was bombarded from three sides. On 25 July, with no hope of rescue from France or Quebec, the French surrendered. This earned Wolfe promotion to major-general and the command of a military and naval expedition against Quebec.*

- *Wolfe's scaling of the Heights of Abraham on 12 September 1759 was a risky strategy, which most of his officers opposed. However, on the Plains of Abraham, the battle lasted less than a hour. Wolfe was wounded three times, the last proving fatal. He died knowing victory was his. Montcalm was also mortally wounded and died the following day. Because of the circumstances of his death, Wolfe became an instant hero. Inflated claims of what he might have achieved if he had lived soon circulated, but the state of his health meant that he was unlikely to have survived much longer.*

SHAKA ZULU

c. 1787–1828

CHRONOLOGY

c. 1787 Born.

1802 Joins the army of Dingiswayo, chief of the Mtetwa.

1816 Becomes chief of the Zulu; begins reorganization of army.

1817 After the death of Dingiswayo, begins expansion of Zulu Empire.

1819 Defeats Ndwandwe.

1820 Begins the Mfecane (the Crushing) devastating Natal.

1827 Death of his mother leaves him plainly psychotic.

1828 Murdered by half-brothers on 23 September.

SHAKA WAS A ZULU CHIEFTAIN who reorganized his army into an invincible force which dominated southern Africa for fifty years.

Born the illegitimate son of the Zulu chief Senszangakona, he was driven out with his mother Nandi, a Langeni, which the Zulu considered an inferior clan. Even his name was an insult – 'iShaka' was an intestinal parasite thought to be responsible for menstrual irregularties and said, by Zulu elders, to be the true cause of Nandi's pregnancy.

▸ OUTCAST

Shaka was brought up an outcast among both the Zula and the Langeni. But when he was sixteen, he was taken under the protection of Dingiswayo, king of the Mtetwa, and was trained in his army. He excelled in single combat, using the heavier shield he had developed to force his opponent to expose his side to the thrust of his assegai, which he also redesigned, and which resembled more the short stabbing sword of the Roman legionary than the traditional light throwing assegai of the Zulu.

When Senzangakona died, Shaka returned to

To create his empire, Shaka had an estimated two million people killed

the Zulu – then numbering just 1,500 – as their chief. He quickly reorganized his army and went after the people who had made his childhood a misery, impaling them on the sharpened stakes of their own *kraal* fences. Any opposition resulted in instant death.

▶ FORGING THE ZULU NATION

Shaka set about destroying all the tribes around him, integrating any survivors into the Zulu nation which, within a year, had quadrupled in number. Together with Dingiswayo, he fought the Ndwandwe at the Battle of Gqokli Hill. Then when Dingiswayo died, Shaka began to take over the Mtetwa Empire.

In his fight against the Ndwandwe, he introduced a tactic new to Africa: scorched earth. The Ndwandwe were finally defeated in a two-day battle at the Mhlatuzi fords.

In 1820, Shaka began the Mfecane – 'the Crushing' – arbitrarily wiping out clans across the plateau of Natal. The devastation was so complete that the Boer's Great Trek of the 1830s was able to pass through an uninhabited landscape.

The Zulu nation grew to 250,000 with an army of 40,000 and occupied territory that stretched from the Cape Colony north to modern-day Tanzania. To create this empire, it is estimated that Shaka killed over two million people, often in mass executions.

When Shaka was wounded in 1824, he was treated by a visiting Englishman. In recompense, he allowed English traders to operate out of Port Natal and a *kraal* 100 miles to the north at Bulawayo, and even tried to exchange ambassadors with King George.

In 1827, his mother died. In grief, he killed 7,000 Zulus. No crops were planted for a year and milk – a Zulu staple – was banned. Milch cows were slain so that calves could know what it felt like to lose a mother and pregnant women were slain with their husbands.

Enforced chastity had already dispirited Shaka's army. When they were sent further and further from home to find lands to conqueror, they rebelled. Two of Shaka's half-brothers, Mhlangana and Dingane, murdered him. He died without dignity, begging his assassins for mercy. They buried him in an unmarked grave near the village of Stanger in Natal. But Zulu power did not die with him. Fifty years later the Zulu army was still effective enough as a fighting force to beat British regulars in the Zulu War.

BUILDING THE ZULU NATION

- *Before Shaka, the Zulu were armed with oxhide shields and light throwing spears, and battles were desultory affairs which broke off before there were many casualties. Shaka rearmed his men with murderous short-bladed assegais for stabbing at close quarters.*
- *He instituted a regimental system, with each regiment or impi housed in a separate kraal. They were distinguished by different head-dresses and markings on their shields.*

Officers directed battles by hand signals, while Shaka sent instructions by runner. They dispensed with their oxhide sandals and could run as much as 50 miles a day.
- *He developed the famous 'buffalo' formation, with the men forming the 'chest' pinning the enemy down while the 'horns' encircled him. The 'loins' were the reserve, who sat looking away from the action to prevent them from becoming unduly excited.*

SIR COLIN CAMPBELL

1792–1863

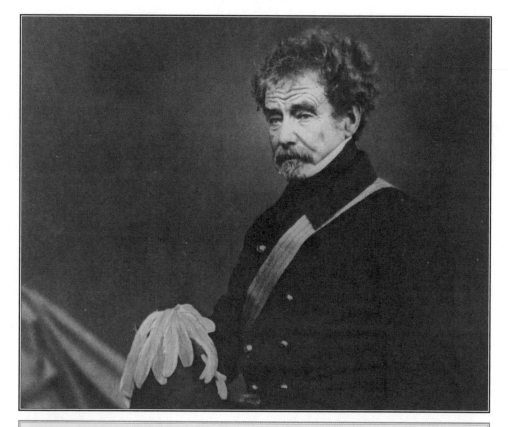

CHRONOLOGY 1792 Born 20 October in Glasgow • 1807 Commissioned as ensign
• 1808 Fights with Wellington at Roliça and Vimiero • 1809 Fights in
Moore's Corunna campaign • 1810 Fights at Barossa and Tarifa • 1814 Fights in War of 1812
against United States • 1813 Fights with Wellington at Vittoria • 1823 Helps put down Demerara
uprising • 1835 Given command of 9th Regiment of Foot • 1841–1843 Serves in Opium War
• 1848–1849 Fights in Second Sikh War; knighted for services • 1854 Fights at Alma and Balaclava
in the Crimea • 1857–1858 Puts down Indian Mutiny • 1858 Created Baron Clyde of Clyesdale
• 1860 Promoted Field Marshal • 1863 Dies 14 August at Chatham, Kent

O NE OF THE LONGEST-SERVING
British military leaders of the nineteenth century, Sir Colin Campbell
became a national hero for his command of the 'Thin Red Line' at Balaclava, and
for putting down the Indian Mutiny.

▶ INTO ACTION WITH WELLINGTON

Born on 20 October 1792, he was the son of
Glasgow carpenter John Macliver. His paternal
grandfather was the Laird of Ardnave, who lost
his lands in the Jacobite Rebellion of 1745. He
took his mother's name, Campbell, when his

'You must die where you stand'

uncle introduced him to the Duke of York, then commander-in-chief of the army, as a candidate for a commission.

At the age of fifteen, he became an ensign in the 9th Regiment of Foot and was sent to Portugal, where he saw his first action under Sir Arthur Wellesley, later **Duke of Wellington**, at Roliça and then Vimiero. He was with Sir John **Moore's** retreat to Corunna.

Serving in the Low Countries, he came down with 'Walcheren Fever', an ague which troubled him for the rest of his life. After recuperating in England, he returned to the Peninsular as a lieutenant and fought with gallantry at Barossa in 1810. The following year he served with the Spanish and took part in the defence of Tarifa. He fought at Wellesley's great victory at Vittoria and was wounded three times – and mentioned in despatches – at the siege of San Sebastian.

Surviving the ill-fated British attack on New Orleans in 1814, he served in British Guiana, putting down the Demerera uprising in 1823.

He was given command of the 9th Foot, but then transferred to the 98th to fight in the Opium Wars in China. Again he was mentioned in despatches, made a Companion of the Bath and became a household name in Britain.

From 1848 to 1852, he commanded a division in India and fought on the northwest frontier. He was in semi-retirement in England when the Crimean War broke out in 1853. Given command of a Highland regiment, he attacked the heights at Alma and distinguished himself at Balaclava. Promoted to command a division, he took part in the storming of Sevastapol.

Returning to India, he was commander-in-chief when the Indian Mutiny broke out. Inside a year, he had restored British control of the sub-continent. Returning to England in 1860, he received a hero's welcome, a peerage and a field marshal's baton. He died at the age of seventy in Chatham, Kent, on 14 August 1863 and was laid to rest in Westminster Abbey.

THE THIN RED LINE

- *After being wounded twice at San Sebastian in 1813 – 'while all around him died' – he left his quarters before his wounds were healed to lead his regiment in a night attack on the French batteries. After fording a river, he was seriously wounded again. He was reprimanded for leaving his quarters without permission, promoted and given a pension.*
- *At Balaclava on 25 October 1854, Campbell deployed his 93rd Highlanders in a 'Thin Red Line' to face a massive cavalry charge by the Russians. 'There is no retreat from here, men,' he told his Highlanders. 'You must die where you stand.' His troops were itching to break and charge, but Campbell yelled,*

'Damn all that eagerness!' The line held and the Russians were driven off by musketry. The 'Thin Red Line' passed into history and Campbell became a national hero.
- *In India in 1857, Campbell was known as 'Sir Crawling Camel' or 'Old Cautious' for the slow and methodical way he reasserted British authority. He relieved Lucknow in November, taking the garrison to Cawnpore, where the garrison had been massacred, and smashed the rebel forces. Returning to Lucknow in March 1858, he succeeded in capturing the city. After British control of northern India had been restored in May, he was promoted to full general.*

CHARLES GORDON

1833–1885

CHRONOLOGY — 1833 Born 28 January in Woolwich • 1852 Commissioned in the Royal Engineers • 1853–56 Fights in Crimea • 1859 Promoted captain; goes to China • 1860 Occupies Peking • 1862 Defends Shanghai • 1873 Appointed governor in Sudan • 1884 Sent to Khartoum to evacuate Egyptian forces • 1885 Dies 26 January in Khartoum

GENERAL CHARLES GEORGE GORDON is best known as Gordon of Khartoum for his famous death in the Sudan in 1885. But before his death he was known to the public as 'Chinese Gordon' for his military feats in China.

Born in Woolwich on 28 January 1833, he was the son of an officer in the Royal Artillery. He joined the Royal Military Academy in

Woolwich as a cadet in 1848. In 1852, he was commissioned as a second lieutenant in the Royal Engineers. In 1854, he was sent to the war in the Crimea. During the siege of Sevastopol, he was mentioned in despatches by the British and decorated for bravery by the French.

▸ **THE CHINESE OPIUM WAR**

In 1859, he volunteered to join the British forces

After his death, 'Chinese Gordon' became 'Gordon of Khartoum' and a national hero

fighting the Second Opium War in China. During the occupation of Peking in October 1860, he led the burning of the emperor's summer palace. Then in May 1862, he supervized the strengthening of the defences of Shanghai, which was under threat during the Taiping Rebellion. Gordon then went to work for the Chinese emperor as commander of the 'Ever-Victorious Army', a force of 3,500 peasant mercenaries led by European officers.

Gordon resigned when the Manchus executed the leaders of the rebellion. When the British begged him to go back, he went, and was promoted to the rank of Mandarin in the Chinese army, though he turned down 100,000 gold pieces offered by the emperor. This gave him the reputation of being incorruptible. The British rewarded him with a promotion to lieutenant-colonel and he became a Companion of Honour.

However, when he returned to England in 1865, the British army would not trust him to command fighting troops. For the next five years, he commanded Royal Engineers renovating forts at Gravesend and Tilbury.

▶ DEATH IN THE SUDAN

Finally promoted to full colonel in 1871, he was sent to Sudan in 1873 as governor, where he set about suppressing the slave trade. In 1880, he went to India as secretary to the viceroy and served in China, Mauritius and South Africa, where his championing of home rule for Botswana, South Africa and Ireland soon made him unpopular with the authorities.

King Leopold of Belgium offered him the governorship of the Congo. But in 1884, the Muslim fundamentalist leader, Muhammad Ahmad al-Mahdi, began a revolt against Anglo-Egyptian rule in Sudan. There was public clamour to send Gordon to lead an orderly withdrawal of the British and Egyptian forces. He arrived in the Sudanese capital Khartoum in February 1884, where he almost at once found himself besieged by the Mahdi .
The government delayed sending a relief column until October. The relief arrived two days after the city had fallen: Gordon – and the city's garrison – were dead.

GORDON OF KHARTOUM

- *Gordon made his reputation in China, leading the Ever-Victorious Army into battle from the front carrying only a walking stick. When Gordon refused to allow his men to loot captured cities, the Ever-Victorious Army mutinied. Gordon responded by shooting dead one of its ringleaders, then threatening to shoot one mutineer every hour until the mutiny was over. It was over within the first hour.*
- *When Gordon arrived in Khartoum on 18 February 1884, he found there were not enough boats to withdraw the Anglo-Egyptian forces. Nevertheless, he succeeded in evacuating 2,000 women and children, along with the sick and wounded, before the*

siege began on 13 March. The British government, feeling that Gordon had disobeyed orders, refused to help, until public opinion and the urgings of Queen Victoria forced them to send a relief column under General Wolseley from Wadi Halfa in October. Wolseley won two notable victories on the way, but an unexplained delay allowed the Mahdi's men to break through a gap in Gordon's defences caused by the seasonal fall in the level of the Nile. The exact circumstances of Gordon's death are not known, but the British people blamed the government's delay. By popular acclaim Chinese Gordon was renamed 'Gordon of Khartoum' and honoured as a national hero.

GEORGE WASHINGTON

1732–1799

1732 Born 22 February in Virginia • 1754 Fights with the Virginian militia against the French • 1755 Aide-de-camp to General Braddock; escapes from 'Braddock's massacre' • 1756 Takes command of Virginia frontier in Seven Years' War • 1758 Becomes a member of the Virginia House of Burgesses • 1775 Appointed commander-in-chief of rebel forces • 1776 Forces British out of Boston; defeated at Battle of Long Island but is victorious in New Jersey • 1777 Withdraws to Valley Forge • 1778 France enters war against the British • 1781 Accepts British surrender at Yorktown • 1789 Elected President of the United States • 1797 Retires after two terms • 1799 Dies 14 December at Mount Vernon.

GEORGE WASHINGTON was not a great general in terms of tactics and strategy, but he took an army 'composed of men sometimes half-starved, always in rags, without pay and experiencing, at times, every species of distress which human nature is capable of undergoing', as he described them, and defeated the well-trained, well-equipped army of one of the most powerful nations on earth – with a little help from the French.

Born in Virginia in 1732, Washington was the son of a tobacco farmer and grandson of an immigrant from Northamptonshire. Between the ages of sixteen and nineteen he surveyed the largely unexplored Shenandoah Valley. In 1754, he had his first taste of combat as a major in the

'To be prepared for war is the most effective way of preserving peace'

Virginia militia leading an expedition against the French on the Ohio River.

▶ FIGHTING FOR THE BRITISH

The following year, as a lieutenant-colonel and aide-de-camp to General Edward Braddock, he escaped with his life when his column was ambushed by the French, killing Braddock. Promoted to colonel, Washington took command of the British defences along the frontier of western Virginia during the Seven Years' War.

After being refused a commission in the regular British forces at the end of the war, he returned to his home at Mount Vernon, entered politics and was elected to the Virginia House of Burgesses in 1858. When the British sought to tax the colonists to pay for their defence, he opposed it and represented Virginia at the Continental Congress in 1774.

▶ COMMANDING THE AMERICAN ARMY

After the battles of Lexington and Concord, which began the American Revolutionary War, he appeared before the congress in his militia uniform and offered his services. Appointed commandeer of the Continental Army by a unanimous vote, he besieged the British in Boston in July 1775, forcing them to withdraw the following March.

Turning his attention to New York, he was defeated at the Battle of Long Island on 27 August and retreated into Pennsylvania with just 3,000 men. On Christmas night 1776, Washington famously crossed the ice-filled Delaware and attacked the British Hessian garrison at Trenton, taking 900 prisoners. He scored another minor victory over a British column at Princeton on 2 January 1777.

These victories boosted morale and Washington began a campaign of attrition, hoping to wear the British down. But after another defeat at Brandywine, he withdrew to Valley Forge, where his men suffered a winter of terrible privation. However, his representatives in Europe had recruited the Prussian officer Baron von Steuben who drilled the revolutionary troops into a disciplined fighting force.

In 1778 France entered the war against Britain. Their fleet provided a counterweight to the Royal Navy, which had given the British the advantage. After a series of battles in the Carolinas, the British under General Cornwallis retreated into the peninsular at Yorktown, Virginia, while Washington kept General Henry Clinton bottled up in New York. Besieged by an overwhelming Franco-American force, Cornwallis surrendered. It was the only decisive battle of the war.

INDEPENDENCE DAY

- *Despite some initial successes, by 1776 Washington had realized that he could not defeat the British in conventional campaigns. Instead, he decided, the American strategy should be 'on all occasions to avoid general action'. In what he called a 'war of posts', the British should be forced to pursue him in the hope that this would exhaust them and over-stretch their resources. Indeed, he won no clear victory until Yorktown.*

- *In 1781, General Cornwallis withdrew his 7,500 British troops into the peninsular of Yorktown in Virginia, in order to maintain communication by sea with General Clinton in New York. He was besieged there by 7,000 Americans and 7,000 French regulars. A French fleet of thirty-six ships prevented a smaller British fleet from getting through to rescue them. Short of food and outnumbered two to one, Cornwallis surrendered.*

ANDREW JACKSON

1767–1845

CHRONOLOGY 1767 Born 15 March • 1781 Captured by the British • 1787 Called to the bar • 1796 Elected first congressman from Tennessee • 1802 Elected major-general of Tennessee militia • 1812 Fights Creek Indians • 1815 Defeats British at the Battle of New Orleans • 1817 Takes Florida from the Spanish • 1828 Elected President • 1845 Dies 8 June near Nashville, Tennessee

ANDREW JACKSON leapt to national fame during the War of 1812 as the victor of the Battle of New Orleans. His invasion of Florida in 1817 set him on the road to the White House.

▶ ELIGIBLE PRESIDENT?

Jackson was said to have been the first president to have been born in a log cabin. However, there is some evidence that he was actually born on the ship that brought his immigrant parents from northern Ireland, making him ineligible to run for the presidency.

Brought up in the Carolinas, he became a mounted courier for the rebel cause when he was thirteen. Captured by the British in 1781, he was

'Take time to deliberate, but when the time for action arrives, stop thinking and go in'

struck across the face with a sabre when he refused to shine the boots of a British officer. This left him with a life-long hatred of the British.

At the age of twenty, he was called to the bar and moved to the area west of the Appalachians that would soon become Tennessee. In 1796, he helped draft the constitution of the new state and became Tennesee's first representative in Congress, serving only one term. Back in Nashville, he was appointed a judge of Tennessee's supreme court and, in 1802, was elected major-general of the Tennessee militia.

▶ MILITIA LEADER

In 1812, he raised a volunteer force to invade Canada and, when war broke out with the British, Jackson offered his militia to the federal government. They were sent to Natchez, Mississippi to support General James Wilkinson, but were soon disbanded. On the gruelling march back to Tennessee, Jackson won his nickname 'Old Hickory'.

The Creek Indians, who were allies of the British, massacred settlers at Fort Mims in the Mississippi Territory. Jackson raised 5,000 men, wiped out two Indian villages and crushed the Creeks at the Battle of Horseshoe Bend.

Fearing a British attack at New Orleans, he took Mobile, Alabama, then swept into Spanish-held Florida, when he heard that British troops had landed at Pensacola. From there he marched on New Orleans, where he defeated the British on 8 January 1815. Soon after the battle, news came that a peace treaty had already been signed in Ghent on 24 December 1814, but Jackson was now a national hero.

Jackson retired to his home at the Hermitage, near Nashville, but was called back into active service in December 1817 after a series of attacks along the border of Georgia. He responded by invading Florida. This caused a political crisis. The government denied authorizing Jackson's invasion, but the Spanish ceded Florida to the United States two years later.

Jackson was persuaded to run for President in 1824, but a split vote gave the White House to John Quincy Adams. However, Jackson's brand of rough-hewn popularism unseated the incumbent in 1828.

CAREER HIGHLIGHTS

- *In the spring of 1814, hundreds of Creeks held up on a peninsular in the Tallapoosa River at Tohopeka, Alabama. Jackson turned up in overwhelming force, with cannon. At the Battle of Horseshoe Bend on 27 March 1814, he demolished the Creeks' defences, slaughtered 800 braves and took 500 women and children prisoner. In the peace treaty, the Creeks were forced to cede 23 million acres, comprising part of southern Georgia and over half of Alabama.*

- *With fifty British ships in the Gulf of Mexico ready to take New Orleans, Jackson rushed to the defence of the city. His force of between 6,000 and 7,000 men, including the local pirates, faced 7,500 British regulars. But*

Jackson had time to prepare earthworks and barricades of cotton bales, and the American riflemen behind them cut down the advancing British formations. The British suffered 2,000 casualties – 289 dead – while the Americans lost thirty-one dead and forty wounded.

- *In 1817, Seminole Indians and runaway slaves hiding out in Spanish-held Florida made a series of attacks along the border with Georgia. Jackson pursued the attackers back across the border into Spanish Florida, taking St Marks and Pensacola and executing two British subjects in the process. This caused furore in the government, but the Spanish ceded Florida to the United States in 1819.*

ROBERT E. LEE

1807–1870

1807 Born 19 January in Stratford, Virginia
1825–1829 Attends West Point.
1846–1848 Fights in Mexican War.
1859 Captures John Brown at Harpers Ferry.
1861 Resigns from US Army to head Virginia's secessionist forces.
1862 Takes command of Army of North Virginia; turns back Northern advance with the Seven Days' Battles; expels Northern forces at the Second Battle of Bull Run; defeats Burnside at Fredericksburg.
1863 Defeats Hooker at Chancellorsville; stopped at Gettysburg.
1864 Fights series of defensive actions at Wilderness, Spotsylvania and Cold Harbor.
1865 Appointed general-in-chief of Confederate forces; defeated at Five Forks 1 April; surrenders at Appomattox 9 April.
1870 Dies 12 October in Lexington, Virginia.

he was the son of Henry 'Light-Horse Harry' Lee, a brilliant cavalry leader in the US War of Independence. He graduated from West Point in 1840, second in his class without a single demerit. He did not drink, smoke or swear, and was deeply religious.

▶ EARLY CAREER

Commissioned a second lieutenant in the Engineers, he served in the Mexican War of 1846–48. His commanding officer said that Lee was 'the very best soldier I ever saw in the field' and he was promoted three times for gallantry.

After serving as superintendent of West Point, he spent six years with the 2nd Cavalry in Texas. On a furlough in the east when John Brown seized the arsenal at Harpers Ferry in October 1859 with the intention of sparking a slave rebellion, Lee took command of the detachment of US Marines that captured Brown.

Lee was recalled to Washington when Texas

ROBERT E. LEE was the most skillful general of the American Civil War. He transformed the Confederate forces from an empty boast to a real threat to the North. But even his strategic and tactical brilliance could not defeat the Union's manpower and industrial might.

Born 19 January 1807 in Stratford, Virginia,

'It is well that war is so terrible, else we would grow too fond of it.'

seceded in February 1861 and he was offered command of the new army being formed to force the states that had seceded back into the Union. He declined. Although he was opposed to slavery and to secession, when his home state of Virginia seceded in April, he resigned his commission and joined the Confederate forces.

▶ LEADING THE CONFEDERATE ARMY

He began building an army and it was a full year before he took command in the field. When General Johnston was wounded at the Battle of Seven Pines – which initially halted General McClellan's Army of the Potomac seven miles east of the Confederate capital, Richmond, Virginia – Lee took over as commander of the Army of North Virginia. In the Seven Days' Battles of 25 June to 1 July, he threw McClellan back. He then defeated General Pope at the Second Battle of Bull Run in August. Richmond, with its industry and armaments factories, was saved.

Lee then took the war to the North. He was under no illusion that he could defeat the Union, but he felt that an invasion might prompt recognition and aid from Britain or France. In early September, he crossed the Potomac to be met by McClellan at Sharpsburg, Maryland. Casualties at the resulting Battle of Antietam on 17 September exceeded 23,000 in one day and Lee was forced back into Virginia.

Burnside replaced McClellan and pursued Lee back towards Richmond. Lee won a stunning victory at Fredericksburg on 13 December, saying famously, 'It is well that war is so terrible, else we would grow too fond of it.' He then defeated General Hooker at Chancellorsville.

Lee invaded the North again, meeting the Union forces at Gettysburg. He failed to win the victory he needed and lost a third of his force. His army was now depleted and he fell back into Virginia. He no longer had the strength to defeat **Grant** who was advancing from the west or to halt **Sherman** who was circling to the south. He fought a series of brilliant defensive actions, but was only delaying the inevitable. He surrendered at Appomatox Court House on 9 April 1865.

After the war, he returned to Virginia a paroled prisoner and became president of Washington College (now Washington and Lee University), and died in Lexington on 12 October 1870. Because of his Confederate command, he had been stripped of his citizenship. It was restored by Congress in 1975.

DEFYING THE UNION

- In June 1862, McClellan was still intent on capturing Richmond and ending the war. Lee spotted that this left his right flank dangerously exposed. In a series of bloody encounters – Oak Grove on 25 June, Mechanicsville 26 June, Gaines's Mill 27 June, Peach Orchard and Savage's Station 29 June, and Frayser's Farm 30 June – he turned back the Union forces, inflicting heavy casualties. Only with support from Union gunboats on the James River was Lee halted at Malvern Hill on 1 July. 'Under ordinary circumstances the Federal Army should have been destroyed,' he wrote.

- In May 1863, Lee's army of 60,000 men was caught in a pincer movement by Hooker's force of 130,000. He left a third of his force to hold Hooker's left wing at Fredericksburg. The rest went west, then divided, striking Hooker's right wing in two directions at Chancellorsville. Casualties were 29,000 on both sides, including the Confederates' irreplaceable General T.J. 'Stonewall' Jackson, but the Union Army was sent reeling again.

WILLIAM T. SHERMAN

1820–1891

1820 Born 8 February in Lancaster, Ohio • 1836–1840 Attends West Point • 1840 Fights Seminole Indians in Florida • 1847 Sent to California as administrative officer • 1853 Resigns from Army; becomes banker in San Francisco • 1860 Heads military academy in Louisiana • 1861 Quits Louisiana to join Union army at the outbreak of Civil War; sees action at the Battle of Bull Run • 1862 Becomes Grant's second in command; victorious at Shiloh • 1863 Destroys Confederate supplies at Jackson • 1864 Takes Atlanta and begins 'march to the sea' • 1865 Takes Columbia and Goldboro • 1869 Promoted to full general • 1869–1883 General in chief of US Army • 1891 Dies 14 February in New York.

WILLIAM TECUMSEH SHERMAN was one of the Union's greatest commanders during the Civil War, famed for his 'march to the sea' through Georgia and the Carolinas in 1864 and 1865 which encircled the South.

The son of a judge in Ohio, he was named Tecumseh after a Shawnee chief. But when his father died when he was nine, he was adopted by a local politician who added William to his name. He was sent to West Point at sixteen and graduated sixth in a class of forty-two.

'I can make Georgia howl'

Commissioned in the 3rd Artillery Regiment, he was sent to fight the Seminole Indians, but missed fighting in the Mexican War.

▶ ADMINISTRATOR

Instead he was sent to California as an administrative officer, arriving at Monterey on 28 January 1847, two days before Yerba Buena was renamed San Francisco. He quit the army in 1853 and joined a bank, but the Panic of 1857 ended his business career. Seeking work, friends got him a job as superintendent of a new military academy in Louisiana in 1860, but when the American Civil War broke out the following year, he returned to the north and joined the US Army as a colonel.

He was in command of a brigade at the disastrous Battle of Bull Run in July 1861. This shattered his nerve. He was sacked after rumours that he was insane. However, Ulysses S. **Grant** took him as his second in command and, under Grant's guidance, he won the Battle of Shiloh in April 1862. Promoted to major-general, he took part in Grant's campaign to take Vicksburg, seeing defeat at Chickasaw Bluffs but redeeming himself by taking Fort Hindman in Arkansas, then crucially destroying the Confederate supplies at Jackson.

▶ THE ARMY OF TENNESSEE

Succeeding Grant as commander of the Army of Tennessee, he joined in the campaign to take Chattanooga in November 1863. He then struck out for Atlanta. From there he marched towards the coast, announcing, 'I can make Georgia howl.'

As his 62,000 men swept through the south they terrorized the inhabitants, slaughtered cattle and confiscated foodstuffs, leaving famine in their wake. He reached the sea in December, taking Savannah on the 25th. On 17 January 1865, Congress passed a vote of thanks to Sherman for his 'triumphal march'.

Sherman then turned northwards through the Carolinas. General Johnston could only offer token resistance and the last battle was fought at Bentonville, North Carolina on 19–21 March. Lee surrendered at Appamatox on 9 April, leaving Johnston's position hopeless. Sherman accepted his surrender near Durham, North Carolina, on 26 April. Despite the brutal reputation he had gained during his march to the sea, the terms he offered were generous.

Unlike Grant, Sherman had no political ambitions. When asked to run for the presidency, he said, 'I will not accept if I am nominated and will not serve if I am elected.'

Instead, he rose to be Command in General of the US Army, serving in that position for fourteen years. He published his *Memoirs* in 1875 and died in New York City on 14 February 1891.

GENERAL OF THE UNION

- *In May 1864, Sherman led 100,000 men from Chattanooga towards Atlanta. He fought running battles with the Confederates under General Joseph E. Johnston at Dalton, Resaca and Cassville. Then on 27 June, he launched a disastrous frontal assault on Kenesaw Mountain, Johnston's position in front of Atlanta. This cost him 3,000 casualties. However, Johnston was replaced by*

General Hood and Sherman broke through on 1 September after Confederate forces had pulled out.
- *On 16 November, Sherman began his 'march to the sea' some 300 miles away. He reached the Atlantic on 22 December, wiring Lincoln soon after: 'I beg to present you, as a Christmas gift, the city of Savannah, with 150 guns, plenty of ammunition, and 25,000 bales of cotton.'*

ULYSSES S. GRANT

1822–1885

CHRONOLOGY
1822 Born 27 April at Point Pleasant, Ohio.
1839–1843 Attends West Point.
1846–1848 Fights in Mexican War under General Zachary Taylor and General Winfield Scott.
1854 Retires from army.
1861 Rejoins at the outbreak of the Civil War.
1862 Takes Fort Donelson, the first Union victory of the war; beats back Confederates at Shiloh.
1863 Vicksburg surrenders, giving Union control of the Mississippi.
1864 Appointed general in chief of Union forces.
1865 Confederates surrender.
1869–1877 President of the United States.
1885 Dies 23 July at Mount McGregor, New York.

U LYSSES S. GRANT rose to command the Union Army during the American Civil War, giving the Federal government victory over the Confederacy. He went on to become President.

Born the son of a tanner, Grant showed little interest in becoming a soldier, but went to West Point in 1839 when no other avenue seemed open to him. He graduated twenty-first out of a class of thirty-nine in 1843. Although the only thing he excelled at while at the academy was horsemanship, he was commissioned as a lieutenant in the 4th Infantry.

▸ THE MEXICAN WAR

When the Mexican War broke out in 1846, his regiment joined General Zachary Taylor on the Rio Grande, with Grant winning commendation for his bravery under fire at the Battle of Monterrey. Under General Winfield Scott, he fought at Cerro Gordo, Churubusco, Molino del Rey and Chapultepec. By the time Mexico City

'I need this man. He fights.'

ABRAHAM LINCOLN ON GENERAL GRANT

had fallen, Grant had been promoted to captain, though he had profound misgivings about the war that he thought was being waged to extend the system of slavery which he hated.

After the war, he was sent to the Pacific coast without his family, first to Oregon, then California. He quit the army in 1854 and returned to Missouri, where he failed both as a farmer and a businessman.

When the American Civil War began in April 1861, he tried to get his commission in the US Army back. Instead, he took command of the 21st Illinois Volunteers. His force was used for defensive and diversionary purposes, but Grant began to believe that the war would be won in the western theatre, rather than in Virginia where the early battles had been.

▸ ON THE OFFENSIVE

After a limited victory at Belmont, Missouri, he got permission to go on the offensive and in January 1862 he began to move on the chain of forts guarding the Tennessee and Cumberland rivers with a fleet of gunboats and soldiers from Cairo, Illinois. They took Fort Henry on 6 February and Fort Donelson ten days later. However, the Confederates counter-attacked at Shiloh on 6 April, costing 13,000 of his 63,000 men to drive them off.

Nevertheless, Grant, now commander of the Army of Tennessee, remained on the offensive, taking Memphis and Corinth. When the 30,000 men trapped inside Vicksburg surrendered on 4 July, Grant took control of the Mississippi, cutting the Confederacy in two. Now in command in the west, he relieved Chatanooga and opened the way for General **Sherman** to march through Georgia to the sea, encircling the South.

When advised against making Grant general in chief of the Union forces, Abraham Lincoln replied, 'I need this man. He fights.' Directing the war by telegraph, Grant sent General Sheridan to clear the Shenandoah Valley, destroying the railroads to paralyses further resistance, while Grant himself marched on the Confederate capital of Richmond with General Meade. The Confederate General Robert E. **Lee** fought a brilliant defensive campaign, but the north's manpower and industrial might meant a Union victory was inevitable. Lee surrendered at Appomattox Court House on 9 April 1865.

Hailed the conquering hero, Grant was elected president for two terms but headed a notoriously corrupt administration. Later he went bankrupt, but his bestselling memoirs, published posthumously, kept his family from penury. Now he lies in a magnificent tomb in New York.

'UNCONDITIONAL SURRENDER'

- *Fort Donelson controlled the water-borne route to Nashville. On 12 February 1862, Grant closed in on it, using a combined army and navy force. The Confederate forces tried to break out. When they failed, they asked for terms. Grant replied, 'No terms, except unconditional and immediate surrender.' Some 15,000 Confederate troops laid down their arms, earning him the nickname 'Unconditional Surrender' Grant.*

- *At Vicksburg, Grant waited from January to March 1863 for the level of the Mississippi to drop, so that he could cross the river and take up a position between the Vicksburg garrison and the Confederate force at Jackson. After beating the Jackson force back, he defeated the Vicksburg garrison at Champion Hill on 16 May.*

THOMAS 'STONEWALL' JACKSON

CHRONOLOGY

1824 Born 21 January at Clarksburg, (West) Virginia.

1842–1846 Attends West Point Military Academy.

1846–1851 Officer in the US Army, including service during the Mexican War.

1852 Resigns commission to take up lecturing post at the Virginia Military Institute.

1861 Appointed commander of Harpers Ferry on the outbreak of the US Civil War; promoted to brigadier-general in the Confederate Army shortly afterwards; First Battle of Bull Run.

1862 Achieves success against the Union Army during the Shenandoah Valley Campaign; Second Battle of Bull Run; Antietam.

1863 Defeats the right wing of Hooker's army at Chancellorsville; shot by accident by own soldiers while returning from intelligence-gathering. Dies of pneumonia 10 May 1863.

Thomas 'Stonewall' Jackson was one of the most successful Confederate generals of the US Civil War, second perhaps only to Robert E. Lee as a military strategist, although on Jackson's death Lee himself said that 'for the good of the country, I would rather have been struck down in Jackson's place'.

Born in Clarksburg, in what was then Virginia (now West Virginia) on 21 January 1824, by the time he was 7 years old Jackson was an orphan, having lost first his father then his mother. He was left to be brought up by an uncle.

In 1842 he entered West Point Military Academy. He initially found the going extremely difficult due to his lack of any real formal education, but showed the dogged perseverance that would characterize his military career, sticking to his task and eventually graduating 17th out of his class of 59, no small achievement.

For the next five years he served in the US Army, beginning as a 2nd Lieutenant, and distinguishing himself during the Mexican War (1846–1848), most notably at Vera Cruz and Chapultepec. Promoted to major as a result of his exploits, he resigned his commission in 1852 to take up a lectureship at the Virginia Miltary Institute.

▶ A CONFEDERATE OFFICER

In 1861, however, the US Civil War broke out. Although opposed to the war, as a loyal Virginian, Jackson felt he had no choice but to join the newly-formed army of the Confederacy, and in April 1861 Governor John Letcher ordered Jackson – now a full colonel – to take command at Harpers Ferry. It was during this posting that Jackson began to organize the troops of the soon-to-be-famous 'Stonewall Brigade', most of whom hailed from the Shenandoah Valley region of Virginia. In June

'There stands Jackson, like a stone wall.'

GENERAL BERNARD BEE AT THE FIRST BATTLE OF BULL RUN, JULY 1861

1861 Jackson was promoted to brigadier-general, and the following month his brigade played a crucial part in the First Battle of Bull Run, where they were described as 'standing like a stone wall' by Jackson's fellow officer, General Bee, earning Jackson his nickname.

Promoted to major-general in October of 1861, Jackson was given command of Confederate troops in the Shenandoah Valley of Virginia. Following a successful campaign, which included victories at Cross Keys and Port Republic, he was ordered to join General Lee in the Peninsula (Eastern Virginia). Operating in unfamiliar terrain, and with exhausted troops, Jackson was not up to his usual high standards as a leader, and his reputation within the army suffered, especially after the Seven Days Battle at the end of June 1862.

On his return to the Shenandoah Valley in July 1862, however, Jackson quickly re-established his reputation at the Second Battle of Bull Run, where he completed a forced march of almost sixty miles in two days in order to mount a surprise attack on the Union troops under General Pope.

▶ **FINEST HOUR**

After the Battle of Antietam on September 17, regarded by many as a tactical victory but a strategic defeat for the Confederacy, Jackson was promoted to lieutenant-general and given command of the new Second Corps, comprising half of Lee's Army of Northern Virginia.

Jackson again distinguished himself at the Battle of Fredericksburg on 13 December 1862, but his finest hour would come in May 1863, at the Battle of Chancellorsville.

While General Lee faced Hooker's army from the centre, Jackson worked his way around and fell upon Hooker's right wing, virtually wiping it out. While reconnoitering with his officers, Jackson was accidentally fired upon by his own troops. Struck by three .57 caliber bullets, he was taken to a field hospital near the battlefield, where his left arm was amputated. Although Jackson survived the surgery, he developed pneumonia while in the hospital, and died on 10 May 1863. Stonewall Jackson is buried in the cemetery at Lexington, West Virginia, the town that was his home during his years as lecturer at the Virginia Military Institute.

MYSTIFY, MISLEAD AND SURPRISE:
THE SHENANDOAH VALLEY CAMPAIGN, 1862

Jackson's Shenandoah Valley campaign of 1862 is a demonstration of how a numerically inferior force can defeat larger forces by swift movement, surprise attack, and intelligent use of terrain. Jackson's two objectives in the Valley were to prevent any Union occupation, and to tie down as many opposing forces as possible. Jackson's attack at Kernstown on March 23, although a tactical defeat, convinced Lincoln of the Confederate threat to Washington, and McClellan was denied reinforcements as he was poised to attack Richmond. When in June the Union armies began a two-prong offensive against

Jackson, he concentrated his forces near the bridge at Port Republic, taking up position between two Union columns separated by mountains and the in-spate Shenandoah River. Jackson attacked first one, then the other, and forced a Union retreat from Shenandoah. In a matter of a few weeks, Jackson's 'foot cavalry' had marched more than 650 miles and inflicted over 7,000 casualties, at a cost of only 2,500. Jackson's campaign had also tied up Union forces three times his strength, and his victories had brought new hope and enthusiasm for the Confederate cause.

COCHISE

1812–1874

CHRONOLOGY 1812 Born in Arizona • 1861 Imprisoned for abducting a child; escapes • 1862 Faces General Carlton at Apache Pass • 1863 Becomes Apache war chief • 1871 Captured by the army, but escapes • 1872 Surrenders • 1874 Dies 8 June in Arizona

A S CHIEF OF THE CENTRAL Chiricahua in southeastern Arizona, Cochise led Apache resistance to the white man's expansion into the southwestern United States in the 1860s.

Nothing is known of Cochise's parentage, birth or early life, but it is known that his people lived in peace with the incoming white settlers through the 1850s. He worked as a woodcutter at the

Apache Pass stagecoach station of the Butterfield Overland line until 1861, when a raiding party drove off cattle belonging to a white rancher and abducted the son of a ranch hand.

▶ ACCUSED

An inexperienced army officer named Lieutenant George Bascom ordered Cochise and five chiefs to appear for questioning. They denied guilt or com-

'When god made the world, he gave one part to the white man, one part to the Apache'

plicity – it was later discovered that another band of Apaches was responsible – but Bascom ordered his men to seize Cochise and the other Apaches.

In the ensuing struggle, one Apache was killed. Cochise suffered three bullet wounds, but escaped by cutting through the side of a tent. He abducted a stagecoach driver and two passengers to exchange for the Apache captives, but Bascom retaliated by hanging the hostages, including Cochise's brother and two nephews.

▸ ON THE WARPATH

To avenge their deaths, Cochise went on the warpath, attacking dozens of white settlements and killing over 150 settlers in two months. During the following year, the marauding Apache bands forced many whites to flee the region. And when the army was withdrawn to fight in the US Civil War in 1861, Arizona was abandoned to the Apaches.

Confederate troops rode into Arizona, and were welcomed by the remaining settlers. In response the Union sent an army of 3,000 California volunteers under General James Carleton to Arizona. In 1862, he marched to Apache Pass to maintain land communication with the East Coast and prevent Confederate attacks. By this time Cochise had joined his uncle Mangas Coloradas. In July, the two chiefs led 700 braves in an ambush, but the Apaches were put to flight by howitzers.

Mangas Coloradas surrendered to General Joseph West and was murdered the following year, and Cochise became the leader of the Apaches. But with the end of the Civil War, the government began a war of extermination against the Native Americans. Cochise and his 200 followers eluded capture for more than ten years by hiding out in the Dragoon Mountains of Arizona, waging a hit-and-run campaign from their mountain strongholds, but when 128 unarmed Apaches were slaughtered by Arizonans in 1871, General George Crook was sent in to stop the killing. He won the allegiance of a number of Apache scouts and brought many others on to reservations. Cochise surrendered but, unhappy with the transfer of his people to the Tularosa Reservation in New Mexico, escaped in the spring of 1872.

General Oliver O. Howard arrived the following year with full powers to make peace. In September 1872, Cochise agreed to go on to the reservation provided his friend Thomas Jeffords was made Indian agent. The war had cost the United States 1,000 dead and $40 million.

Cochise died on the Chiricahus Apache Reservation on 8 June 1874 with Jeffords by his side. He was succeeded as chief by his son, Taza, but it was another Apache named Geronimo who renewed the conflict the following decade. Today, the southeasternmost county of Arizona bears the name of Cochise.

GUERRILLA WAR

- To avenge the death of his brother, nephews and other Apache hostages, Cochise blazed his way through more than a dozen white settlements, killing more than 150 people, in just two months.
- For ten years, Cochise mounted a guerrilla war against the white man, but he was always prepared to make peace. After fourteen mail drivers were lost in sixteen months,

the mail superintendent Thomas Jeffords, a six-foot tall New Yorker with a flaming red beard, marched into the middle of Cochise's camp, dropped his guns and demanded a parley. Cochise and Jeffords became firm friends and the Apache stopped attacking Jeffords' drivers. However, when Mangas Coloradas was murdered, Cochise redoubled the war.

RED CLOUD

1822–1909

CHRONOLOGY

1822 Born on Platte River, Nebraska • **1841** Kills Bull Bear, chief of the Koya Oglalas • **1842** Leads first war party; marries Pretty Owl • **1866** Wipes out eighty US soldiers at Fort Phil Kearny • **1867** Attacks US troops at Wagon Box Fight • **1868** Signs Second Treaty of Fort Laramie • **1870** Visits Washington • **1873** Settles at Red Cloud Agency on the White River • **1876** Arrested after Lakota, Cheyenne and Araphoes defeat Custer at the Battle of the Little Bighorn • **1878** Moves his people into Pine Ridge Agency • **1890** 150 Lakotas killed at Wounded Knee • **1909** Dies 10 December at Pine Ridge, South Dakota

RED CLOUD WAS ONE of the most important Lakota leaders of the 19th century, who successfully resisted the US government's attempt to fortify a road across the plains to the newly discovered goldfields in the Montana Territory.

Born Mahpius Luta near the forks of the Platte River, near what is now North Platte, Nebraska, in 1822, he was a Oglala Teton Dakota. His mother was an Oglala and his father, who died

'They made many promises, but kept only one; they promised to take our land and they took it'

in Red Cloud's youth, was a Brulé Red Cloud. With no hereditary title, he was raised in the household of his maternal uncle, Chief Smoke.

▶ CHIEF OF THE LAKOTA

Much of his early life was spent at war, fighting the neighbouring Pawnee and Crow, as well as other Oglala, and he rose to prominence due to his bravery in battle. In 1841 he killed one of his uncle's primary rivals, Bull Bear, chief of the Koya Oglalas, an event which divided the Oglala for the next fifty years. But he gradually rose to the leadership of the Lakota nation in territorial wars with the Pawnees, Shoshones, Crows and Utes.

In 1865, the US Army had begun building forts along the Bozeman Trail, which ran through the heart of Lakota territory, from Fort Laramie in present-day Wyoming to the gold-fields of Montana. Red Cloud led the Sioux and the Cheyenne against this project, taking construction workers hostage and attacking the soldiers guarding them. The garrisons were kept in constant fear of attack.

Red Cloud's harassment was so effective that the US government had to abandon the forts and the road itself. After the garrisons had been withdrawn and the forts burnt, Red Cloud signed the Second Treaty of Fort Laramie on 29 April 1868. Under it the US government agreed to the closing of the Bozeman Trail and guaranteed the Lakota their land in what is now the western half of South Dakota, including the Black Hills, along with much of Montana and Wyoming.

Red Cloud then laid down his arms. He visited Washington in 1870 to negotiate a trade agreement, then settled in the Red Cloud Agency on the White River, in Nebraska. However, the peace did not last. Red Cloud's son and other followers scorned treaties with the white man and left to continue the struggle.

▶ AFTER LITTLE BIGHORN

General George Armstrong Custer's Black Hills expedition in 1874 brought war to the northern Plains again. However, Red Cloud did not join Crazy Horse, Sitting Bull and other war leaders in the Lakota War of 1876–77, but he found himself arrested after Custer and his men were wiped out at the Battle of Little Bighorn.

After the eventual defeat of the Lakota nation, Red Cloud moved with his people to the Pine Ridge Agency in South Dakota, but he continued to fight for people. Throughout the 1880s Red Cloud struggled with the Pine Ridge Indian Agent over the distribution of government food and supplies and the control of the Indian police force, eventually securing the agent's dismissal.

Fearing the army's presence on his reservation, Red Cloud would not endorse the Ghost Dance movement, and lived to see 150 Lakotas killed at Wounded Knee.

He died on 10 December 1909 at the Pine Ridge Agency. Though he had maintained his struggle to preserve Native American ways, he and his wife were baptised as Christians, taking the names John and Mary, a few years before his death.

A SUCCESSFUL CAMPAIGN

- *Red Cloud's campaign against the Bozeman Trail was the most successful war fought by an Indian nation against the United States. As caravans of miners and settlers began to cross Lakota land, he launched a series of assaults on the forts, taking construction workers hostage. In December 1866, he wiped out Lieutenant-Colonel William Fetterman and a column of eighty men just outside Fort Phil Kearny, Wyoming.*

CRAZY HORSE

C. 1842–1877

CHRONOLOGY **c. 1842** Born near present-day Rapid City, South Dakota • **1865** Joins Red Cloud in struggle against the Bozeman Trail • **1866** Helps wipe out eighty US soldiers at Fort Phil Kearny • **1868** Refuses to abide by Second Treaty of Fort Laramie and takes off • **1876** Forces withdrawal of General Crook; joins Battle of Little Bighorn • **1877** Surrenders to Crook; dies 5 September at Fort Robinson, Nebraska

FAMED FOR HIS FEROCITY in battle, Crazy Horse was a leader in the Sioux Wars of the 1860s and 1870s. He was seen by his people to be a visionary leader who was committed to preserving the Lakota way of life and defending them against the white man's invasion of the northern Plains.

Born Tashunka Witco (meaning 'his horse is crazy') near present-day Rapid City, South Dakota, he was the son of a medicine man and the nephew of Spotted Tail, the Sioux chief who tried to negotiate the mineral rights when gold was discovered in the Black Hills, only failing when he set the price too high at $60 million.

▶ A YOUNG WARRIOR

Even as a young man, Crazy Horse was a legendary warrior. Before he was twelve, he had killed a buffalo and was given his own horse. On 19 August 1854, he witnessed the killing of the Brulé leader in Conquering Bear's camp in northern Wyoming. The following year he witnessed US troops destroying Native American tepees and possessions during General William S. Harney's punitive expedition along the Oregon Trail. By that time he was stealing horses from the Crow tribe, traditional enemies of the Sioux, and, at 20, led his first war party.

Crazy Horse's reputation grew when he joined

By the age of twenty, Crazy Horse was leading his own war party

Red Cloud's war to fight the building of the fortified Bozeman Trail from 1865 to 1868 and played a key role in destroying William J. Fetterman's brigade at Fort Phil Kearny in 1867.

▸ WAR CHIEF

But Crazy Horse would not lay down his weapons after the Second Treaty of Fort Laramie in 1868 and took off into unceded buffalo country. Crazy Horse found himself the war chief of the Oglalas, with some Brulé followers as well. They hunted, fished and fought other Native Americans, in an effort to preserve the Lakota way of life. He married both Cheyenne and Oglala women.

Crazy Horse resisted American encroachment on Lakota lands following the Fort Laramie Treaty, attacking a surveying party sent into the Black Hills by General Custer in 1873. Then in 1874, gold was discovered.

On 31 January 1876, the nomadic tribes were ordered back to the reservation. Crazy Horse refused to go and General George Crook came to get him. But Crazy Horse retreated into the hills, then drove Crook back with a surprise attack at Rosebud Creek. After that, Crazy Horse joined Sitting Bull for the Battle of Little Bighorn on 25 June.

Following the Lakota victory at Little Bighorn, Sitting Bull retreated to Canada, but Crazy Horse stayed behind to fight General Nelson Miles that winter. On 8 January 1877, at Wolf Mountain on the Tongue River in southern Montana, Crazy Horse led 800 braves in a surprise attack. But Miles had disguised his howitzers as wagons and opened fire with them. The Indians withdrew to bluffs and, when the soldiers counter-attacked, retreated under the cover of a snowstorm.

The situation was hopeless, however. On 5 May 1877, Crazy Horse led some 800 weary and starving followers to Fort Robinson on the Red Cloud Agency in northwest Nebraska. He refused to go to Washington, D.C. for a meeting with President Rutherford Hayes.

He left the reservation to take his sick wife to her parents. Fearing that he was going back on the warpath, Crook had him arrested. Crazy Horse did not resist, but when he realized that he was being taken to the guardhouse, he began to struggle and a soldier ran him through with a bayonet.

THE BATTLE OF ROSEBUD CREEK

- *When the War Department ordered all Lakota bands on to their reservations in 1876, Crazy Horse became a leader of the resistance. In March 1876, when his scouts discovered an Indian trail, General George Crook sent a detachment under Colonel Joseph Reynolds to locate the Indian camp along the Powder River in southeast Montana. At dawn on 17 March, Reynolds ordered a charge. The Indians retreated to surrounding bluffs and fired at the troops who burned the village and rounded up the Indian horses. Crazy Horse regrouped his warriors and, during a snowstorm that night, recaptured the herd. Closely allied to the Cheyenne by marriage, he gathered a force of 1,200 Oglala and Cheyenne at his village and turned back General George Crook on 17 June 1876, as Crook tried to advance up Rosebud Creek toward Sitting Bull's encampment at Little Bighorn.*
- *After his victory at Rosebud Creek, Crazy Horse joined forces with Sitting Bull and, on 25 June, led his braves in the counter-attack that destroyed Custer's 7th Cavalry at Little Bighorn, flanking Custer's men from the north and west as Hunkpapa warriors led by Chief Gall charged from the south and east.*

FREDERICK THE GREAT

1713–1786

CHRONOLOGY

1713 Born 24 January in Potsdam.

1740 Accedes to the throne of Prussia; seizes Silesia.

1741 First victory at Battle of Mollwitz.

1742 Victory at Chotusitz; Austria cedes Silesia to Prussia.

1744 Captures Prague, starting Second Silesian War.

1745 Victories at Hohenfriedburg and Sohr.

1746 Victories at Hennesdorf and Kesseldorf.

1756 Invades Saxony, starting Seven Years' War; victory at Lobositz.

1757 Victory at Prague; defeat at Kolin; victory at Rossbach; victory at Leuthen.

1758 Victory at Zorndorf; defeat at Hochkirchen.

1759 Defeat at Kundersdorf.

1760 Victories at Liegnitz and Torgau.

1762 Victories at Burkesdorf and Freiberg.

1763 Peace of Hubertusburg ends Seven Years' War.

1786 Dies 17 August in Berlin.

his accomplice, a close friend, before being jailed. Released eighteen months later, he was reconciled with his father and joined the Prussian troops who were fighting in the War of the Polish Succession.

▶ KING OF PRUSSIA

When his father died on 28 May 1840 and Frederick acceded to the throne, he inherited an army of 80,000 men. He immediately went to war, seizing Silesia, then part of the Austrian Empire. The Austrians counterattacked at Mollwitz on 10 April 1741. The cavalry was routed and Frederick left the battlefield with them. The Prussian infantry, however, managed to win the battle and Frederick vowed never to flee again. He improved his cavalry and was seen at the thick of the fighting from then on.

FREDERICK THE GREAT made Prussia a great military power. In most of his campaigns he was outnumbered both in men – once by twenty to one – and nations allied against him, but through bold and offensive action, he nearly always won.

The son of Frederick William I of Prussia, he was an artistic youth, and when forced to join the grenadiers, he attempted to flee to France with a fellow officer at the age of twenty. Frederick was forced to watch the execution of

'Were he still alive, we should now not be here in Prussia' NAPOLEON BONAPARTE

After victory at the Battle of Chotusitz on 17 May 1742, the Austrians signed the Treaty of Breslau, ceding Silesia to Prussia. But in 1744, Frederick suspected that Austria aimed to take back its lost province and he marched 80,000 men into Bohemia, taking Prague on 2 September 1744. He defeated the Austrians in Silesia at Hohenfried on 4 June 1745, then invaded Bohemia again. When this failed, he inflicted 8,000 casualties on an Austrian force blocking his retreat at Sohr. He threw back invading columns at Hennersdorf and Kesseldorf, signing the Treaty of Dresden confirming Silesia as Prussian in December 1745.

▶ THE SEVEN YEARS' WAR

In August 1756, Frederick began the Seven Years' War by attacking Saxony – it is said he had a life-long hatred of Saxony after contracting a sexual disease in the Saxon Court as a youth. He now faced an alliance of Saxony, Austria, France and Russia. He defeated the Austrians at Lobositz and Prague, but lost the battle at Kolin on 18 June 1757. Even so, he moved quickly to the west to block a French advance. Then he turned to face the Austrians coming from Bohemia and the Russians who were crossing East Prussia. Meanwhile, the Swedes were advancing from Pomerania.

He defeated a Franco-Austrian force at Rossbach, smashed the Austrians at Leuthen and Breslau, and knocked out the Russians at Zorndorf on 25 August 1758. However on 14 October, he was beaten by the Austrians at Hochkirchen, where he was outnumbered 90,000 to 37,000. He was beaten by the Russians at Kundersdorf on 12 August 1759, and the enemy occupied his capital, Berlin.

Frederick spent time rebuilding his exhausted army with light infantry and mobile, horse-drawn artillery. He won hard-fought victories at Liegnitz and Torgau. Elizabeth of Russia died and her successor Peter III made peace. Then Frederick knocked Sweden out of the war. After further victories at Burkersdorf and Freiberg in 1762, the war ended with an armistice.

Frederick ruled for another 23 years. When he died, Prussia still had a standing army of 190,000 and the center of power in Germany had moved irrevocably from Vienna to Berlin.

WAR WITH AUSTRIA

- *On 5 November 1757, Frederick's 22,000-man Prussian army met a combined Franco-Austrian force of 41,000 at Rossbach in Saxony. The two-hour battle cost Frederick 550 men; his enemies lost 7,000.*
- *After the Battle of Rossbach, Frederick marched 13,000 of the survivors 170 miles into Silesia in just twelve days. Reinforced to 35,000 with 167 guns, he met an Austrian force of 65,000 with 210 guns deployed along a 5-mile front. At 5 a.m. on 5 December Frederick sent his advance guard to make a feint to the left, then marched his main force in two columns behind wooded hills to the*

right. They made an oblique attack on the Austrians extreme right wing and rolled up the line. The Austrians held at the village of Leuthen. Frederick threw in his reserves and took it, but the Austrians formed up again behind it. Siege guns saw off the Austrian cavalry to the left, while a three-pronged cavalry charge routed the horse to the right. The Austrian infantry then broke and fled. Against 6,400 Prussian casualties, they had lost 22,000 men including 12 prisoners, 131 guns and 46 regimental colors (flags). Two weeks later, Frederick hit the Austrians at Breslau, taking 17,000 men and 81 guns.

GRAF HELMUTH VON MOLTKE

1800–1891

could be deployed by road and railways and receive orders by telegraph.

Born on 26 October 1800 in Mecklenburg, Molke moved with his family to Holstein, then a Danish possession, as a child. He studied with the Royal Cadet Corps in Copenhagen and joined the Danish infantry. At twenty-one, he returned to Prussia to join the Life Guards, supporting himself by writing. He wrote a number of books and translated Edward Gibbon's *Decline and Fall of the Roman Empire* into German.

His grasp of military theory and the tactical skills he demonstrated in manoeuvres at the Prussian military academy set him apart, and in 1828 he was given leave to serve with Sultan Mahmud's army in the Russo-Turkish War. He distinguished himself at Nazib the following year when his artillery unit held back an infantry assault. His account of the action was a bestseller in Prussia. Now financially secure, he married an English girl, the stepdaughter of his sister, twenty-five years his junior. He later returned to Turkey to help modernize their army and was on hand when they fought the Egyptians in Syria.

▸ RE-ORGANIZING THE ARMY

When he became chief of the general staff in

HELMUTH VON MOLTKE created the modern Prussian army which forcibly united Germany. He developed new systems to control huge armies that

Moltke's re-organized Prussian army would be a key factor in the unification of Germany

1857 he set about re-organizing the Prussian army too. An efficient army, he believed, was vital to Prussia, a country with no natural frontiers and surrounded by enemies. It would be a key factor in the unification of Germany.

Under Moltke's new system, the head of any major formation had to be a graduate of the military academy and those in charge of transport, supplies and other non-combat units had to be trained in those disciplines. He had also studied how railroads and the telegraph had been used during the American Civil War. He realized that modern artillery and new, more accurate breech-loading rifles that were quicker to reload needed new battlefield tactics.

Prussia was on a war footing. The conscript army and its civilian reserve were trained in Moltke's new tactics. Its railway system was expanded and industrial capacity was upped to supply the army.

▶ THE SEVEN YEARS' WAR

Moltke's first opportunity to put his new tactics into operation came in 1864, in a war against Denmark over Schleswig-Holstein. Kaiser Wilhelm I was so impressed by his Chief of Staff that he handed over battlefield control to him.

Moltke found that old-fashioned frontal assaults were costly and developed new flanking and encircling manoeuvres. These were employed in the Seven Weeks' War against Austria and the Catholic German states, who were beaten decisively in the Battle of Königgrätz in 1866. However, his encircling manoeuvres were not totally successful and he set about modifying them.

New steel, breech-loading artillery was introduced and Moltke doubled the size of the Prussian army. Within three weeks he could mobilize 500,000 superbly equipped troops – and put three times that number in the field within six months. Prussia then led a coalition of the German army into a war with France, winning a decisive victory at Sedan just six weeks after war had been declared.

After the war, Moltke realized the vital role the railways had played in the victory at Sedan. He developed a new mobilization plan that fitted with the train timetable and could be set in motion with a single telegram. His fame was such that a copy of his portrait, 'The Great Silent One', showing him calmly weighing the situation during the Battle of Königgrätz, appeared in every Prussian schoolroom.

THE BATTLE OF KÖNIGGRÄTZ

- *In the Battle of Königgrätz, the Prussian army equipped with breech-loading needle rifle and deployed by railroad (the first time in a European war) faced an Austrian army with muzzle-loading rifles who depended for their effectiveness on bayonet charges. Moltke took the opportunity to test his tactics. On 3 July 1866 he had assembled a force of 250,000 men to face 230,000 Austrians. The Austrians lost 40,000, including nearly*

- *20,000 who were taken prisoner. The Prussians lost 15,000 and the Austrians were forced to withdraw.*
- *In the first week of the Franco-Prussian War, Moltke assembled three armies on the French border. They surrounded the ill-prepared French army at Sedan, forcing it to surrender. Over 100,000 French prisoners were taken, including the French emperor Napoleon III. He was deposed and went into exile in England.*

PRINCE OTTO VON BISMARCK

1815–1898

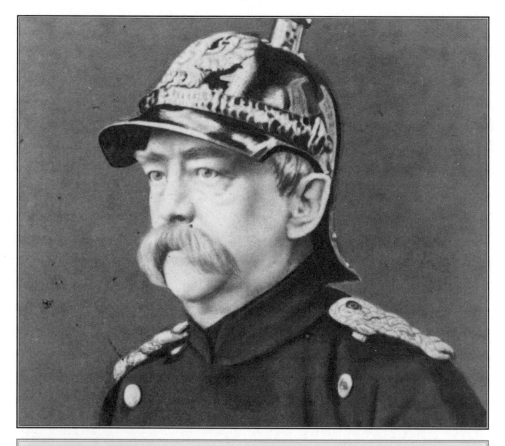

CHRONOLOGY 1815 Born 1 April in Brandenburg • 1847 Attends Prussian United Diet • 1851 Attends Federal German Diet in Frankfurt • 1859 Ambassador to Russia • 1862 Ambassador to France; becomes prime minister • 1863–1866 Institutes military reforms • 1866 Invades Holstein; defeats Austria in Seven Weeks' War • 1870 Provokes Franco-Prussian War • 1871 Becomes first chancellor of united Germany • 1890 Steps down as prime minister • 1898 Dies 30 July

OTTO VON BISMARCK was the Prussian statesmen who, by the skilful manipulation of war, united Germany. He was born in Schönhausen, Brandenburg, on 1 April 1815. After reading law at the Universities of Göttingen and Berlin, he became a judicial administrator at Aachen. He entered the Prussian Parliament as an ultra-royalist totally opposed to democracy. And in 1851 he represented Prussia at the Federal German Diet in Frankfurt.

In 1859 he went to St Petersburg as ambassador to Russia. Then in 1862, he went to the court of Napoleon III as ambassador to France. Later

'The great questions of the day will not be settled by speeches but by iron and blood'

that year, he was recalled to become prime minister of Prussia, and set about uniting Germany with Prussia as its head, supporting Kaiser Wilhelm I's plans to vastly expand the army.

▶ THE SEVEN YEARS' WAR

A short war in 1864 put the duchies of Schleswig and Holstein in German hands. Schleswig was administered by Prussia; Holstein by Austria. On 9 June 1866, Bismarck sent troops into Austria, provoking the Seven Weeks' War which inflicted a major defeat on the Austrians and the Catholic German states allied to her. These were forcibly taken into the North German Confederation, though Austria was left outside as Bismarck did not want any challenge to Prussian supremacy. The Confederation granted universal suffrage for men, though the Kaiser (and Bismarck) maintained control of military spending.

In France, Napoleon III was already worried about the growing strength of his neighbour and, in 1870, Bismarck deliberately provoked the Franco-Prussian War. A swift victory at the Battle of Sedan ended the Second Empire in France and sent Napoleon III into exile in England. The remaining independent German states joined Bismarck's Northern Confederation to form a German Empire, which also took the provinces of Alsace and Lorraine from France. This was a bone of contention between France and Germany, until they were returned in 1918.

▶ FIRST CHANCELLOR OF GERMANY

As first chancellor of the new German Empire – a position he held for nineteen years – Bismarck then went about making peace. He presided over the Congress of Berlin in 1872, putting Germany on a level with the great powers of the day – Russia, Austria, France and Great Britain. He negotiated the Dreikaiserbund (the 'Three Emperors' League') with Russia and Austria. This did not survive the Russo-Turkish War of 1877. So to counteract the danger of Russia and France joining forces against Germany, he formed a Triple Alliance with Austria and Italy in 1879.

Inside Germany, he developed a central bank, a common currency, and a single legal code. Bismarck also became the first statesman in Europe to devise a comprehensive scheme of social security, offering workers insurance against accident and sickness, as well as old age benefits. This was a political move to counter the growing movement for socialism. Meanwhile he repressed trade unions.

But by 1890 his policies began to come under attack. With his Prussian manner, he was seen as old-fashioned and outdated in a modern industrial state. On 18 March 1890, two years after Emperor Wilhelm II's accession, he was forced to resign, and devoted his last years to writing his memoirs, before dying in 1898.

NORTH GERMAN ALLIANCE

- *After the defeat of Austria in the Seven Weeks' War, the peace treaty scarcely demanded a thing from Austria. But Hanover, Hesse-Kassel, Nassau, and Frankfurt, which had all fought against Prussia, were annexed. The king of Hanover was removed, along with the ruling house in Hesse, and the North German Confederation, an alliance of seventeen German states, was formed in 1867.*

- *Victory in the Franco-Prussian War prompted the kingdoms of Bavaria, Württemberg, Baden and Hesse to join the North German Alliance. This led to the declaration of the German Empire (Deutsches Reich) in 1870. Kaiser Wilhelm I of Prussia was proclaimed German Emperor in Versailles in 1871. Bismarck was appointed imperial chancellor, not responsible to parliament but to the emperor.*

ALFRED VON TIRPITZ

1849–1930

CHRONOLOGY   1849 Born 19 March at Küsten, Prussia • 1865 Enlists in Prussian Navy • 1895 Promoted to rear admiral • 1896 Heads squadron in East Asia • 1897 Becomes secretary of state for the navy • 1898 First Fleet Act starts building high-seas battle fleet • 1900 Second Fleet Act expands ocean-going fleet • 1916 Resigns • 1930 Dies 6 March at Ebenhausen

ALFRED VON TIRPITZ was the admiral chiefly responsible for the build-up in strength of the German navy in the run-up to World War I. The son of a civil servant, Tirpitz signed up with the Prussian navy in 1865 as a midship-man. He attended the Kiel Naval School and was commissioned in 1869. He commanded a flotilla of torpedo boats and went on to become inspector general of the torpedo fleet. During this time he became a keen advocate of the use of submarines in warfare.

He was known as 'Tirpitz the Eternal' for his ability to hold on to his job

▶ SECRETARY OF STATE

Becoming a rear admiral in 1895, he took command of a cruiser squadron in East Asia in 1896. The following year, he was appointed Secretary of State of the Imperial Navy Department and the Kaiser was very receptive to his plans for a much-enlarged German fleet.

This expansion was set in motion by the First Fleet Act in 1898 which envisaged a high-seas battle fleet capable of taking on the French or Russian fleets. The Second Fleet Act in 1900 outlined an ambitious plan to construct a fleet capable of challenging the British Royal Navy by 1917.

Tirpiz's plan was counterproductive. While its aims were unrealistic, it alerted Britain to Germany's intention to threaten her position as the dominant sea power. She began a ship-building programme of her own in 1905, famously launching the massive HMS *Dreadnought* in 1906. At that time Britain had a lead of seven capital ships over Germany. Indeed, the German ship-building programme began a global naval arms race, which saw even Turkey and Chile massively enlarging their fleets.

The British rapidly pulled ahead and, by the time war was declared in the summer of 1914, Germany had twenty-nine battleships while the British had forty-nine. The German fleet never became a real challenge to the British fleet.

The only encounter between the two fleets occurred at the Battle of Jutland which raged from 31 May to 1 June 1916. The British suffered heavy losses, but retained control of the North Sea. The German Navy returned to port unmolested and both sides claimed victory.

▶ SUBMARINE WARFARE

As such direct challenges were untenable, Tirpitz concentrated on building submarines. His aims were to chip away at the British fleet until it was weak enough to be attacked by his battle fleet. However, attacking Atlantic shipping – such as the sinking of the *Lusitania* in May 1915 – had risks of its own. Attacking civilian shipping, with the consequent loss of American lives, turned public opinion in the United States against Germany. As a result the US joined World War I on the side of Britain and France in 1917.

Tirpitz had been promoted to grand admiral in 1911, and became commander of the German navy on the outbreak of war in 1914. He was known as 'Tirpitz the Eternal' because of his ability to hold on to his job while others lost theirs. This was because of the high level of support he received from Wilhelm II. Even the Kaiser's brother, Heinrich, was pushed out after quarrelling with Tirpitz. However, in March 1916, Tirpitz tendered his resignation after his controversial policy of the unrestricted use of U-boats was challenged. To his surprise, it was accepted by the Kaiser.

In 1917, he became co-founder of the right-wing Fatherland Party, which aimed to curb the collapse of morale on the home front. He served as a deputy in the Reichstag from 1924 to 28, but without the navy behind him he was never seen as a significant political figure. He died in Ebenhausen, near Munich, on 6 March 1930.

THE FLEET ACTS

- *The First Fleet Act of 1898 provided for the construction of one flagship, sixteen battleships, nine large cruisers, twenty-six small cruisers and eight armoured vessels by 1904.*

- *The Second Fleet Act of 1900 provided for the construction of a battlefleet of two flagships, thirty-six battleships, eleven large and thirty-four small cruisers by 1917.*

PAUL VON HINDENBURG

1847–1934

PAUL VON HINDENBURG was the leading German military figure in World War I, and became president of Germany in the crucial inter-war years.

Born on 2 October 1847 at Posen (now Poznan in Poland) he was the son of an aristocratic Prussian family and became a cadet at the age of eleven. Joining the 3rd Guards Regiment in 1866, he fought in the Seven Weeks' War between Prussia and Austria. He then fought in the Franco-Prussian war.

After graduating from the Prussian military academy, he joined the general staff. Later he commanded the 91st Regiment, then the IVth

In 1918, Hindenburg was seen by the Allies as the man to hold Germany together in defeat

Corps at Magdeburg, retiring at the age of sixty-four after an undistinguished career.

▸ VICTORY IN THE EAST

Recalled to service at the outbreak of World War I, he became **Ludendorff's** boss. The two of them met for the first time on Hanover railway station and discussed Ludendorff's plan to halt the Russian advance in East Prussia. They were aided by the fact that the Russians were sending messages uncoded, so it was easy to establish their positions and intentions. As the Russian First Army was halted until its supply column caught up with it, the Germans left a cavalry division as a screen while rushing the infantry by train to attack the Second Army.

As a native of East Prussia, Hindenburg knew how difficult it would be for the Russians to advance in good order through the swampy and forested terrain. The Germans fell back, luring the Russians into a trap at Tannenberg.

This victory in the east came at a time when the Schlieffen Plan, the operation to deliver a knock-out blow to France through Belgium, had failed. Hindenburg was seen as the saviour of his country.

He went to the aid of the Austro-Hungarian army in Galcia in September and advanced into Poland to thwart a Russian assault on the indus-trial area of Silesia in November. As a result he was given overall command in the east. A new two-pronged offensive began in February 1915. By June the Russian army was about to collapse.

▸ THE WESTERN FRONT

In the summer of 1916, Hindenburg and Ludendorff were transferred to the Western Front. They planned to shorten the German line and create a strong reserve. And in March 1917, the Germans pulled back to strong defensive positions known as the Hindenburg Line.

In 1918, when it was plain that the war was lost, it fell to Hindenburg to take charge. He participated in the new republican government after the abdication of the Kaiser, oversaw the withdrawal of the German army from France and Belgium, and put down left-wing uprisings in Germany.

He retired again in 1919, but in 1925 he was again seen as the only man who could hold Germany together in the face of economic depression and political violence and was elect-ed president of the Weimar Republic.

On 30 January 1933, in the face of a constitu-tional crisis, he appointed Adolf Hitler chancellor. He died on 2 August 1934 at Neudeck (now in Poland) before the worst excesses of the Nazi regime became apparent.

CAREER HIGHLIGHTS

- *In August 1914, two Russian armies invaded East Prussia, but failed to make contact with each other. The Germans attacked the Second Army at Tannenberg on 26–30 August. With 32,000 casualties and 92,000 taken pris-oner, the Russians lost an entire army along with 400 cannon at the cost of 13,000 Prussian casualties. Then Hindenburg turned back to in finish off the First Army. The Russians lost 250,000 men in all at a cost to Germany of 40,000. Although the plan had*
- *been Ludendorff's, Hindenburg, as his commander, got the credit.*
- *In November 1918 it fell to Hindenburg to tell the Kaiser he should abdicate. Ludendorff had already been forced to resign as the Allies would not sign an armistice if he remained in position. Hindenburg, however, was seen as a man the Allies could deal with, and, because of his reputation, he was thought to be a man that could hold Germany together in defeat.*

JOHN JOSEPH PERSHING

1860–1948

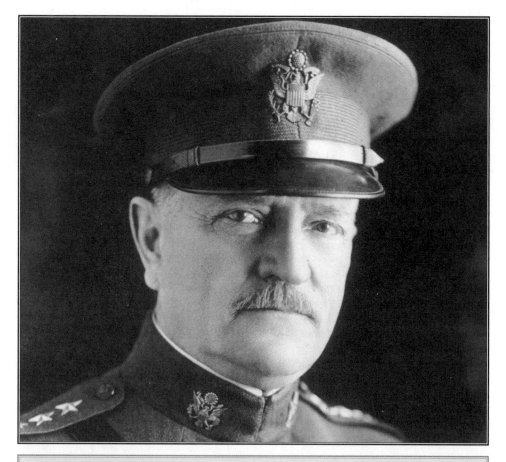

CHRONOLOGY   1860 Born 13 September in Laclede, Missouri • 1886 Graduates from West Point • 1886–1989 Fights Sioux and Apache • 1898 Fights in Spanish-American War • 1903 Fights in Philippines Insurrection • 1916 Commands expedition against Pancho Villa • 1917 Heads American forces in Europe • 1921–1924 Serves as Chief of Staff • 1948 Dies 15 July in Washington, D.C.

JOHN 'BLACK JACK' PERSHING led the American Expedition Force on the Western Front during World War I. Born in a rural community in Missouri on 13 September 1860, Pershing worked as a school teacher before passing the entrance exam to West Point. He graduated with the highest cadet rank,

president of his class. He joined the cavalry and fought the Sioux and Apache. At the same time, he studied law, graduating in 1893. He was decorated for bravery, fighting in the Philippines during the Spanish-American War. This brought him to the attention of Theodore Roosevelt who promoted him to brigadier-general. He helped

'I will not be coerced'

put down the Philippines Insurrection of 1903 and gained further military experience as an observer with the Japanese Army in the Russo-Japanese War of 1904–1905, then served in the Philippines again from 1906 to 1913.

▶ RAIDING INTO MEXICO

In 1916, he led a raid into Mexico against the guerrilla leader Pancho Villa. Pershing had already earned the nickname 'Black Jack' from serving with a Black regiment. It now summed up his mood. While he was in Mexico he learned that his wife and daughters had been killed in a fire at their home.

He followed his Mexican adventure by becoming a military instructor at West Point and at the University of Nebraska at Lincoln.

In 1917, he was chosen to lead the AEF in France. He insisted on having a force large enough to operate as an independent command, rather than have his men used to reinforce British and French units that had been depleted by the fighting.

'We came American,' he told the commanders in Europe, 'We shall remain American and go into battle with Old Glory over our heads. I will not parcel out American boys.'

Nevertheless, he did cede command to the French commander Marshal Foch when the German spring offensive in 1918 threatened Paris. However, he fought an independent action against the St-Mihiel salient and led the Allied Meuse-Argonne offensive which destroyed German resistance in 1918. His greatest achievement was creating a two-million-man army in under two years.

▶ GENERAL OF THE ARMY

In 1919, he was made general of the armies of the United States and served as chief of staff from 1921 until his retirement in 1924. In that role he was a staunch champion of national preparedness as he was already pessimistic about the possibility of having another war with Germany. In 1923, he said, 'We never really let the Germans know who won the war. They are being told that their army was stabbed in the back, betrayed, that their army had not been defeated. The Germans never believed they were beaten. It will have to be done all over again.'

He published his two-volume memoirs, entitled *My Experiences in the World War*, in 1931, which won the Pulitzer Prize for history the following year. Throughout World War II, the chief of the general staff General George Marshall sent him detailed reports. He died in Washington, D.C., in 1948 and is buried in Arlington National Cemetery.

CAREER HIGHLIGHTS

- In early 1916 the Mexican bandit-revolutionary Pancho Villa executed sixteen US citizens at Santa Isabel and attacked a US Cavalry post at Columbus, New Mexico. President Woodrow Wilson sent an expedition under Pershing to track him down. This proved impossible as Villa knew the terrain and the Mexican government disliked having US troops on their territory. However, Pershing did succeed in dispersing Villa's guerrilla army and his ten-month campaign brought

- him to national attention.
- When the US joined World War I, it was envisaged that only a small force of troops would be sent to Germany. Pershing insisted on having a million men under his command by 1918, with a planned rise to three million by 1919. He also insisted that the AEF operate as an independent command. When European politicians insisted he hand over command to the French, he replied, 'I will not be coerced.'

EARL DOUGLAS HAIG

1861–1928

1861 Born 19 June in Edinburgh • **1895** Graduates from Sandhurst • **1898** Fights at the Battle of Omdurman • **1899–1902** Fights in the Boer War • **1906–1909** As director of training, helps reorganize the British Army • **1914** Leads I Corps in northern France • **1915** Commands First Army; becomes commander-in-chief of British Expeditionary Force • **1916** Somme offensives cost 420,000 British casualties; promoted to field marshal • **1917** Leads failed Passchendaele Campaign • **1918** Leads British forces to victory • **1919** Created Earl • **1928** Dies 29 January in London

FIELD MARSHAL DOUGLAS HAIG was the commander-in-chief of the British Expeditionary Force in France and Flanders during most of World War I.

Born on 19 June 1861 in Edinburgh, Haig was the son of a wealthy family of whisky distillers. In 1895, he graduated with first-class honours from the Royal Military Academy at Sandhurst and joined the 7th Hussars. He fought in Sudan under Lord Kitchener and saw action with the Egyptian cavalry at the Battle of Omdurman in 1898.

The following year he was appointed chief of staff to General Sir John French in South Africa. He was also given field commands. Towards the

'Every position must be held to the last man; there must be no retirement'

end of the war, he mounted operations against the Boer guerrillas.

After spending time in India, he was called to the War Office in London where, as director of military training, he helped the Liberal war minister Richard Burdon Haldane reorganize and re-equip the army that was subsequently deployed in World War I.

▸ TO FRANCE

In 1914 Haig went to France as commander of the I Corps, which was expanded into the First Army the following year. No one had anticipated the size of the forces needed in World War I and it soon became obvious that his former commander Sir John French was not capable of leading such a large army. Haig wrote to King George V, a long-standing friend, and voiced his concerns. As a result French was replaced with Haig. However, he was constantly at loggerheads with the secretary of state for war and then Prime Minister David Lloyd George, who called him 'brilliant to the top of his riding boots'.

While Haig insisted that World War I could only be won in the west, Lloyd George considered the situation stalemated there and favoured flanking attack from the near east. Haig was also criticized for his tactics of attrition. His stated aim was 'to kill more Germans', but massive British casualties also resulted. In his first major action – the Somme Offensive of July-November

1916 – 20,000 men were lost on the first day. In all there were 420,000 casualties for a gain of little more than eight miles.

The following year the Passchendaele Campaign failed to reach its objective – the U-boat bases along the Belgium coast. Rain and the destruction of the drainage system through shelling left the advance bogged down in mud. But Haig continued the offensive into November at a massive cost of 300,000 casualties.

▸ HOLDING THE LINE

Despite Haig's failure, Lloyd George found he could not replace him. Instead he starved him of reinforcements. This left the British Army vulnerable when the final German attack came the following spring. In March 1918 **Ludendorff** tried to force a wedge between the British and French armies. Fearing that the French commander Field Marshal Petain was more interested in defending Paris than maintaining the line, Haig and Lloyd George engineered the appointment of Marshal Foch as Allied generalissimo. The line held and the British use of mass tanks and the arrival of fresh American troops gave the Allies their victory.

After the war, Haig started the British Legion, a welfare organization for ex-soldiers, and began the 11 November Poppy Day appeal to raise money for a welfare fund that still bears his name. He died in 1928.

BUILDING THE RESERVE

- *Under war minister Richard Burdon Haldane, Haig created a general staff and an expeditionary force ready for any future European war. Since the Crimean War of 1853–1856, the British Army had only been used in colonial wars and was unused to facing modern artillery and small arms. He also created the Territorial Army as a reserve. Without Haig, there would have been no British Army to send to Flanders in 1914.*

- *In the face of Ludendorff's spring offensive in 1918, the British, Haig famously announced, now had their 'backs to the wall'. But Haig showed himself a more able commander in defence. He frustrated and delayed the German advance until 8 August when General Rawlinson staged his counterstroke which, effectively, won the war.*

VISCOUNT EDMUND ALLENBY

1861–1936

CHRONOLOGY   1861 Born 23 April in Brackenhurst, Nottinghamshire • 1882 Joins
Inniskilling Dragoons • 1884–1885 Joins expedition to
Bechuanaland • 1888 Sees active service in Zululand • 1899–1902 Fights in Boer War •
1910–1914 Serves as inspector general of cavalry • 1915 Commands Third Army on Western Front
• 1917 Fights in Battle of Arras; takes command of Egyptian Expeditionary Force; defeats Turks at
Gaza; captures Jersulem • 1918 Victorious at Battle of Megiddo; takes Damascus and Aleppo •
1919–1925 High commissioner for Egypt • 1936 Dies 14 May in London

FIELD MARSHAL Edmund H. Allenby forced the surrender of the Turks during World War I with the last large-scale victory by horse-mounted cavalry. He ended Ottoman power in Syria, allowing the British and the French to reshape the Middle East.

Born on 23 April 1861 to a landed family in East Anglia, he attended Sandhurst before joining the 6th Inniskilling Dragoons in Africa as a cavalry lieutenant. He served for six years in Bechuanaland and Zululand. After a brief return to England, he fought in the Boer War, gaining a reputation as a cavalryman.

▶ CAVALRY COMMANDER

From 1910 to the outbreak of World War I, he was inspector general of the cavalry. He then became commander of the cavalry in the British Expeditionary Force in France and Flanders, until it became clear that mounted troops had no

Allenby's capture of Jerusalem in 1917 was the last large victory by horse-mounted cavalry

role in trench warfare. In 1915, he distinguished himself as a corps commander at the Battle of Ypres and was given the Third Army, which he commanded at the Battle of Arras.

In the east, the Turks were allied with the Germans and had resisted several offensives by the British in Palestine. In the summer of 1917, he was sent to Egypt with the order to 'take Jerusalem before Christmas'.

He moved his headquarters from Cairo up to the front line. To supplement his regular cavalry, he raised camel detachments and integrated them into a Desert Mounted Corps. In October, he began his offensive with the feint towards Gaza. Allenby's intelligence officer Colonel Richard Meinertzhagen, seemingly by accident, dropped a bloodstained haversack in front of a Turkish patrol. The haversack contained fake plans to take Gaza. Frantic radio messages talking of court-martialling Meinertzhagen for negligence convinced the Turks that the plans were genuine. Instead, Allenby moved against Beersheba, whose water supply was vital to any offensive. Once the infantry had breached its defences, the Australian Cavalry Brigade took the city on 21 October. He then pushed the retreating Turks out of Gaza and captured Jerusalem with two weeks to spare.

The critical situation on the Western Front meant that much of Allenby's victorious army was transferred to France. He held the Turks

back with Lawrence and his Arab guerrillas.

▸ ENTERING MEGIDDO

More Arabs were recruited by the simple device of rendering his name as El Nebi, Arabic for 'the promised one of God'. Nevertheless, by the time his army was up to strength again, it faced an in-depth line of 40,000 men and 350 artillery pieces which stretched from the Mediterranean to the Jordan. Using a simple piece of deception, Allenby breached the line on 19 September. The next day his cavalry entered Megiddo.

For this action he became Viscount of Megiddo which amused him. According to biblical prophesy, Megiddo is the place where the last battle between good and evil is to be fought.

By 22 September, Allenby was moving swiftly. Damascus fell on 1 October; Aleppo on 25 October. An armistice signed on 30 October ended Turkey's participation in the war. In just thirty-eight days, Allenby had advanced over 360 miles of deserts, defeating three Turkish armies in the process. More than 80,000 Turks, Germans and Austrians had been captured or killed for 853 Allied dead and 4,480 wounded.

Allenby became high commissioner in Egypt, but after falling out with the foreign secretary in 1925 he resigned, returning to England to pursue his life-long passions for orniothology and botany. He died, aged seventy-five, on 14 May 1936 and is buried in Westminster Abbey.

THE CAPTURE OF JERUSALEM

- *After capturing the water supply at Beersheba, Allenby hit and divided the Turkish Seventh and Eighth Armies, which pulled back to avoid being trapped. The Germans sent General von Falkenhayn to assist the Turks, but he could not halt the advance. Jerusalem fell on 9 December with Allenby entering the captured city on foot.*

- *In September 1918, Allenby used spare tents and dummy stores to build a huge camp facing the western end of the Turkish line. With the Turks' attention fixed there, he began a devastating artillery barrage on the other end of the front. The infantry then breached the enemy line and the Desert Mounted Brigade rode through with the support of the Royal Air Force.*

SIR HENRY RAWLINSON

1864–1925

1864 Born 20 February at Trent Manor, Dorset • 1884 Joins the King's Royal Rifles in India • 1886 Sees first action in Burma • 1889 Joins Coldstream Guards as captain • 1898 Joins Lord Kitchener on advance to Omdurman; mentioned in despatches • 1899–1902 Fights in Boer War • 1914 Divisional comander on Western Front • 1915 Corps commander on Western Front • 1916 Evacuates Gallipoli; fights in Battle of the Somme • 1917 Commands British left on Western Front • 1918 Takes command of Fourth Army; wins victory at the Battle of Amiens with massed tanks • 1919 Evacuates Allied force from northern Russia • 1920 Appointed commander-in-chief in India • 1925 Dies 28 March in Delhi

S IR HENRY SEYMOUR RAWLINSON, Baron Rawlinson of Trent, was a career soldier who, by the use of tanks and air-craft, brought World War I to an end and began a new era of mobile armoured warfare.

Born on 20 February 1864 at Trent Manor, Dorset, he was the elder son of Sir Henry

Creswicke, the army officer and celebrated Orientalist who deciphered Mesopotamian script and greatly expanded knowledge of the ancient Middle East. He was educated at Eton and Sandhurst and joined the King's Royal Rifles in India in 1886. He accompanied the commander-in-chief in India, Lord Roberts (a friend of his

'With our backs to the wall we shall, I know, give a good account of ourselves'

father) to Burma during the guerrilla war that followed the capture of Mandalay, seeing his first action as a mounted infantryman in the Rifle Brigade. He won the Burma medal and was mentioned in despatches.

▶ AFRICAN SERVICE

Returning to England on the death of his mother in 1889, he transferred to the Coldstream Guards. In the winter of 1897, he took his wife to Egypt for her health. In Cairo, Kitchener, who was preparing his advance on Omdurman, offered him a job on his staff. He served at the battles of Atbara and Omdurman and was mentioned in despatches.

In 1899, he went to South Africa. He was responsible for bringing up the naval guns that prevented the Boers taking Ladysmith. After the siege was lifted, he commanded a mobile column until the end of the war, being mentioned in despatches five times.

In 1903, he was promoted to lieutenant-general and made commandant of the Army Staff College. He was a major-general by the outbreak of World War I and served on the Western Front from 1914, serving with both the infantry and cavalry. When he fell out with his superiors over tactics, he was sent to evacuate the British and ANZAC troops stranded on the Gallipoli Peninsula in Turkey.

Returning to the Western Front, he persuaded his commander-in-chief, Earl **Haig**, to mount a night attack on the Somme – the first night attack of the war. It was successful. Rawlinson was promoted to full general and took over the British left wing in November 1917.

▶ INNOVATION IN THE WEST

After a period on Supreme War Council, he was put in charge of the remnants of the British Fifth Army, which he reconstituted as the Fourth. During training, he practised co-ordinating the movements of troops and the latest tanks. He used them successfully on a small-scale attack on Hamel on 4 July 1918. Haig and the French commander Marshal Foch approved Rawlinson's plan to use them in a large-scale attack. On 8 August, Rawlinson launched an attack that co-ordinated tanks and aircraft, sending the enemy reeling. Although World War I dragged on for three more months, it was won by Rawlinson's innovative tactics at the Battle of Amiens. The Armistice was signed on 11 November.

Both Houses of Parliament passed a vote of thanks. By that time Rawlinson was on his way to Archangel to evacuate the Allied Intervention Force from northern Russia. In 1920, he returned to India as commander-in-chief. After playing polo and cricket on his sixty-fifth birthday, he was taken ill and died after an operation on 28 March 1925. His body was returned home and buried at Trent.

CAREER HIGHLIGHTS

- *On 8 August the British Fourth Army under Rawlinson attacked at Amiens. The entire Tank Corps was there, nearly 600 armoured vehicles. At 0420hrs, they moved out through the darkness and mist behind a creeping barrage. After dawn 500 aircraft joined the fray. Surprise was total. German troops dropped their weapons and surrendered. On the first day, a hole 11 miles wide was punched in the German front line. Seven German divisions were thrown into confusion. The advance was so rapid, Corps headquarters was overrun. Some 40,000 Germans were captured during the first three days. The German commander Erich von Ludendorff said, '8 August was the black day for the German Army in the history of the war.' Then and there he decided that the war must be ended.*

ERICH LUDENDORFF

1865–1937

ERICH LUDENDORFF was the master planner behind much of the German strategy in the closing years of World War I who very nearly won the war for

the Central Powers with an all-out assault on the Western Front in spring 1918.

Born in Kruszewnia near Posen in East Prussia (now Poznan in Poland) on 9 April 1865,

'8 August [1918] is the black day of the German Army'

Ludendorff was the son of a cavalry officer. Educated in the cadet corps, he became an infantry officer and was quickly promoted to the general staff. He was responsible for updating the Schlieffen Plan for an attack on France. Key to this was the taking of the fort at Liège, thought to be impregnable. At this very fort, Ludendorff would later demonstrate his personal courage. And contrary to custom, he got involved in politics, calling for a strengthening of the army in the run-up to World War I.

▸ ON THE EASTERN FRONT

After the initial assault in the West, Ludendorff was sent to the Eastern Front as chief of staff to the elderly General Paul von **Hindenburg**. Together they dealt the Russians a serious blow at the Battle of Tannenberg, pushing the Russians back until they were no longer a threat to German territory.

After the failure of the German offensive at Verdun in August 1916, Ludendorff was transferred to the Western Front, again under Hindenburg. The German war effort was already suffering from the British naval blockade. Ludendorff backed all-out submarine warfare, even engineering the downfall of a chancellor who opposed it. But instead of causing the collapse of the British, it eventually prompted the United States to enter the war.

Ludendorff's plan was to go on the defensive on the Western Front. To prevent any further problems on the Eastern Front, he organized the return of the Bolsheviks, including the then unknown Lenin, in a sealed train to Russia to throw the country into chaos. Meanwhile he tried to force Italy, which was on the Allied side throughout World War I, to capitulate.

▸ WESTERN OFFENSIVE

He planned a great offensive on the Western Front for the spring of 1918. It very nearly succeeded. But the Allies held and the German army was left exhausted. The Americans had entered the war on the Allied side, making the outcome inevitable. In August, the British deployed tanks *en masse* for the first time, breaking the deadlock of trench warfare. Germany sought terms and an Armistice was called on 11 November.

After the war, Ludendorff sought refuge in Sweden. When he returned to Germany he marched in the front ranks of the failed Nazi beer-hall putsch in Munich in November 1923. In 1924 he was elected to the Reichstag as a Nazi, holding his seat until 1928. By then he had become disillusioned, turned to religion and become something of a recluse. He died in Munich on 20 December 1937.

CAREER HIGHLIGHTS

- *In the opening days of World War I, the German advance was halted by heavy enemy fire from a fortress at Liège in Belgium, which was thought by some to be impregnable. Although he was a staff officer, Ludendorff walked calmly through heavy Belgian fire down the road to the fortress, inspiring his men, who resumed their advance.*
- *On 21 March 1918, Ludendorff threw 67 divisions back by 3,000 guns against a* *British line comprising 26 divisions and 1,000 artillery pieces. As the British fell back, he threw 40 divisions towards Paris in an attempt to win the war once and for all. Once again, the French held them on the Marne, but in weeks, Ludendorff had reversed all the Allied advances over the last years. The German army was now exhausted, however. Rawlinson's attack with mass tanks on 8 August threw the Germans back, forcing them to seek terms in October.*

PAUL VON LETTOW-VORBECK

1870–1964

CHRONOLOGY
1870 Born 20 March in Saarlouis, Prussia.
1900 Fights in the Boxer Rebellion.
1914–1918 Fights British, Belgians and Portuguese.
1918 Invades northern Rhodesia.
1919 Returns to Germany to hero's welcome.
1929–1930 Serves as deputy in Reichstag.
1964 Dies 9 March in Hamburg.

June, an international relief force of 2,100 marched on the city from the northern port of Tientsin, taking the capital on 14 August.

▸ COLONIAL WARS

Lettow-Vorbeck was with the South West Colonial Forces which put down the Herero and Hottentot uprisings in Namibia, then a German colony, giving him valuable experience in bush fighting. Returning to Germany, he joined the general staff in Berlin and taught colonial warfare in staff college.

In 1884, Germany had also established a colony in east Africa – *Deustch-Ostafrika* or German East Africa – which comprised present-day Burundi and Rwanda, mainland Tanzania and part of Mozambique. This was surrounded by Portuguese, Belgian and British colonies.

After World War I broke out, Lettow-Vorbeck was appointed commander of the German East African Colonial Force, known as the *Schutztruppen*. It comprised 2,700 German offices and 11,400 askaris or native Africans. Leaving a small detachment to screen the Belgians to the west, Lettow-Vorbeck marched north into Kenya and captured the small border town of Taveta. His actions panicked the British colonists who demanded that London send an army to protect them.

In fact, they were in little danger. Lettow-Vorbeck's force was too small to invade the country. Instead he turned to guerrilla warfare,

P AUL VON LETTOW-VORBECK was the commander of Germany's small East African force during World War I. He fought continuously throughout the war, holding down much larger forces and preventing them serving on the Western Front. At the end of the war, he was the only German general who was undefeated.

Born the son of a Prussian general in Saarlouis, Rhine Province, Prussia on 20 September 1870, he went to China in 1900 as part of the expedition that crushed the Boxer Rebellion, a peasant uprising that aimed to drive all foreigners out of the country. When the foreign legations were beleaguered in Peking on 20

'An army that had not lost capitulated to an army that had not won'

making cross-border raids to blow up the Ugandan railway.

The British sent an Anglo-Indian force with the aim of taking Moshi, which they believed to the German military base, in a pincer movement. Two brigades were to be landed at the German port of Tanga. The first did so successfully and marched northwest towards Moshi, 170 miles inland. Its lead battalions were attacked by Lettow-Vorbeck's *Schutztruppen*, sending the Indian troops fleeing for the beaches.

Lettow-Vorbeck then took a bicycle ride to reconnoitre Tanga. He reinforced his garrison there with askaris and greeted the second British brigade with well-aimed fire. The British rallied and almost overwhelmed the *Schutztruppen* until two companies of reinforcements arrived by train. Joining battle, they routed the British. Lettow-Vorbeck then turned and finished off what remained of the northern pincer, leaving Kenya unprotected.

▸ GUERRILLA WARFARE

In 1915, the South African General Jan Smuts arrived with two divisions. On 8 March, he attacked Taveta. But Lettow-Vorbeck had deployed a thin outpost line, allowing the main force to slip away. In another encounter on 20 March, the *Schutztruppen* main body again slipped away before they could be encircled.

Soon three British divisions overran German East Africa, but Lettow-Vorbeck and his men constantly eluded them. Smuts tried to starve them

out by seizing their supply center at Kibata, but the *Schutztruppen* took it back at bayonet-point.

However, these encounters were costly. After winning a tactical victory at Lindi in October 1916, the *Schutztruppen* were down to 267 German officers and 1,700 askaris, armed with thirty heavy and seven light machine-guns, and a couple of mountain guns. With nowhere to run to in German East Africa, they invaded the Portuguese colony of Mozambique. The British held the frontier with 30,000 men, while a Portuguese force of 80,000 scoured the countryside for them.

It seemed that the *Schutztruppen* were trapped on 28 September 1918, but Lettow-Vorbeck escaped again. In the first week of November he invaded northern Rhodesia (now Zambia). By 12 November, he was 150 miles inside the country when he captured a British despatch rider and discovered the war was over. On 25 November, his remaining force of 155 Germans and 1,168 askaris surrendered. This was said to be 'the capitulation of an army that had not lost to an army that had not won'.

Returning to Germany in 1919, Lettow-Vorbeck was given a hero's welcome. In July of that year, he led the right-wing forces that occupied Hamburg, preventing it being taken by the left-wing Spartacists. He was elected to the Reichstag as a right-wing deputy. Never a Nazi, he tried unsuccessfully to rally the conservative opposition to Hitler.

CAREER HIGHLIGHTS

- *With the defeat of the Tanga expedition, the British fled so swiftly that they left behind their wounded, along with much needed machine guns and ammunition. Thus equipped, Lettow-Vorbeck began making raids deeper into Kenya.*
- *At Lindi, the only port left in German hands,*

in October 1916, eighteen companies of Schutztruppen with six artillery pieces smashed two British divisions.
- *In all, it is estimated that Lettow-Vorbeck's tiny force of 14,000 men held down British, Belgian and Portuguese forces of between 130,000 and 300,000.*

KEMAL ATATURK

1881–1938

CHRONOLOGY 1881 Born 12 March in Salonika • 1899 Enters War College in Istanbul • 1902 Graduates as second lieutenant • 1905 Graduates as captain from General Staff College; sent to Syria • 1911 Fights Italians in Libya • 1912–1913 Fights in the Balkan Wars • 1915 Throws back Allied force landing at Gallipoli; hailed as 'Saviour of Istanbul' • 1916 Promoted to general; defeats Russians on the Eastern Front • 1918 Oversees Ottoman withdrawal from Syria • 1919 Calls for Turks to fight for independence and lands on coast of Anatolia • 1920 Establishes provisional government in Ankara • 1921 Defeats Greeks at Battle of the Sakarya • 1922 Expels Greeks; abolishes sultanate • 1923 Becomes president of the new Republic of Turkey • 1934 Given the title Ataturk • 1938 Dies 10 November in Istanbul

ATATURK MEANS 'Father Turk' and the Turkish general Kemal Ataturk is seen as the father of modern Turkey. He rescued the Turkish rump of the Ottoman Empire at the end of World War I and repulsed the British, French, Italians and Greece to establish a modern state.

Born Mustafa Rizi on 12 March 1881 at

Salonika (now Thessaloniki in Greece), his father, a lieutenant during the Russo-Turkish War of 1877–1878, hung his sword over his son's cradle and dedicated him to a military career. Although he died when Mustafa was seven, at his insistence, his son was educated in a secular school.

At twelve Mustafa began his military train-

After the Turkish victory at Gallipoli, Ataturk was hailed as the 'Saviour of Istanbul'

ing and picked up the nickname Kemal, which means 'the perfect one'. As Mustafa Kemal, he went to military school in Monastir (now Bitola, Macedonia) in 1895, moving on to the War College in Istanbul the following year, graduating in the top 10 out of 450. At General Staff College he graduated fifth in a class of 57 in 1905, but he was already involved in radical politics and sent to a remote posting in Syria.

▸ DEFENDING GALLIPOLI

In 1911, he went to fight the Italian invasion of Libya, then a province of the Ottoman Empire. In the Balkan Wars of 1912–1913, he defended Gallipoli, but saw the Ottoman Empire lose much of its European territory, including Salonika and Monastir.

Although he opposed German influence in Istanbul – to the point of alienating war minister Enver Pasha – he fought in World War I when Turkey was allied with the Central Powers. He defended Gallipoli again against the ill-fated British, Australian and New Zealand landings. Without waiting for German reinforcements, he took personal command, holding the high ground above the landing beaches and holding the Allies back to a narrow coastal strip. Making no progress, they withdrew.

In 1916, he was promoted to general and given the title Pasha after being the only Turkish general to win an action against the Russians. As commander of the Seventh Army in Syria, he organized an orderly retreat in the face of Allenby's onslaught.

▸ POLITICAL CONTROL

At the end of World War I, the victorious Allies sought to divide Turkey up between them. The sultan appointed Kemal head of a small force to suppress protest during the occupation. Instead Kemal called for Turks to fight for their independence and on 19 May 1919, he declared a provisional government in Ankara and was elected president the following year. The French and the Italians who had troops in Armenia were persuaded to withdraw. The Russians withdrew their support from an independent Armenia and the province was taken.

For the next two years, he fought the Greeks, finally expelling them in 1922. He then set about introducing surnames, the Latin alphabet, western clothing and emancipating women. A lifelong drinker, he died from cirrhosis of the liver, exacerbated by gonorrhoea, on 10 November 1938 in the Dolmabahçe palace in Istanbul. He now lies in a magnificent mausoleum in Ankara.

CAREER HIGHLIGHTS

- *During the defence of Gallipoli, Kemal was hit by a piece of shrapnel, but the fob watch he kept in his top pocket saved his life. After the Turkish victory at Gallipoli, he was promoted to colonel and hailed as 'the Saviour of Istanbul'.*
- *In June and July 1920, the Greeks were advancing on Ankara. They were halted on 10 January 1921 by the First Battle of Inonu. A second battle raged from 27 March to 1 April and on the evening of 6 April the*

Greeks retreated. But they advanced again in July 1921, pushing the Turks back to the Sakarya River, so close to Ankara that the sound of gunfire could be heard in the capital. Ataturk then took personal command, defeated the Greeks at the Battle of Sakarya which raged from 23 August to 13 September 1921, finally pushing the Greeks into the sea at Izmir the following year and establishing his uncontested authority over the country.

CARL GUSTAV MANNERHEIM

1867–1951

Born at Villnäs on 4 June 1867, when Finland was still part of Russia, Mannerheim was of aristocratic Swedish ancestry. In 1889, he joined the Russian Army as a lieutenant in the cavalry. He was part of the honour guard at the coronation of Czar Nicholas II in 1895 and he saw action in the Russo-Japanese War of 1904–1905 as a major. By the outbreak of World War I, he was a lieutenant-general and commanded a corps fighting the Germans.

▸ FIGHTING FOR FINLAND

After the October Revolution in Russia in 1917 and the collapse of the army, he returned home and joined the movement that declared the independence of Finland on 6 December 1917. The following January, Mannerheim took command of the anti-Bolshevik forces in the Finnish Civil War. With German help, he defeated the Bolsheviks and pushed the Russians out, securing Finnish independence.

The Russians were defeated and, in 1918, the

CARL GUSTAF EMIL MANNERHEIM led Finland's independence movement in World War I and ensured his country's survival as an independent nation during World War II.

Mannerheim is today considered the 'George Washington of Finland'

Germans withdrew as part of the Armistice agreement ending World War I. Mannerheim was named regent of Finland and continued mopping up pockets of Communist resistance until Finland declared itself a republic on 17 June 1919 and Mannerheim stepped down.

In 1931, Finland faced a renewed threat from the Soviet Union and the sixty-four-year-old Mannerheim was recalled to head the national defence council. Over the next eight years, he oversaw a line of fortifications across the rugged terrain of the Karelian Isthmus facing Leningrad which was called the Mannerheim Line. It was near completion when the Red Army attacked on 30 November 1939 with a million men.

Finland had an army of just 300,000, only 50,000 of them regulars. But the Finnish soldiers had warm winter clothing, white outer garments that blended in with the snow and skis for mobility. They had also been well trained to man the fortifications.

Many of the Soviet soldiers attacking them were from the Ukraine and unused to the cold weather in the north. They were ill-equipped, poorly trained and lightly clad. But by 1 February 1940, the Soviets had committed fifty-five divisions (750,000 men), overwhelming the Mannerheim line at Summa. Finnish deaths soon topped 25,000. Although the Soviets lost ten times that number, along with 400,000 wounded, Finland could not replace their losses and surrendered on 12 March 1940.

▶ GERMAN ALLIES

Then when the Germans attacked the Soviet Union in June 1941, Finland allied itself with Germany and Mannerheim went on the offensive again. But when the Russians were forced out of Finland, Mannerheim refused to join the siege of Leningrad. Having won a second war of independence, Mannerheim was named marshal of Finland.

In 1944, when the tide had turned against Germany, the Soviets renewed their attack. Once more Mannerheim's army performed superbly against a vastly superior force. But when the Soviets signed a peace treaty with Germany on 4 September 1944, Finland changed sides. Mannerheim then fought a last campaign to drive his former German allies out of Lapland.

As president of Finland, Mannerheim walked a tight rope between East and West in the immediate post-war era. He stepped down at the age of seventy-nine in 1946 due to ill-health, dying in Switzerland on 27 January 1951. Mannerheim is considered the George Washington of Finland.

CAREER HIGHLIGHTS

- *After Mannerheim took command of the 'White' forces in Finland on 16 January 1918, he moved south against the pro-Communist Red Guard. He captured the Russian garrison at Vasa, along with much-needed arms and ammunition. But his offensive stalled at Tampere on 16 March. The Germans came to his aid, taking Helsinki on 18 April and dividing the Russians. He then moved eastwards cutting off the Karelian Isthmus from Russia.*
- *From December 1939 to January 1940, Mannerheim fought a masterful defensive action at the Battle of Suomussalmi. He let the weather and the terrain slow the Red Army while ambushing its supply lines and destroying individual units by artillery and sniper fire. During the attack, the Soviets lost 27,500 men, many frozen to death, against the Finns' 900.*

GERD VON RUNDSTEDT

1875–1953

CHRONOLOGY 1875 Born 12 December at Aschersleben, Prussia • 1983 Becomes infantry officer • 1914–1918 Serves in World War I • 1938 Retires • 1939 Recalled to duty to lead army group in Poland • 1940 Leads army group in the Battle of France • 1941 Oversees invasion of the Ukraine; dismissed after Soviet counter-offensive • 1942 Recalled to command in France • 1944 Dismissed after failing to halt Allied invasion; recalled for the Ardennes offensive • 1945 Dismissed a third time; captured by US troops; held by British as a war criminal • 1949 Released on the grounds of ill health • 1953 Dies 24 February in Hanover

FIELD MARSHAL Gerd von Rundstedt was one of Hitler's ablest generals. He played a crucial role in Germany's early advances on both the western and eastern fronts.

Born the son of a general at Aschersleben near Magdeburg on 12 December 1875, he was sent to the cadet academy at Potsdam before becoming an infantry officer. He rose steadily through the ranks and joined the general staff in 1907. He

was sent to reorganize the Turkish army and served as a staff officer during World War I.

▶ RE-ARMING THE REICH

Remaining in the army after the war, he was active in Germany's clandestine re-armament programme both before and after Hitler came to power. By 1938, he was commander of the First Army Corps in Berlin. That year Hitler dismissed

'Make peace, you idiot'

his war minister, Werner von Blomberg, and his commander-in-chief of the army, General Werner von Fritsch. This precipitated the so-called Blomberg-Fritsch crisis. When Hitler replaced von Fritsch with his own favourite, Field Marshal Walter von Reichenau, the high command were outraged. They chose von Rundstedt to be their spokesman and tell Hitler that he had picked the wrong man. Eventually Hitler backed down and appointed Field Marshall Walter von Brauchitsch instead.

Von Rundstedt himself retired on the grounds of age. But he was recalled the following year to lead an Army Group in the attack on Poland. He showed considerable skill in using a fast mobile assault to cut the Polish western armies off from Warsaw, and then destroy them.

He backed von **Manstein's** plan to attack France through the Ardennes. When Hitler agreed, von Rundstedt was put in charge of Army Group B and the German army gained total victory in France in just six weeks. The only error made during this lightning assault was stopping before Dunkirk, allowing the British to evacuate much of their army.

▶ INVASION OF THE SOVIET UNION

The following year, von Rundstedt was in command of Army Group South during the invasion of the Soviet Union. He swept through the Ukraine, arriving at the River Don in October 1941. By this time the Red Army was putting up a stout resistance and von Rundstedt made a strategic withdrawal – the first German retreat of the war. He stoutly defended his decision, but suffered a heartattack and was relieved of duty.

In July 1942, he was made Supreme Commander in the West and fortified the coast against the expected Allied invasion. But his failure to halt the Normandy landings and push the Allies back into the sea earned him the sack again.

He was recalled once again to command the Ardennes offensive in the winter of 1944 – known to the Allies as Battle of the Bulge – although he had made his view that it was ill-timed clear. When the offensive failed, von Rundstedt organized the retreat to the Rhine, but was sacked once again in March 1945.

Although he was from Junker stock and looked down on Nazism, he never participated in any of the plots against Hitler. He was captured by US troops and held by the British as a war criminal, but was released in May 1949 on the grounds of ill-health. He died four years later. General Eisenhower praised him as the most able of Germany's generals in World War II.

CAREER HIGHLIGHTS

- *On 20 May 1940, the Panzers leading von Rundstedt's Army Group B in the invasion of France reached the English Channel just ten days after crossing the German frontier and a week after entering France.*
- *During the German invasion of the Soviet Union in 1941, von Rundstedt's Army Group South completed the largest encirclement in military history, killing or capturing over a million men.*

- *After D-Day, the head of the German armed forces high command Field Marshal Wilhelm Keitel asked glumly, 'What shall we do now?' Von Rundstedt answered, 'Make peace, you idiot.' His advice, which proved to be correct, was not taken and von Rundstedt was dismissed, only to be recalled later when Hitler needed him.*

DOUGLAS MACARTHUR

1880–1964

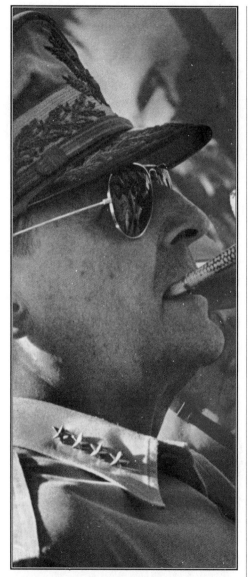

MacArthur, later the army's ranking officer. He graduated top of his class from West Point in 1903 and was commissioned as a second lieutenant in the Corps of Engineers. In 1904–1905, he went with his father as an observer to the Russo-Japanese War. He also served in Korea and the Philippines early in his career and was military aide to President Theodore Roosevelt.

▶ **THE SEVEN YEARS' WAR**

He saw his first active service as a captain on the US's punitive expedition which occupied Vera Cruz in Mexico in 1914. Sent to World War I with the 42nd Division, he saw action at the Battle of the Marne and, towards the end of the

DOUGLAS MACARTHUR was the US Army general who oversaw the Allied victory in the Pacific in World War II. Born on 26 January 1880 in Little Rock, Arkansas, he was the son of Arthur

'I will return'

war, became the US Army's youngest divisional commander.

After the war he remained in Europe as part of the force occupying the Rhineland. Returning home, he became the youngest superintendent of West Point, made another tour in the Philippines and served as army chief of staff from 1930 to 1935. He then returned to the Philippines as an army advisor in the run-up to independence.

He retired from the US Army in 1937, but stayed on in Manila as a field marshal in the Filipino army. However, as war clouds gathered, he was recalled as commander of the US Army Forces in the Far East and was told to prepare the Philippines' defences for a Japanese attack.

▸ DEFENDING THE PHILIPPINE

The Japanese landed on 22 December 1941 and pushed MacArthur's 130,000 men back into the Baatan Peninsular and the fortified island of Corregidor. On 11 March 1942, on the direct orders of President Roosevelt, MacArthur reluctantly fled the Philippines, vowing, 'I will return.'

From his base in Australia, MacArthur co-ordinated a series of amphibious invasions to 'island hop' US forces back across the Pacific. Victory came when airbases within flying distance of the Japanese mainland were secured and atomic bombs were dropped on Hiroshima and Nagasaki. After accepting the Japanese surrender in Tokyo Bay on 2 September 1945, he stayed as commander of the occupation forces.

When the Korean War began in 1950, MacArthur was given command of the United Nations forces. MacArthur managed to turn the tide of the war. With the North Koreans almost beaten, the Chinese entered the war, pushing MacArthur back beyond Seoul. He had turned the tide again when he was relieved of command on 11 April 1951 for advocating a direct attack on China, possibly with atomic bombs.

Returning to America a hero, he addressed a joint secession of Congress. After that it was quickly forgotten. He died on 5 April 1964 at the Walter Reed Army Medical Center in Washington, DC and is buried in Norfolk, Virginia.

GREATEST US GENERAL

- *During World War I, MacArthur showed conspicuous courage. Disdaining both a gas mask and a steel helmet he led his men over the top armed only with a riding crop, professing the belief that no enemy could harm him. He earned four silver stars for bravery and Pershing said of him, 'MacArthur is the greatest leader of troops we have.'*
- *During the retreat into the Baatan Peninsular, MacArthur frequently exposed himself to fire in actions that slowed the Japanese advance. Although only 22,400 of his 130,000-strong army were trained, they held out until May 1942.*

- *After the dropping of the atomic bomb on Hiroshima and Nagasaki brought the Pacific war to a close, newly-created general of the army Douglas MacArthur was chosen to receive the Japanese surrender on board the USS Missouri in Tokyo Bay.*
- *North Korea's invasion of the South seemed unstoppable until MacArthur halted them at Pusan. Then a daring amphibious landing at Inchon cut of the Communist invaders. The retreat turned into a rout.*
- *In 1951, MacArthur returned to the US for the first time since 1937. At a welcome-home parade in New York, a crowd of seven million turned out – the largest in history.*

ARCHIBALD WAVELL

1883–1950

FIELD MARSHAL Archibald Wavell was the commander whose early victories against the Italians in North Africa against enormous odds put heart into the British war effort when the country was facing its darkest hour.

Born the son of a major-general in Colchester on 5 May 1883, he studied at Sandhurst for six

'The best soldier has in him a seasoning of devilry'

months before joining the Black Watch in time to see action in the Boer War. In 1903, he returned to India where he had spent his early childhood and in 1908 he saw action in the Bazar Valley.

▸ THE FIRST WORLD WAR

After attending staff college in 1911, he spent a year with the Russian Army. He was working in the War Office when World War I broke out, but managed to get overseas. At Ypres in June 1915, he lost an eye and was awarded a Military Cross.

In 1916 he was sent as liaison officer to the Russian army fighting in Turkey. Then he was posted to Palestine and joined Allenby's staff in 1918. The inter-war years were spent in various staff jobs. In 1937, he was posted back to Palestine, to quell the troubles there. Then, after a period as head of Southern Command, he went back to the Middle East in July 1939 to head a new command there.

On 13 September 1940, the Italian Tenth Army took the small border port of Sollum. They then advanced a further 50 miles into Egypt and occupied the British base at Sidi Barrani on 16 September. Six weeks later Wavell's British Western Desert Force started a 'five day raid' which pushed the Italians back across the border on 10 December. Reinforced by Australians, the Western Desert Force continued to advance pushing the Italians out of Cyrenaica.

▸ SUCCESS IN THE DESERT

By the time the Italians surrendered on 7 February, the British had driven them back 500 miles, taking over 130,000 prisoners, along with 400 tanks and 1,290 guns. Meeting no further resistance, the Western Desert Force could have gone on to take Tripoli, but their supply lines were already over-stretched and Churchill wanted to divert men and resources to Greece.

Meanwhile **Rommel** had arrived in Tripoli. His Afrika Korps quickly reversed the situation. Both Greece and Cyrenaica fell and Wavell faced problems on three sides. Rashid Ali in Iraq had sided with the Axis. Syria was occupied by Vichy forces, who were harbouring Germans, and the British garrison at Tobruk was under siege. Although he protested that he did not have the resources to tackle all three, he invaded Iraq in early June and the French in Syria asked for an armistice in July. But his attempts to relieve Tobruk had failed and he was replaced.

He was sent to India as commander-in-chief, but when the Pacific war broke out he found himself commander-in-chief of Southeast Asia. There was little he could do to prevent the fall of Malaya, Singapore and Burma. Created a viscount, he was appointed viceroy of India, a position he held until 1947.

VICTORY AND DEFEAT IN AFRICA

- *When Italy came into the war in 1940, Wavell's 30,000 men faced ten times that number under Marshal Graziani in North Africa. Wavell forced Italians in Ethiopia and Somaliland to surrender and Graziani's men in Libya were only saved by the intervention of Rommel and the Afrika Korps.*
- *When the Afrika Korps pushed the British back towards Egypt, Wavell held on to*

Tobruk. This prevented Rommel throwing his full weight against the British in Egypt, possibly taking the Suez Canal and driving on to the oilfields of Arabia. Although Wavell was replaced in July, Tobruk (by then a symbol of hope to the Allies) held out until it was relieved in December. The following year, Rommel was on the border of Egypt again, but this time strength was with the British.

VISCOUNT ALANBROOKE

1883–1963

CHRONOLOGY 1883 Born 23 July at Bagnères-de-Bigorre in France • 1902
Graduates from Royal Military Academy at Woolwich • 1906 Goes to
India • 1914–1918 Serves as artillery officer in France • 1939 Commands corps in France • 1940
Evacuated from Dunkirk • 1941 Appointed chief of the Imperial General Staff • 1944 Promoted to
field marshal • 1963 Dies 17 June at Hartley Wintney, Hampshire

A LAN BROOKE, later Viscount
Alanbrooke, was the chief of the
Imperial General Staff and Winston
Churchill's principal military advisor
during World War II.

Born to an Anglo-Irish family on 23 July
1883 at Bagnères-de-Bigorre in France, he was
brought up in the south of France where his
family had a villa. Educated in the local school,

he spoke both French and German before he
learnt English. After graduating from the Royal
Military Academy at Woolwich in 1902, he
served with the Royal Field Artillery in Ireland
for four years.

▸ **THE CREEPING BARRAGE**

In 1906 he was posted to India and joined the
Royal Horse Artillery in 1909. During World

'He must be classed as a brilliant soldier'

GENERAL DWIGHT D. EISENHOWER ON ALANBROOKE

War I, he commanded various artillery units in France, rising from lieutenant to lieutenant-colonel. He was credited with producing the first 'creeping barrage' during the Battle of the Somme. Awarded the Distinguished Service Order, he was mentioned in despatches six times.

Between the wars, Brooke held a number of staff and regimental jobs, including director of military training and head of the School of Artillery. In 1939, Brooke took command of II Corps of the British Expeditionary Force in France. He fought a series of delaying action, co-ordinating the retreat with frequent visits to the frontline. After his men were evacuated from Dunkirk, he went to Cherbourg, then Brittany to organize the evacuation of other Allied forces from western ports.

In July 1941, he took command of the home forces and in December became chief of the Imperial General Staff. Although he modestly recorded that his role was to translate Churchill's ideas into military reality, in fact many of the big ideas of the war were his. He came up with the 'Europe First' strategy which Churchill later agreed to with Roosevelt, where the Allies would defeat Hitler first, before turning their full force on Japan. He was also the architect of the southern strategy – fighting the Germans across North Africa, then up through Sicily and Italy, while

Bomber Command reduced German industry, and its cities, to rubble.

▶ SUPREME COMMAND DENIED

Brooke was Churchill's first choice for Supreme Commander of the Allied Expeditionary Force, overseeing the invasion of Europe. But, for political reasons, the job had to go to an American. Eisenhower said of the man he replaced, 'Brooke did not hesitate to differ sharply... but this never affected the friendliness of his personal contacts or the unqualified character of his support. He must be classed as a brilliant soldier.' However the sentiment was not reciprocated. Brooke's diaries were used as the basis of Sir Arthur Bryant's *Turn of the Tide*, published in 1957, and *Triumph in the West*, published in 1959, which provoked controversy due to their criticism of Eisenhower's ability as a commander. This was all the more controversial as Eisenhower was US President at the time.

Like Churchill, Brooke foresaw the Soviet hegemony in Europe but, by that time, America was in the ascendancy and there was nothing they could do to stop half of the Continent from swapping one tyranny for another.

After the war, honours were heaped on him. He was created a baron in 1945 and Viscount Alanbrooke of Brookeborough in 1946.

• CAREER HIGHLIGHTS •

- Throughout World War II, Brooke and Churchill made a winning combination. While publicly Brooke said that Churchill was 'the most wonderful man I have ever met', he wrote in his diary that his prime minister was 'the most difficult man to work with I have ever seen'. Churchill said that, despite their differences, he never thought of replacing him.
- Crucially, Brooke retained the respect of both

Stalin and Roosevelt. His American counterpart General George C. Marshall said that he was 'determined in his position, yet amenable to negotiation, generous in his judgements and delightful in his friendship'.
- As well as being decorated by Britain, Alan Brooke was also honoured for his wartime service by France, Belgium, Poland, Czechoslovakia, Greece, Denmark, Portugal, Ethiopia, Sweden and the Soviet Union.

YAMAMOTO ISOROKU

1884–1943

CHRONOLOGY — 1884 Born 4 April in Nagaoka, Japan • 1904 Graduates from naval academy; sees action in Russo-Japanese War • 1919–1921 Attends Harvard University • 1924 Serves as instructor at naval air station • 1926–1927 Naval attaché in Washington, D.C. • 1929 Commands aircraft carrier *Akagi* • 1935 Becomes deputy navy minister • 1938 Commands 1st Fleet • 1941 Becomes commander-in-chief of Combined Fleet; plans attack on Pearl Harbor • 1942 Defeated at the Battle of Midway • 1943 Dies 18 April when his plane is shot down over the Solomon Islands

ADMIRAL ISOROKU YAMAMOTO was the commander-in-chief of the combined fleet of the Japanese Imperial Navy which helped vastly expand the Japanese Empire in the early days of World War II. He was also the architect of the attack on Pearl Harbor which brought the US into the war in 1941, although he himself was against the attack.

Born Isoruku Takano at Nagaoka, Japan on 4 April 1884, the son of an impoverished samurai family, Yamamoto would later change his surname to that of his adopted father. After graduating from naval academy, he served as an ensign on the battleship *Nissin* at the Battle of Tsushima, where the Russian navy was crushed in 1905. He was wounded, losing two fingers from his left hand.

By 1915, he was already advocating the development of ships capable of launching and recovering aircraft. From 1919 to 1921, he attended Harvard, returning to the US as naval

'I fear we have only awakened a sleeping giant, and his reaction will be terrible.'

attaché to Washington, D.C. in 1926, after serving at a naval air station.

▸ FIRST COMMAND

Back in Japan, he became head of the aviation branch of the naval general staff. In 1929, he was given command of the aircraft carrier Akagi, later the flagship of the task force that attacked Pearl Harbor. As deputy navy minister in 1935, he travelled widely, inspecting navies in Europe and America.

By 1938 he was commander of the 1st Fleet and in August 1941 took overall command of the combined fleet of the Imperial Navy. Japan was already at war with China and America was refusing to supply Japan with oil and other supplies. The Japanese high command decided that they must seize the oilfield in Borneo and take over the British, French and Dutch colonies in the Far East, along with the Philippines which was under US control, establishing a 'Greater East Asia Coprosperity Sphere' – in other words, a Japanese overseas empire.

Such a move would invite the intervention of the US. This meant its Pacific Fleet must be neutralized. Yamamoto suggested destroying it while it lay in Pearl Harbor, though he was against the idea of bringing America into the war. Having spent many years in the US, he knew that Japanese industrial production could never rival that of the US. When he drew up his plan for a surprise attack on Pearl Harbor, he warned that he could only promise to keep America at bay for six months. The high command felt that this would be long enough to muster the raw materials of its new overseas empire to fight a prolonged war which, with the aid of the Germans, it felt it could win.

▸ SIX MONTHS' SUCCESS

After the success of the attack on Pearl Harbor and the rapid Japanese advance through southeast Asia, Yamamoto sought to consolidate his position in the Pacific with an invasion of Midway Island. On 3–4 June the US carriers that had escaped damage at Pearl Harbor knocked out four Japanese carriers, including the Akagi. The high command had had its six months.

Yamamoto was launching the remains of his carrier force against the beleaguered American foothold on Guadalcanal in the Solomons in April 1943 when his plane was shot down. By this time Yamamoto was seen as a great hero in Japan. His loss was a serious blow to morale and to the continued Japanese war effort.

CAREER HIGHLIGHTS

- *On 7 December 1941 a Japanese fleet comprising six aircraft carriers, two battleships, three cruisers, and eleven destroyers arrived 275 miles north of Hawaii. From there, 360 planes were launched. The battleship Arizona was destroyed. The Oklahoma capsized. The Nevada, California and West Virginia sank and three other battleships, three cruisers and three destroyers were damaged. Some 188 aircraft were destroyed. There were 3,581 US military casualties, including over 2,300 killed. The Japanese lost thirty planes and fifty-five men.*

Although Yamamoto's plan had succeeded brilliantly, the US aircraft carriers were not in port at the time. They would take their revenge at Midway six months later.
- *On 18 April 1943, Yamamoto was promoted to Admiral of the Fleet. However, on that same day, a message was intercepted, telling the Americans that he was on a tour of inspection in the Solomon Islands. Sixteen fighters took off from the beleaguered Henderson's Field on Guadalcanal and shot down the two bombers carrying Yamamoto and his staff.*

GEORGE S. PATTON

1885–1945

1885 Born 11 November at San Gabriel, California.

1909 Graduates from West Point.

1916 Aide de camp to Pershing on his Mexican expedition.

1918 Leads the 1st US Tank Brigade at St Mihiel.

1942 Lands in Morocco.

1943 Leads II US Corps, pushing Axis forces out of North Africa; commands Seventh Army in capture of Palermo.

1944 Leads Third Army in sweep across northern France; fights in the Battle of the Bulge.

1945 Dies 21 December in Heidelberg, Germany, after an automobile accident.

GENERAL GEORGE S. PATTON was the outstanding American tank commander during World War II. Nicknamed 'Old Blood and Guts' by his men – 'our blood, his guts' – and sporting ivory-handled pistols, he could inspire his soldiers like few others.

The son of a Virginian family with a long military tradition, Patton graduated from West Point in 1909 and joined the cavalry. An outstanding horseman, he represented the US in the first modern pentathlon (running, riding, swimming, shooting and fencing) in the Stockholm Olympics in 1912. After a year at the French Cavalry School, he wrote the official US Army manual on the sabre and was a keen student of the US Civil War.

He joined **Pershing** on his expedition into Mexico in pursuit of Pancho Villa. Having swapped his horse for motorized transport, Patton famously charged a mounted band of Villa supporters in his car, killing several with his revolver.

'Dear Ike, today I spat in the Seine.'

GENERAL PATTON, REPORTING HIS ARRIVAL IN PARIS TO EISENHOWER, 1944

‣ ARMOURED WARFARE

Accompanying Pershing to France in 1917, he quickly saw the need for tanks to break the deadlock of trench warfare. As commander of the first US armoured unit, he schooled his men in tank warfare in Langres in November 1917, seeing action at their head the following year.

During the inter-war years, Patton continued to command the US's fledgling armoured force, though the Depression starved it of funds. However, witnessing the success of the German blitzkrieg at the beginning of World War II, the US began to build up its armoured forces. Patton became commander of the 1st Armored Brigade in July 1940, which became the 1st Armored Division the following July.

After studying desert warfare in Arizona, he went to North Africa with **Eisenhower** in Operation Torch. But his unit landed on the Atlantic coast of Morocco, where there was no fighting. However, in March 1943, he was given command of the II US Corps in Tunisia and, within two months, Axis forces had been pushed out of North Africa.

‣ PAPER COMMAND

He rose to fame during the Anglo-American invasion of Sicily in July 1943, but after he slapped two shell-shocked enlisted men, calling them cowards, he was transferred to England

and took no part in the invasion of Italy. Once he had publicly apologized for the slapping incident, his notoriety was used to good effect. He was given a 'paper' command as part of the operation to deceive the Germans into thinking that the invasion would be in the Pas de Calais.

Montgomery was in command of the landings in Normandy and in July 1944 he gave Patton field command of the Third Army which was to break out westwards from the beachhead. Sweeping around to the south he stormed across France, reaching the Meuse before he ran out of fuel.

When the Germans counter-attacked in the Battle of the Bulge, Patton turned northwards, reaching the front in a matter of hours. He attacked the south of the salient while Montgomery hit the north.

In a surprise attack, he crossed the Rhine on 22 March 1945. Four days later, he was 100 miles further east and, by the end of the war, had swept into Austria and Czechoslovakia.

Removed from his command for criticizing the denazification programme, he had an automobile accident near Mannheim on 9 December 1945 and died in hospital in Heidelberg on the 21st. He was buried in the American cemetery in Luxembourg alongside the men who had died in his race across Europe.

CAREER HIGHLIGHTS

- *In September 1918, Patton led the 1st US Tank Brigade into action at St Mihiel. Later, supporting the Meuse-Argonne Offensive, he was wounded and was awarded the Distinguished Service Cross for bravery.*
- *In July 1943, Patton commanded the Seventh Army in the invasion of Sicily. After taking Palermo, he beat the cautious*

Montgomery in the race for Messina, bringing him fame at home and the antagonism of Montgomery.
- *Patton led the breakout from the Normandy beachhead on 1 August. Within two weeks he had surrounded over 100,000 German soldiers in the Falaise gap. By the end of the month, he had reached the Saar River.*

ERICH VON MANSTEIN

1887–1973

CHRONOLOGY 1887 Born 24 November in Berlin • 1906 Joins the 3rd Guards Regiment • 1914–1918 Serves on Western, Eastern and Balkan Fronts • 1939 Chief of staff to von Rundstedt during invasion of Poland; developes plan to attack France through the Ardennes • 1940 Leads XXXVIII Infantry Corps in invasion of France • 1941 Leads LVI Panzer Corps in invasion of Soviet Union • 1942 Captures Sevastopol • 1943 Fails to relieve Stalingrad; recaptures Kharkov • 1944 Dismissed by Hitler • 1945 Captured by the British; tried for war crimes • 1953 Released on grounds of ill-health • 1973 Dies 11 June in Irshenshausen near Munich

ERICH VON MANSTEIN was considered one of the finest German strategists and field commanders of World II. His great contribution to the German war effort was the development of the plan to attack France through the Ardennes.

Born in Berlin on 24 November 1887, the son of an artillery officer, he was adopted by General Georg von Manstein after the death of his parents. In 1906, he joined the 3rd Guards Regiment

'In sum, he had military genius'

BASIL LIDDELL HART

as an officer. In November 1914, he was wounded near Ypres. Afterwards he served as a staff officer on the Western, Eastern and Balkan Fronts.

▶ A CONTROVERSIAL PLAN

Between the wars, he worked for, among others, General Gerd von **Rundstedt** and was his chief of staff during the invasion of Poland in 1939. He devised a controversial plan to attack France through the Ardennes. This was opposed by the Army High Command, but Hitler favoured it. When it was put into action, von Manstein led the XXXVIII Corps which spearheaded the battle for France.

When his plan was brilliantly successful, he was chosen to command Operation Sea Lion, the planned invasion of England. But when that was cancelled, he headed the LVI Panzer Corps on its race to Leningrad. Then with Army Group South he took 430,000 Soviet prisoners, withstood the Red Army's winter counter-offensive and took Crimea in July 1942.

He conceived Operation Winter Storm to relieve the German Sixth Army that was surrounded at Stalingrad. He put it into effect in December 1942 and almost succeeded. Then in February 1943, he managed to hold the Don crossing, allowing the German Army in the Caucasus to be withdrawn.

▶ DISAGREEING WITH HITLER

Manstein then wanted to evacuate Kharkov, hoping that the Red Army would exhaust itself pursuing him. He would then turn and destroy it. But Hitler wanted Kharkov to be held to the last man. There was a row, but Manstein got his way. He lured the Red Army westwards until it ran out of fuel then turned and attacked, recapturing Kharkov. It was Manstein's last victory. The Red Army and its T34 tanks that were coming off the Soviet production lines in ever increasing numbers were unstoppable. At Kursk in July 1943, the Soviets won the biggest tank battle in history. In March 1944, Hitler sacked him and he retired to his estate.

He was offered command again by Hitler's successor Admiral Doenitz, but the war had come to an end. Captured by the British, he was accused of war crimes, but was acquitted of the most serious charges and was freed in 1953 on the grounds of ill-health. Later he advised the new West German government on the structure of its armed forces. He published his memoirs, *Lost Victories*, in 1955 and died in 1973.

CAREER HIGHLIGHTS

- *Manstein's plan for the invasion of France replaced the Schlieffen Plan, which had failed in World War I but was still favoured by the German Army High Command. It envisaged advancing through the Ardennes Forest, thought by the Allies to be impassable. It was brilliantly successful.*
- *In the invasion of the Soviet Union, Manstein's LVI Panzer Corps advanced 200 miles to the Dvina river in four days. He* *almost took Leningrad and began a siege that lasted for 900 days.*
- *Early in 1943, Manstein destroyed the Red Army's winter offensive. He realized that if he simply fell back, evacuating Kharkov, the Soviets would keep on driving westwards until they were told to stop. When Manstein heard that they had run out of fuel, he turned and launched a massive counter-attack, retaking Kharkov in the most successful German counter-offensive of the war.*

BERNARD LAW MONTGOMERY

1887–1976

FIELD MARSHAL Bernard Law Montgomery was the inspirational British commander in World War II. He gave Britain its victory in North Africa and went on to command Allied ground troops from D-Day to the German surrender in May 1945.

Born in London on 17 November 1887, the son of a priest, he attended Sandhurst, but failed to score high enough to fulfil his ambition to join the Indian Army. Instead he took a commission in the Royal Warwickshire Regiment and served on the Northwest Frontier.

▸ YPRES AND THE SOMME

In World War I he showed conspicuous courage. Within three days of landing, he was reported missing in action. Later wounded three times and left for dead, he fought at Ypres and the

'Before Alamein, we never had a victory. After Alamein, we never had a defeat' WINSTON CHURCHILL

Somme. Awarded the Distinguished Service Order and the Croix de Guerre, he was mentioned in despatches six times.

Between the wars, Montgomery served in Ireland and Palestine and taught at the British Army's Staff College with Alan **Brooke**. By the outbreak of World War II he had risen to the rank of major-general. In September 1939 he landed in France and was given command of a division. Fighting a rearguard action through Belgium, he emerged with an enhanced reputation. One of the last out of Dunkirk, he returned to England to help organize the defence of the south coast.

In August 1942, he was given command of the Eighth Army in North Africa after Winston Churchill's first choice for the position General W.H.E. 'Strafer' Gott was killed in an air crash. Morale among new command was low; they had just been pushed back all the way across the Western Desert by Erwin **Rommel**. However, Montgomery inspired confidence in them and they stopped Rommel's Afrika Korps at the Battle of Alam Halfa on 31 August–3 September 1942, then threw them back at El Alamein seven weeks later. By 12 May 1943, he had met up with an Anglo-American force invading from the west, and together they drove the Germans out of North Africa completely.

▶ EIGHTH ARMY IN ITALY

Now under the command of Dwight D. **Eisenhower**, Montgomery continued to lead the Eighth Army during the invasions of Sicily and Italy. Again under the overall command of Eisenhower, Montgomery was put in charge of land forces at D-Day and it was his battle plan that proved ultimately successful.

Criticized for being over-cautious, Montgomery planned an uncharacteristic dash through northern Holland into the heart of Germany itself. It faltered when paratroopers well ahead of the main force failed to hold the bridge at Arnhem. He redeemed himself, however, during the Battle of the Bulge in the winter of 1944, when he took command of the Anglo-American forces to the north, preventing the Germans reaching Antwerp.

Driving on into Germany, it was Montgomery who accepted the German surrender. He later headed NATO before retiring in 1958.

VICTORY IN THE DESERT

- Having witnessed the carnage of World War I, Montgomery only attacked when he had overwhelming force. At El Alamein (23 October 1942) he had vastly superior forces while Rommel was at the end of a long supply line. A disciplined attack following a meticulous battle plan resulted in total defeat for the revered 'Desert Fox'. Some 59,000 men were killed or captured and over 500 German tanks destroyed. Winston Churchill said, 'Before Alamein, we never had a victory. After Alamein, we never had a defeat.'
- Put in charge of the D-Day landings, Montgomery vastly expanded the invasion force, making it the largest seaborne invasion in history. His strategy was to hold Germany's main force – its Panzers – at the eastern end of the beachhead with experienced British forces, while the Americans broke out to the west. It took longer than anticipated, but the operation was undoubtedly a success.
- Montgomery was also in charge of crossing the Rhine, in force, in March 1945. But he was denied his final ambition – the chance to make a dash on Berlin. However, it was in his tactical headquarters on Luneberg Heath that Germany's unconditional surrender was signed.

HEINZ GUDERIAN

1888–1954

CHRONOLOGY

1888 Born 17 June in Kulm, Germany.

1900 Enters cadet school.

1907 Commissioned in 100th Hannover Jaeger Battalion.

1912 Joins radio company.

1914–1917 Commands radio communications for 5th Cavalry Division.

1918 Serves on general staff.

1922 Joins the Inspectorate of Motorized Transport in Berlin.

1932 Starts large-scale armoured manoeuvres.

1934 Comes to the attention of Hitler.

1935 Starts Panzer divisions.

1937 Publishes *Achtung – Panzer!*

1939 Leads Panzers in Poland.

1940 Leads Panzers in France.

1941 Leads Panzers in Russia.

1943 Becomes inspector general of armoured troops.

1944 Becomes Hitler's acting chief of staff.

1945 Resigns; captured by US forces.

1954 Dies 14 May in Schwangau bei Fussen, West Germany.

G ENERAL HEINZ GUDERIAN was Germany's leading theorist of tank warfare, who was responsible for the development of the Panzer divisions and the blitzkrieg method of attack used during World War II.

Born in Kulm on 17 June 1888, the son of a Pomeranian infantry officer, Guderian was sent to cadet school at the age of twelve. At seventeen, he was commissioned as a lieutenant in the 100th Hannover Jaeger Battalion, which his father commanded. However, he became interested in radio communication and, during World War I, commanded a radio post for the 5th Cavalry Division, giving him an interest in battlefield mobility.

'If the tanks succeed, then victory follows'

▶ PANZER THEORY

In 1922, he joined the Inspectorate of Motorized Transport in Berlin. At that time, German military vehicles were only supposed to be used for carrying supplies, but he was asked to produce a report on the possibility of using them to deploy troops. Taking ideas from British tank theorists, he began to develop strategies that employed large numbers of armoured vehicles, supported by aircraft, that would make lightning attacks, encircling huge numbers of troops and paralysing enemy nations.

By 1932, he was developing these ideas with large-scale manoeuvres. When Hitler saw one of these demonstrations in 1934, he realized that Guderian had developed a new way to wage aggressive warfare and, the following year, the first three Panzer divisions were created.

In 1937, Guderian published *Achtung – Panzer!*, a handbook of tank tactics which he hoped would win over the conservative elements in the high command who still thought that tanks should support cavalry and foot soldiers. Guderian saw no role for cavalry and believed that motorized infantry should support tanks.

His theories were put to the test in Poland, France and Russia. Guderian and those Panzer commanders that followed him believed in commanding from the front, using radios in each tank to co-ordinate operations. Poland and France fell in a matter of weeks.

▶ THE PRODUCTION RACE

His strategy brought huge gains in Russia too, initially. But the German army found itself at the end of a long supply line when the Russian winter struck. Germany then found that it could not compete with Soviet industry which out-produced them with their superior T34 tank. This was the very thing that Guderian had warned Hitler about before his Russian adventure.

Guderian also noticed that the British had learnt to defeat his Panzers in the Western Desert with deep screens of anti-tank guns which were cheaper and easier to produce than tanks. After D-Day, Allied air superiority made it almost impossible for the Panzers to move during the day in good weather without being attacked.

Guderian suggested new tactics that would at least slow the Allied onslaught, but Hitler was wedded to the mobile Panzer warfare that had made such gains at the beginning of the war. Guderian fell out with him and was allowed to resign on the grounds of ill-health on 5 March 1945.

PANZER LEADER

- *When Guderian's Panzers rolled over the border into Poland on 1 September 1939, they were untested in combat. Even when they had been deployed on the unopposed takeover of Austria and Czechoslovakia, many had broken down. But Hitler's faith in Guderian paid off. Poland was taken in just twenty-eight days.*
- *Guderian led the surprise attack through the Ardennes Forest on 10 May 1940. Three days later, he had captured Sedan. By 23 May, he had taken Calais and Bologne and was halted in front of Dunkirk, though he had faced numerically superior forces. By the time the French surrendered on 22 June, he had reached the Swiss border.*
- *Hitler ordered Guderian to lead the invasion of the Soviet Union in June 1941, though Guderian thought it a mistake. Initially, his strategy worked superbly. His Panzers penetrated hundreds of miles into enemy territory, encircling millions of men.*

DWIGHT D. EISENHOWER

1890–1969

GENERAL DWIGHT DAVID Eisenhower commanded the largest multinational military force ever assembled. With over four million men under his command, he led the invasion of Western Europe during World War II, overseeing the fall of Hitler and Nazi Germany.

Born on 14 October 1890 in Denison, Texas,

Eisenhower grew up in Abilene, Kansas. Unable to afford college, he applied to West Point and was accepted. In his class of 164, he graduated 61st academically and 125th in discipline. His class of 1915 was to produce fifty-nine generals.

Commissioned in the infantry, he found himself in command of a tank training center. World War I ended shortly before he was due to be sent

'I hate war as only a soldier who has lived it can, one who has seen its brutality, its stupidity.'

overseas. In the inter-war years, he took a number of staff posts and in 1935 he went to the Philippines to help reorganize their army.

▸ WAR GAMES

In 1941, he came to the attention of army chief of staff General George C. Marshall for his role in planning a large-scale war game. When the United States entered the war that December, he was assigned to the group in Washington planning the invasion of Western Europe.

Promoted to major-general in June 1942, he was given command of US troops in Europe. A month later, he was put in charge of Operation Torch, the Anglo-American invasion of French North Africa. Eisenhower's skill was to keep control of the flamboyant commanders under him, such as **Montgomery** and **Patton**. He also maintained the vital unity between the battle-hardened, well-trained and experienced British, who considered the raw Americans civilians in uniform, and the Americans, who found the British condescending.

▸ ONTO THE BEACHES

With Patton and Montgomery, he staged landings on Sicily and in Italy. Then in December 1943, he was appointed Supreme Commander of the Allied Expeditionary Force that was going to invade France. Churchill conceded that an American must lead this force for political reasons. Although there would be equal numbers of British and Americans on the beach on D-Day, most reinforcements would come from the US, so the AEF would end up overwhelmingly American. Nevertheless, Eisenhower did appoint Britons as his deputy and as commanders of the air, sea and land forces. Montgomery as leader of the land forces was often given free rein, despite the complaints of Eisenhower's own officers.

In December 1944 Eisenhower became the first US General of the Armies since **Pershing**. To the end, he had to contend with the rivalry of Montgomery and Patton, who both wanted the lion's share of supplies to pursue their own 'narrow front' advance. Eisenhower insisted on a 'broad front' approach satisfying neither man.

Sparing with men's lives, Eisenhower let the Soviets take Berlin, over the complaints of Churchill. He returned to the US in June 1945 to a hero's welcome. Retiring from active service in 1948, he became president of Columbia University, before becoming Supreme Commander of Nato in 1950.

Elected President in 1953, he negotiated an end to the Korean War. After two terms in office, he left the White House in 1961 and retired to his farm in Gettysburg, Pennsylvania to work on his memoirs.

D-DAY COMMANDER

- With General Montgomery pushing the Afrika Korps back across the Western Desert in 1942, Eisenhower launched the first Anglo-American operation of the war with the invasion of French North Africa to Rommel's rear. Together they forced the Axis forces out of North Africa altogether by May 1943.
- On 24 December 1943, Eisenhower was appointed Supreme Commander of the Allied Expeditionary Forces. Then on 6 June despite the threat of bad weather, he sent a million men in some 4,000 ships across the Channel to Normandy in the biggest amphibious landing in history. On 25 August they had liberated Paris. After reversing a fierce German counter-attack in the Ardennes in December, Allied troops crossed the Rhine on 7 March 1945 and Germany surrendered on 7 May.

ERWIN ROMMEL

1891–1944

joined the 124th Württemberg Infantry Regiment as an officer cadet in 1910. Commissioned lieutenant in 1912, he fought in France, Romania and Italy during World War I, earning the Iron Cross, First Class. Away from the war of attrition being fought on the Western Front, Rommel was the first to perfect *Stosstruppen* (shock troop) tactics in an attack on the Italian mountain stronghold of Caporetto in October 1917.

'I was under the impression that I must not stand still or we were lost,' he wrote.

▸ MASTER OF TACTICS

These small, highly mobile, integrated squads were later used on the Western Front, but the war was lost when the British started deploying tanks en masse.

After World War I, he stayed on in the infantry, in various teaching posts, where he developed these *Stosstruppen* tactics. He went into print with his idea in his book *Infantry*

F IELD MARSHAL ERWIN ROMMEL, known to his enemies affectionately as 'the Desert Fox' was the most highly respected German general of World War II for his tactical skills, his uncanny ability to anticipate his opponents' moves and his genius in handling massed formations of armour.

Born to a middle-class family in Heidenheim in Württemberg, Germany on 15 November 1891, he

'I must not stand still or we are lost'

Attacks, published in 1937, which was based on the lectures he gave as an instructor at the Infantry School in Dresden. Hitler was impressed and appointed him commander of his personal bodyguard and promoted him to major-general.

Rommel himself was impressed by the blitzkrieg tactics used for the first time in Poland in 1939. On 15 February 1940, he was given command of the 7th Panzer Division. In the Battle for France, he showed even greater ability in armoured warfare than his commander. Rather than engaging the enemy on a broad front, he punched a hole through their lines, countering superior numbers and firepower with surprise. Leading from the front, he was a great favourite among his men.

▶ **AFRIKA KORPS COMMANDER**

In February 1942, he was sent with the newly formed Afrika Korps to North Africa where Germany's Italian ally was being comprehensively defeated by the British in Libya. He immediately went on the offensive, pushing the British back all the way to the Egyptian border. Again Rommel inspired his troops, leading from the front and wearing his trademark sun-and-sand goggles, which he had captured from the British. He adapted the Panzer tactics to the open spaces of the desert so that his opponents called him 'the Desert Fox'.

At the end of 1941, the British counter-attacked, pushing Rommel back across the desert. But he regrouped and, by the summer of 1942, was within 60 miles of Alexandria. Hitler ordered an attack on Cairo, but starved Rommel of the tanks he needed as they were fully committed on the Eastern Front. Rommel was soundly beaten by General **Montgomery** and his Eighth Army. But this time as he retreated across the desert he found an Anglo-American force to his rear, which had landed in French North Africa.

Rommel was recalled and, after serving in Italy, was sent to strengthen the French coastal defences. Again he was starved of supplies and when the Allies landed in Normandy, Hitler refused him the Panzer reserve until it was too late to push the invasion force back into the sea. He was relieved of command because he was injured when his car was attacked by British fighter-bombers.

After the attempt on Hitler's life in July 1944 failed, Rommel was implicated in the plot. He was persuaded to take his life with poison on 14 October and was later buried with full military honours.

SHOCK TROOPS

- On 26 October 1917, Rommel led a bayonet charge at the Italian mountain stronghold of Caporetto with just 200 men. They captured 9,000 men and eighty-one heavy guns for few losses of their own. He was promoted to captain and awarded the Pour le Merite, *the highest imperial decoration for bravery.*

- *During the Battle for France, Rommel combined Guderian's theories of armoured warfare with his own 'shock troop' philosophy. His race to the French coast was so swift that Rommel's formation was dubbed* 'the ghost division'. At a cost of 42 Panzers and 2,500 men, Rommel took 100,000 prisoners and destroyed 450 enemy tanks, along with thousands of other vehicles and artillery pieces.

- *The Libyan port of Tobruk was a symbol of British resistance. It had held out against Rommel's siege for 242 days in 1941, the longest siege in British military history. However, in a counter-attack the following year, it fell in just two days. The day after that, Rommel was promoted to field marshal.*

HAROLD ALEXANDER

1891–1969

paigns against **Rommel** and later took command in Italy.

Born in London on 10 December 1891 to a titled Anglo-Irish family, he attended Sandhurst before being commissioned a second lieutenant in the Irish Guards. In 1914, he went to France with the vanguard of the British Expeditionary Force and saw action there continuously for the next four years. Wounded twice, he won the Military Cross and Distinguished Service Order. He commanded a brigade and became the youngest lieutenant-colonel in the army.

▸ BATTLES IN THE BALTIC

In 1919 he commanded a German force which drove the Red Army out of Latvia, winning the Order of St. Anne with swords which he always wore prominently. He spoke German and Russian fluently. When the Soviet Union recognized Latvian independence in 1920 he returned to England. In 1922 he was given command of

HAROLD ALEXANDER, later Earl Alexander of Tunis, was the field marshal in command of Allied forces in the Western Desert during the cam-

'The only man under whom any general would gladly serve' FIELD MARSHAL MONTGOMERY

the army of occupation in Constantinople.

After a number of regimental and staff jobs, he was sent to command the Nowshera Brigade on the Northwest Frontier, one of the most coveted postings in India. There he learnt Urdu.

In 1939, he took the 1st Division to France: acting as rearguard, it held the German advance long enough for the British Expeditionary Force to be evacuated from Dunkirk.

Promoted to lieutenant-general he was given Southern Command, then commanded Force 110 which planned amphibious invasions. In February 1942, he was sent to Burma, though it was too late to save the situation there.

In August 1942, with Rommel only 60 miles from Cairo, Alexander was made commander-in-chief in the Middle East with **Montgomery** as his army commander. Montgomery had little respect for those set above him, even Churchill. But he said later that Alexander was 'the only man under whom... any general... would gladly serve in a subordinate position'. In return, Alexander took no credit for the desert victories, leaving all the glory to Montgomery.

▸ AT CASABLANCA

Alexander attended the Casablanca Conference in January 1943, where he won the confidence of President Franklin Roosevelt. He was put in command of the Anglo-American force in the battle for Tunis. At first he despaired that the Americans 'simply did not know their jobs as soldiers' and 'lacked the will to fight'. However, while American officers found most British officers condescending, everyone had respect for Alexander and under his firm command the Anglo-American First Army began to make the same solid progress as Montgomery's Eighth Army that was advancing from the east. Alexander planned the final battle in the Tunis campaign, employing an elaborate and successful plan of deception. In just two days, a quarter of a million enemy troops were captured.

He was also in overall command of the invasion of Sicily. In the assault phase, his plan called for a larger amphibious force than that deployed at D-Day in Normandy. He went on to command the invasion of Italy, taking Rome on 4 June 1944. By this time he was co-ordinating an army that consisted of units from Britain, the US, India, France, Italy, New Zealand, Poland, Greece and Czechoslovakia. The plan for the final battle in the Italian campaign in April 1945 was another of Alexander's elaborate deceptions. On 29 April Alexander accepted the Germans' unconditional surrender.

·A LEADER OF MEN

- *Alexander first came to prominence during World War I. Author Rudyard Kipling said of him, 'It is undeniable that Colonel Alexander had the gift of handling men on the lines to which they most readily responded... his subordinates loved him... and his men were all his own.'*
- *During the last three days of the Dunkirk evacuation, when Alexander was in command, 20,000 British and 98,000 French were evacuated. Alexander left on the last motor launch after touring the beaches to make sure that there were no British troops remaining.*
- *On 13 May 1943, Alexander cabled Churchill, saying, 'Sir, it is my duty to report that the Tunisian campaign is over. We are masters of the North African shores.'*
- *In April 1945 in Italy, a million Germans laid down their arms in the first mass surrender of the war.*

MAO TSE-TUNG

1893–1976

CHRONOLOGY 1893 Born 26 December in Hunan Province • 1911–1912 Serves as soldier in revolutionary forces to found republic • 1921 Founds Chinese Communist Party • 1931 Founds Red Army; elected chairman of the Chinese Soviet Republic • 1934 To escape Nationalist forces, embarks on the 'Long March' • 1937 Forms alliance with Nationalists to fight invading Japanese • 1945 Fights Nationalists again • 1949 Proclaims People's Republic of China and becomes its chairman • 1976 Dies 9 September in Peking

MAO TSE-TUNG – also known as Mao Zedong – was a Communist guerrilla leader who took over the world's most populous country in an armed struggle that took 22 years, and remained its leader for another 26. Taking his own military inspiration from **Sun Tzu**, he has been an inspiration to other revolutionary leaders the world over.

Born to a well-off, though peasant-class fami-

ly in the village of Shao-shan, Hunan Province on 26 December 1893, he was well educated, studying the lives and works of George **Washington**, **Napoleon** and Sun Tzu, among others. He served briefly as a soldier in the revolutionary movement that overthrew the last imperial dynasty and established the Chinese Republic.

Working as a library assistant in Peking University in 1918–1919 he studied Marx and

'Political power grows out of the barrel of a gun'

Engels. On 1 July 1921, Mao and fellow Marxists founded the Chinese Communist Party in Shanghai. In 1923, the CCP merged with the Nationalist Party or Kuomintang. But when Chiang Kai-shek took over, he expelled the socialists and set about unifying the country under his leadership.

▶ PEASANT SUPPORT

Chiang's Kuomintang had a strong following in the cities, while the CCP found its support among the rural peasantry. In 1927, Mao and his followers began a series of uprisings, the most notable being in the city of Nan-ch'ang. When these were violently suppressed, Mao and a few hundred peasants set up a base in the Chingkang Mountains on the Hunan-Kiangsi border and began guerrilla operations. In 1931, Mao over-ran part of Kiangsi and founded the Chinese Soviet Republic with himself as head. His peasant guerrillas were now the Red Army.

However, the Kuomintang had done better, with Chiang Kai-shek taking over the government in Peking in 1928. He was determined to strangle the Chinese Soviet Republic and surrounded it with 700,000 men. Half of Mao's army was lost. But on 15 October 1934, the remaining 100,000 broke through the Nationalist lines and escaped to the west. Over the next two years, in the 'Long March', they travelled 6,000 miles to the safety of Yenan on the USSR border.

▶ COMMUNIST CONTROL

When the Japanese invaded in 1937, the Communists and Nationalists formed an alliance to fight them. But when World War II was over, they began fighting each other again. During the war years, the Communists had grown to be the stronger force. The Nationalists were defeated and in 1949 Chiang Kai-shek withdrew to the island of Taiwan to form Nationalist China. The mainland was now in the hands of Mao and he proclaimed it a People's Republic, which he ruled until his death in 1976.

While Mao Tse-tung's Communist ideology did much to impoverish China, it made him one of the richest men in the country. His 'Little Red Book' (*The Thoughts of Chairman Mao*) sold in its millions, becoming the bible of the Red Guard during China's 'Cutural Revolution' in the 1960s and 70s and the revolutionary primer for wannabe revolutionaries around the world.

THE RED ARMY

- *Although the Chinese Red Army – or, officially, the People's Liberation Army – was founded in 1931, it traces its origins back to the Nan-ch'ang Uprising of 1927, when Mao's Chinese Communist Party broke away from the Nationalists, took over the city of Nan-ch'ang and held it for several days. At its height, the Red Army numbered over three million, with compulsory military service for all men over eighteen.*

- *By 1934, the Chinese Soviet Republic controlled a population of several million but found itself encircled by Nationalists. That October Mao and his followers set out on a* 6,000-mile trek from their base in southeast China to a remote stronghold in the northwest. Of the 100,000 who set off, only 8,000 arrived. On the way Mao tightened his grip on the Communist Party and the 'Long March' became one of the mythical pillars of the People's Republic.

- *On 1 October 1949, Mao Tse-tung stood at the Gate of Heavenly Peace and read a proclamation announcing China's new People's Republic to a cheering crowd of 200,000. Within hours the Soviet Union recognized the new regime.*

WILLIAM SLIM

1891–1970

CHRONOLOGY 1891 Born 6 August in Bristol • 1914 Joins Royal Warwickshire
Regiment • 1915 Wounded in the Dardenelles • 1916 Wounded in
Iraq • 1917 Posted to India • 1940 Sent to take Gallabat in Eritrea • 1941 Wounded in Eritrea;
fights Vichy French in Iraq; invades Persia • 1942 Commands retreat from Rangoon • 1943
Counter-attacks at Arakan • 1944 Begins re-conquest of Burma • 1945 Retakes Rangoon • 1948
Appointed chief of the Imperial General Staff; promoted to field marshal • 1953–1960 Serves as
governor-general of Australia • 1970 Dies 14 December in London.

WILLIAM SLIM was the British
general who commanded the 'forgotten army' that turned back the
Japanese invasion of India and
beat the invaders in Burma. During his long military career he rose from lance-corporal to field
marshal and chief of the Imperial General Staff.

Born the son of an iron merchant in Bristol on
6 August 1891, he was a member of the Officers'
Training Corps at school. His ambition was to

become an army officer, but his parents could
not afford to send him to Sandhurst.

▶ INTO INDIA

At the outbreak of World War I, he volunteered
and was posted to the Royal Warwickshire
Regiment. He first saw action in the Dardanelles
and was wounded so seriously that it was thought
unlikely that he would ever be fit for active duty
again. Although still officially unfit, he was post-

'Finest general the Second World War produced'

LORD LOUIS MOUNTBATTEN

ed to Mesopotamia where he was wounded again. Evacuated to India, he was given a regular commission and joined the Indian Army.

In 1939, as commander of 10 Indian Infantry Brigade of the 5th Indian Division, he went to Eritrea where he was ordered to take Gallabat and prevent the Italians from invading Sudan. He succeed, but failed to take nearby Metemma. Soon after, he was injured again when his vehicle was shot up by a low-flying plane. On recovery, he was sent back to Mesopotamia.

After his success there, he was posted back to India, where Wavell sent him on to Burma to take control of the two British-Indian divisions retreating from Rangoon. He managed a fighting retreat and got his men back to India, tired and exhausted, before the monsoon. Then he counter-attacked and halted the Japanese advance at Chittagong and Impal.

▶ THE RECONQUEST OF BURMA

Given command of the Fourteenth Army, he planned the re-conquest of Burma, putting Orde Wingate's Chindits and other irregulars in behind the enemy lines. The Japanese Fifteenth Army began another all-out offensive in March and April 1944 to take British strongholds at

Kohima and Impal so they could invade India. After bitter fighting, the enemy were held, then forced back towards the Chindwin valley.

As the war in Europe came to an end, Slim had the supplies to undertake large-scale seaborne, airborne and armoured assaults. In one bold ruse, he used fake radio traffic to encourage the Japanese to attack what they thought was an isolated formation, then slipped his main force around their flank, encircling their Fifteenth and Thirty-third Armies, and isolating the Twenty-eighth.

When he recaptured Rangoon on 2 May, Lord Mountbatten, the Supreme Allied Commander in Southeast Asia, said, 'Slim was the finest general the Second World War produced.'

Before Slim's Fourteenth Army could taste any more victories, the end of the war came with the dropping of atomic bombs on Hiroshima and Nagasaki. Their contribution was overlooked and they became the 'forgotten army'.

Slim went on to become the chief of the Imperial General Staff in 1948, was promoted to field marshal, and served as governor-general of Australia from 1953 to 1960. He published his memoirs *Defeat Into Victory* in 1956 and was created a viscount in 1960.

HOLDING THE LINE IN BURMA

- *In Iraq in May 1941, Slim fought a brief and successful campaign against the Vichy French. Then he invaded Persia, keeping it out of the war. He met up with Soviet troops in Tehran and the rail-link through Persia became an important supply line for the Russians who were now facing Hitler.*
- *Until 1943, the Japanese had an unbroken series of successes. But Slim devised a new strategy to halt them. Instead of simply withdrawing, he left behind well-stocked strongholds which could be supplied by air. If the advancing Japanese army bypassed them,*

they would play havoc with its supply lines or attack them from the rear during any counter-offensive.
- *In early 1944, the Japanese mounted a new attack, believing they could shatter the British on the Burmese border and provoke an uprising in India. But the offensive was held for three weeks; then the Japanese were driven back in disorder. In a disastrous defeat, the Japanese Fifteenth Army suffered over 50,000 casualties, half of them fatal. Slim was awarded the CB and KCB and achieved international fame.*

OMAR BRADLEY

1893–1981

GENERAL OMAR N. BRADLEY was one of the key American generals in World War II, serving with distinction in North Africa, Sicily, France and Germany. A self-effacing man, he was known as the 'GI's General'.

Born to a poor family in Clark, Missouri on 12 February 1893, he graduated from West Point with Eisenhower in the star class of 1915. He served in the 14th Infantry Regiment during World War I, but was not sent to France.

From 1920 to 1924, he taught math at West

190

Bradley's respect for his men's lives earned him the sobriquet 'the GI's General'

Point, then both attended and instructed at the Command and General Staff School at Fort Leavenworth, Kansas and the Infantry Training School at Fort Benning, Georgia, rising to become commandant there.

▶ FIGHTING COMMANDER

With America's entry into World War II in 1941, he commanded the 82nd and 28th Divisions, turning them into tough fighting units. He was assistant to **Eisenhower** in the invasion of French North Africa. Bradley took over command of II Corps when **Patton** was promoted. His corps then occupied Bizerte and took 40,000 prisoners on 7 May 1943, the day the British took Tunis.

Bradley commanded II Corps during the invasion of Sicily, though he was criticized by Patton for not being aggressive enough. But Patton was disgraced by an incident where he slapped two shell-shocked soldiers and Bradley was chosen to be army group commander on D-Day. Bradley went ashore on 9 June. He was in command of the US breakout to the west, with Patton as his spearhead, and they attempted to close the Falaise gap.

After liberating Paris on 25 July, he was put in charge of the Twelfth Army Group, the largest force ever placed under an American army group commander, leading over 1,250,000 men in the field. His forces suffered the counter-attack through the Ardennes in the Battle of the Bulge. When this was thrown back, Bradley pushed on into Germany.

▶ HALT BEFORE BERLIN

With Patton in Czechoslovakia, threatening Prague, and Simpson on the Elbe with his Ninth Army ready to burst out of its bridgeheads and drive on Berlin, Bradley called a halt. He advised Eisenhower against the capture of Berlin. It had already been decided that the German capital would be within the Soviet zone of occupation and Bradley reckoned that it would cost 100,000 Allied lives to take possession of a ruined city and its hungry people – a price he considered too high. Churchill, particularly, was outraged. Bradley had not appreciated the political advantages that taking the city would bring, especially in the forthcoming Cold War.

After the war, Bradley served as head of the Veterans Administration, then replaced Eisenhower as army chief of staff in 1948. The following year he became the first chairman of the newly formed Joint Chiefs of Staff. In 1950, he became one of the few to be promoted to five-star general. His memoirs *A Soldier's Story* were published in 1951 and he retired from active duty in 1953. A second volume of memoirs *A General's Life* was published in 1983, two years after his death. He is buried in Arlington National Cemetery.

BREAKING THE SIEGFRIED LINE

- *After the breakout from the Normandy beachhead, Bradley was put on an equal footing with Montgomery, with overall command of Allied land forces going to Eisenhower. Bradley's army group then pursued the remnants of the German Seventh Army and Fifth Panzer Army that had escaped encirclement at Falaise. They crossed the Seine and liberated Paris on 25 August 1944.*

- *After the Battle of the Bulge, Bradley quickly breached the Siegfried Line – Germany's border defence – and crossed the Rhine over an undamaged railway bridge at Remagen on 7 March 1945, which retreating German troops had failed to blow up. The speed of his advance cornered 335,000 German troops in the Ruhr pocket, who surrendered.*

GEORGY ZHUKOV

1896–1974

GEORGY KONSTANTINOVICH Zhukov was commander-in-chief of the Red Army during World War II. He, more than anyone, was responsible for the Soviet victory over Hitler.

Born to a poor family in the village of Strelkovo 60 miles east of Moscow on 1 December 1896, he first went out to work at the age of eleven. At fifteen, he was an apprentice furrier and in World War I he was drafted into the 10th Novogorod Dragoon Regiment. Acts of bravery led to four decorations and a promotion to corporal.

'Let me defend my country with my rifle and a bayonet in my hand'

▶ REICHSWEHR PUPIL

After the Russian Revolution, he joined the Red Army and fought with the 1st Moscow Cavalry Division. He rose to command the 39th Busulokov Cavalry Regiment and in 1923 was sent to Germany to attend a leadership course run by the Reichswehr. After graduating from the Frunze Military Academy, he was sent to head Soviet forces that secured the Mongolian-Manchurian border against a Japanese invasion.

After serving as chief of staff in the Winter War against Finland in 1939–1940, he was given command of the Kiev military district. And, after winning a war game, Stalin appointed him chief of staff of the Red Army.

When the Germans attacked the Soviet Union in the summer of 1941, Stalin took control as generalissimo with Zhukov as his deputy. Few dared oppose Stalin, but when Zhukov was told that one of his ideas was 'rubbish', he replied, 'If you think that your chief of staff can talk only rubbish, then demote me to a private soldier and let me defend my country with my rifle and a bayonet in my hand.'

After organizing the defences of Leningrad, Zhukov moved to Moscow to direct its defences. He then staged a counter-offensive that winter, which drove the Germans out of central Russia. Planning every major engagement in the war, he effectively became commander-in-chief, though Stalin reserved that title for himself. After overseeing the defence of Stalingrad, he planned the counter-offensive that encircled the Sixth Army and was made Marshal of the Soviet Union.

▶ FROM KURSK TO BERLIN

After defeating the Germans at the Battle of Kursk, he pushed them back through the Ukraine, Belorussia, Poland and Czechoslovakia. Forward elements raced to the Elbe to join up with the Americans there, while Zhukov was in overall command when Berlin was attacked by two Red Army fronts, taking the German capital and winning the war.

Zhukov was greeted as a hero when he returned to Moscow in 1946, but Stalin was a jealous man and sent him into exile as commander of a distant military region. When Stalin died in 1953, Zhukov helped Nikita Khruschev's rise to power and was rewarded with a place on the Communist Party Presidium. But when Khruschev fell in 1964, Zhukov fell with him. He spent his last years writing an account of World War II and died on 18 June 1974.

TAKING BERLIN

- In the fighting along the Khalin Gol river and the Manchurian border in 1939, Zhukov led massed tank units into action, inflicting 60,000 casualties on the Japanese invaders. He was promoted to General of the Army.
- At Kursk in July 1943, the Germans attempted to surround a Soviet salient around the city. Anticipating this, Zhukov pulled his main force back, leaving only anti-tank guns and minefields. The Germans were halted after 10 miles, then thrown back by a counter-attack, losing 125,000 men, 550 tanks and 200 aircraft. The Battle of Kursk was the largest tank battle in history, involving 6,000 tanks, 4,000 aircraft and two million men. The Soviet advance then resumed, pushing the Germans back all the way to Berlin.
- In April 1945 Zhukov commanded the Battle for Berlin and, on 8 May 1945, he represented the Soviet Union at Germany's formal surrender. He remained in Germany as commander of the Soviet occupation force and served as the Soviet representative on the Allied Control Commission.

IVAN KONEV

1897–1973

IVAN STEPANOVICH KONEV was Zhukov's
most able general in World War II, halting
the Germans outside Moscow, pushing the
Germans out of the Soviet Union and being
the first Soviet commander to reach German soil.

Born to a peasant family on 28 December

1897 in Lodein near Archangel, he was con-
scripted into the Czarist Army, serving in an
artillery regiment on the Galician front, where
he was promoted to sergeant for bravery.

After the Russian Revolution, he joined the
Red Army, serving in the Civil War as command-

Konev's 2nd Ukrainian Front were the first Russian troops onto German soil

er of an armoured train and commissar of a rifle brigade. He put down the naval mutiny at Kronstadt, in the Gulf of Finland, in 1921.

▸ DEFENDING MOSCOW

After graduating from the Frunze Military Academy in 1926, he was posted to the Far East, escaping Stalin's purges. When the Germans invaded the Soviet Union, Konev led an army group to Smolensk in an attempt to halt the German advance on Moscow. When that failed, Konev was called back to help defend Moscow under Zhukov. It was his Kalinin Army Group that finally flung the German's back far enough to halt the German reinforcements being sent to Stalingrad.

In 1943, he built up a huge army of reserves that recaptured Kharkov after the Battle of Kursk. Heading the 2nd Ukrainian Front (which was technically subordinate to Zhukov's 1st Ukrainian Front) the two commanders surrounded the German army corps at Korsun in early 1944, capturing or killing over 100,000 men. They then advanced on a 350-mile wide front, driving the Germans from Soviet soil and killing 380,000 and capturing 158,000 on the way.

Konev reached the Oder-Neisse Line on 15 February, but had to halt for supplies. Stalin ordered him to support Zhukov's left wing, while his forward units made a dash to link up with the Americans on the Elbe, halting their advance there.

▸ RACE FOR BERLIN

Realizing that the Battle for Berlin was going to be bitter, Konev insisted that artillery be deployed at a density of 250 guns per kilometre to provide a rolling barrage. He and Zhukov were supposed to race for the city. Zhukov was held up by a spirited defence along the Seelow heights by General Gotthard Heinrici. Consequently Konev was ordered to swing his front around into Berlin and, after a brief battle, he took the city. But, as overall commander, Zhukov took the credit.

When Zhukov became head of the Soviet occupation force in Germany, Konev was given the corresponding post in Austria. But when Zhukov fell from power in 1946, Konev replaced him as commander-in-chief.

As deputy minister of defence in 1955, he became the chief architect of the Warsaw Pact and served as its commander-in-chief from 1955 to 1960, when he retired, returning briefly during the Berlin crisis in 1961.

A dedicated Communist, Konev knew how to retain his rank and power both under Stalin and after him. He remained an advisor to the inspector general of the army until his death at the age of 75 on 21 May 1973. He is buried in the walls of the Kremlin.

A DECORATED HERO

- *Heading the Kalinin Army Group outside Stalingrad, Konev sprang what became known as the 'Konev ambush'. He let his troops at the center retreat, then encircled the oncoming enemy with the flanks. Launching the counter-offensive on 5 December 1941, he pushed the Germans back 100 miles, though with heavy casualties on both sides.*
- *Konev's 2nd Ukrainian Front was the first across the Vistula into Poland in 1944 and the first onto German soil. His advance guard were the first to link up with the Americans on the Elbe and his troops were the first Soviet soldiers into Berlin.*
- *Konev's personal valour and dedicated service won him five Order of Lenins, two Hero of the Soviet Union medals, and the Order of Victory with Diamonds – a decoration only ever awarded to eleven Soviet officers.*

VASILY CHUIKOV

1900–1982

CHRONOLOGY 1900 Born 31 January near Moscow • 1918 Joins Red Army; sees action in Civil War • 1919 Becomes regimental commander • 1925 Graduates from Frunze Military Academy • 1939 Takes part in Soviet invasion of Poland • 1939–1940 Fights in Russo–Finnish War • 1942 Commands Soviet forces at the Battle of Stalingrad • 1945 Accepts surrender of Berlin • 1972 Appointed senior inspector general at the Ministry of Defence • 1982 Dies 18 March in Moscow

General Vasily Ivanovich Chuikov was the Soviet commander who halted the German advance at Stalingrad, destroying the Sixth Army and turning back the German invasion of the Soviet Union in World War II. He pursued the German army back to Germany, taking Berlin and ending the war.

Born the son of a peasant on 31 January 1900 in Serebryannye Prudy, a village just outside Moscow, he joined the Red Army in 1918. He saw his first action in the post-revolutionary Civil War at Tsaritsyn (later named Stalingrad

'We shall hold the city or die here'

and now called Volgograd). He joined the Communist Party and within two years of enlisting was in command of a regiment.

Graduating from the M.V. Frunze Military Academy in 1925, he specialized in Far Eastern studies and was military advisor to the nationalist leader Chiang Kai Sheng in China from 1926 to 1937. He studied new techniques of mechanized warfare and was part of the force that occupied the Soviet zone of Poland when Germany invaded in 1939. He then fought in the Russo-Finnish War of 1939–1940, before returning to China as military attaché.

▶ BATTLE ON THE VOLGA

When Germany invaded the Soviet Union in 1941, Chuikov returned home, and was sent to command the Sixty-second Army as it was being pushed back on to the Volga river. On 25 July Chuikov arrived at the front line to find his army in full retreat in front of the German Panzers and aircraft. Using brute force, he pushed his men back into the line. Stalingrad then found itself besieged by twenty-two German divisions, over 700 planes, 500 tanks and over 2,000 guns and mortars. But Chuikov would not give up. He told his men, 'We shall hold the city or die here.'

Chuikov held a narrow strip of the west bank of the Volga and kept his men supplied by ferrying food, ammunition and fresh troops across the river. The Germans on the other hand found themselves cut off when winter closed in. Their Panzers were vulnerable in the narrow streets of Stalingrad.

▶ URBAN WARFARE

The Red Army fought building by building, blowing up the stairs so that different floors of the same building were occupied by different sides. As the fighting continued, most of the city was reduced to rubble, but this only served to give Soviet troops armed with grenades and anti-tank guns more places to hide. Eventually they were forced to fight in the sewers.

On 19 November 1942, the Red Army counter-attacked with a pincer movement north and south of the city, encircling General Paulus's Sixth Army. A promised airlift brought insufficient supplies. In January 1943, despite Hitler's instructions to fight to the last man, Paulus surrendered.

In April 1943, Chuikov was given command of the 8th Guards and fought with them through the Crimea, across western Russia and Belorussia, and through Poland. His men established the first bridgehead over the River Oder and spearheaded the Soviet push into Germany. He was one of General Zhukov's principal commanders at the final assault on Berlin.

After the war he commanded the Soviet occupation force in Germany. He joined the Central Committee of the Communist Party in 1952 and in 1972 he became the senior inspector general in the Ministry of Defence.

HOLDING STALINGRAD

- Chuikov had held Stalingrad against the German onslaught for eighteen months when, on 31 January 1943, the German commander General Paulus surrendered with his remaining 91,000 troops. The Soviets recovered 250,000 German and Romanian corpses and total Axis losses are estimated to have been 800,000 dead. The official figure for Soviet losses in the campaign to hold Stalingrad includes 1,100,000 dead.
- On 1 May 1945, a delegation from Hitler's bunker approached Chuikov and asked him for his terms for a truce. The following day, General Weidling, the commandant of Berlin, formerly surrendered the city to him.

ORDE WINGATE

1903–1944

CHRONOLOGY 1903 Born 26 February at Naini Tal, India • 1923 Commissioned in the Royal Artillery • 1927 Travels to Sudan • 1928–1933 Serves on Abyssinian frontier with Sudan Defence Force • 1933 Explores Libyan desert • 1935 Italy invades Abyssinia • 1936 Posted to intelligence staff in Palestine • 1939 Serves as major in anti-aircraft unit • 1940 Travels to Khartoum to support Abyssinian rebels • 1941 Captures Addis Ababa and reinstalls Haile Selassie • 1942 Organizes the 'Chindits' in India • 1943 Leads Chindit force into action against the Japanese in Burma • 1944 Dies 24 March in Burma

CHARLES ORDE WINGATE was the leading British 'irregular' leader of World War II. His unconventional force, Wingate's Raiders, more commonly known as the Chindits, harassed a superior Japanese force in the jungles of Burma.

Born in Naini Tal, India, on 26 February 1903, Wingate was the son of a long-serving Indian Army officer. His parents were Plymouth Brethren. He studied at the Royal Military Academy, Woolwich and was commissioned in the Royal Artillery in 1923.

Wingate took command of a force of British, Gurkha and Burmese troops: the Chindits

He learnt Arabic at the School of Oriental Studies in London. In 1927 he went to Sudan to continue his studies, travelling there by bicycle as far as Brindisi. Obtaining a posting in the Sudan Defence Force, he served on the Abyssinian frontier from 1928 to 1933. He then took off into the Libyan desert on foot in search of the legendary oasis of Zerzura.

▶ PALESTINIAN PATROLS

From 1933 to 1936, he served with artillery units in England. Then he went to Palestine as an intelligence officer at a time when the Arabs were rebelling against Jewish immigration. He was outspokenly pro-Jewish and organized Jewish youths into 'night patrols'. He was wounded in a skirmish in 1938 and, when the rebellion was put down, was awarded the DSO.

At the outbreak of World War II, Wingate was a brigade-major with an anti-aircraft unit, but in 1940 he was sent to Khartoum to aid Ethiopian rebels fighting the Italians, who had occupied Abyssinia in 1935. Under Wingate's command, they liberated the country. He returned to England with malaria and attempted suicide.

On recovery, he was called out to India to help reverse the Japanese invasion of Burma. He proposed the use of a 'long range penetration group' to cause disruption behind enemy lines. These would communicate by radio and be supplied by air – innovations at the time.

▶ THE CHINDITS

In June 1942, he was given a force of British, Gurkhas and Burmese to train. They took as their badge the mythical chinthé – the half lion, half griffin figure seen guarding Burmese pagodas – giving them their name, Chindits. He also trained a similar US force known as 'Merrill's Marauders'. In February 1943, the Chindits crossed the Chindwin river in eight columns and for six weeks struck against the Japanese rear. Some had difficulty extricating themselves and Wingate returned to India in May 1943, having lost 1,000 men, a third of his original force. Because of the harsh treatment the Japanese meted out to prisoners, those too badly injured to make the journey back to India were shot.

Preparations were now being made for the reconquest of Burma. He was promoted to major-general and given a much larger force to command. These men would be landed behind enemy lines by glider and transport plane, with only one column infiltrating on foot. Within three weeks, they commanded a wide area 200 miles behind enemy lines.

On 24 March 1944, Wingate was visiting one of his units. Flying in a tropical storm over the Naga jungles of northern Assam, his plane crashed. He is buried in Arlington National Cemetery.

BEHIND ENEMY LINES

- *In January 1941, Wingate crossed the frontier into Abyssinia (now Ethopia) with the exiled Emperor Haile Selassie and some 2,000 British, Sudanese and Ethiopians to face a much larger Italian force. Less than four months later, on 5 May 1941, he entered the capital Addis Ababa and restored the emperor, receiving a bar to his DSO.*

- *When Wingate returned from Burma in May 1943, he was given a second bar to his DSO. It was considered that he had proved his case and he flew with Winston Churchill to Quebec where he explained his new theories of war to President Roosevelt and other war leaders.*

SIR DAVID STIRLING

1915–1990

CHRONOLOGY

1915 Born 15 November in Keir, Stirlingshire.
1939 Joins the Scots Guards Supplementary Reserve.
1941 Volunteers for Guards Commando; sent to Egypt; founds SAS.
1942 Promoted to lieutenant-colonel; awarded DSO.
1943 Taken prisoner in Tunisia.
1943–1945 Escapes four times, ending up in Colditz.
1990 Dies 4 November in London.

▸ COMMANDO TRAINING

Returning to Britain, Stirling joined the Scots Guards Supplementary Reserve as a subaltern, but volunteered for the commandos as soon as he had been commissioned. He joined Layforce (three commando units under his friend Brigadier Robert Laycock) and was sent to the Middle East. The unit was disbanded, however, by the time he reached Egypt.

By this time the war in North Africa had become a series of advances and retreats along the coast. Stirling saw the opportunity to turn the enemy's flanks by sending raiding parties through the supposedly impassable sea of sand inland and destroying targets far behind enemy lines. He joined forces with the Australian Jock Lewes, an officer with the Welsh Guards. Together they would become the nucleus of the Special Air Service Regiment.

Lewes scrounged fifty parachutes and he and Stirling started to make training jumps. Disaster struck when Stirling's parachute snagged on the tail of the aircraft. Injured in the fall, Stirling spent his months in the hospital planning his new unit.

When he was released, he went to see the commander-in-chief in the Middle East, General Sir Claude Auchinleck, slipping past the guard on his crutches. Auchinleck quickly saw the

S IR DAVID STIRLING FOUNDED and led the British Special Air Service in the Western Desert. It went on to become the elite regiment of the British Army.

Born in Keir, Stirlingshire, on 15 November 1915, the son of brigadier-general Archibald Stirling of the Scots Guards, he dropped out of Cambridge with the intention of climbing Mount Everest. After training in Switzerland, he was in North America climbing the Rockies when war was declared in 1939

Stirling inspired his men into raids so daring that they were bound to succeed

potential of the new unit. Stirling was promoted to captain and given a force of sixty-six men, including six officers and as many NCOs. This independent command was to be called L Detachment, Special Air Service Brigade.

▶ FORMING THE SAS

The first mission for the SAS was to jump behind enemy lines on 17 November 1942 to gather intelligence and tie up German forces. They jumped in terrible conditions. Of the sixty-six, only twenty-two made it back.

Abandoning aircraft, the SAS decided to go into battle overland with the Long Range Desert Group, a motorized reconnaissance unit, who would drop them off behind enemy lines and pick them up again at a rendezvous point at a specified time. From their drop-off points, the SAS would walk to their destination, moving at night to avoid air reconnaissance and enemy foot patrols.

They had to travel light and one of the most important innovations came from Jock Lewes. He devised the lightweight Lewes Bomb out of oil and thermite. Placed on top of the wing of an aircraft, it would explode and ignite the fuel inside. Weighing just one pound, one man could carry enough to destroy a squadron of planes. When one of the raiders, Irish rugby player

Paddy Mayne, ran out of Lewes bombs, he ripped out an aircraft control panel with his bare hands.

When the German army stepped up security, the SAS changed tactics. They equipped themselves with jeeps carrying twin Vickers machine-guns. A squadron of jeeps sped onto an enemy airfield and fired tracers at the aircraft, setting them on fire. In the confusion the SAS would disappear back into the desert.

Eventually, Stirling was captured and spent the rest of the war in prisoner-of-war camps. His brother Bill took over command of 2 SAS, while Paddy Mayne took over command of 1 SAS. After the war in North Africa was over, SAS units began establishing bases in France, far behind enemy lines, dropping in the standard squads of four men with limited supplies. They would stage daring raids on German supply depots, rail-lines and strategic positions, providing reconnaissance and tying up hundreds of German troops who otherwise would have been used against the Allies at Normandy.

When Stirling was released, he planned SAS operations against Japan, but the war ended before they could be put into operation. He went on to set up organizations to promote racial integration in Africa and help with the continent's economic problems. He was knighted in 1990.

A NEW FORM OF WARFARE

- *Within two weeks of the beginning of its second mission, the SAS had destroyed ninety enemy aircraft on the ground. Stirling was promoted to major and Hitler issued his infamous Kommandobefehl, instructing his commanders to suspend the Geneva Conventions when they captured Stirling's raiders and other commandos. To his credit, Rommel ignored this.*
- *Stirling inspired his men into raids that were*

so daring that they were bound to succeed. During 1942, they were so successful that he was awarded the DSO. He also became an officer of the Legion of Orange and of the Order of Orange Nassau.
- *Stirling was captured in Tunisia in 1943. He escaped from prisoner-of-war camp four times and was eventually locked up in Colditz Castle, the prison for habitual escapers.*

VO NGUYEN GIAP

B. 1912

of his troops, where Ho Chi Minh quoted Thomas Jefferson in his speech declaring independence and Giap was named minister of the interior and commander-in-chief in Ho's government.

▶ GUERRILLA WAR

The French returned, however, in 1946 and Giap fled. Under his command, the Vietminh then fought a successful guerrilla war following the theories of Mao Tse-tung. But in 1951, he reverted to conventional warfare with the Red River delta offensive, attacking strongly held positions in Hanoi and the port of Haiphong. He was defeated, but afterwards he inflicted a series of defeats on the French, overwhelming the isolated garrisons at Cao Bang and Lang Son. Giap then destroyed what remained of the French colonial army at Dien Bien Phu.

The country was divided along the 17th parallel by the Geneva Accords for administrative reasons until an election could be called. But the US, unwilling to see the south fall to Communism, encouraged Diem to declare a separate republic in South Vietnam.

Giap became commander-in-chief and minister of defence of North Vietnam. In 1961, he published a manual of guerrilla warfare called

VO NGUYEN GIAP was the Vietnamese military leader who beat the French in the Indochina war of 1946–1954 and the Americans in the Vietnam war of 1965–1975

Born in 1912 at An Xa, Vietnam, just north of the 17th parallel which later became the border between North and South Vietnam, he studied law at Hanoi University where he met Ngo Dinh Diem who went on to become president of South Vietnam and Giap's bitter enemy. Vietnam was then part of French Indochina and Giap's anti-colonist views forced him to flee to China in 1939. His wife was arrested and died in a French jail two years later.

In China Giap met fellow Communist Ho Chi Minh. Together they formed the Vietminh in 1941. He returned to Vietnam where he formed 'armed propaganda teams'. With the defeat of the Japanese in 1945, he entered Hanoi at the head

NVA losses in Vietnam were an estimated 900,000 – fifteen times those of the U.S.

People's War, People's Army. He took charge of the war to reunify the country, setting up the North Vietnamese Army, a regular force, in the North, and encouraging a guerrilla army, the Vietcong, in the South.

Again he used classical Maoist tactics. Political cadres would be infiltrated into remote rural areas and would convince the population to support them. Next, guerrilla groups would make hit-and-run attacks on government forces. When the government troops hit back, they would find themselves overextended and vulnerable to attack by conventional forces.

▶ WAR WITH THE US

Giap was not surprised by the commitment of American ground troops in March 1965. Plans had already been laid for a long war. By June, small contingents of North Vietnamese troops were fighting alongside the Vietcong to test American strength and observe US tactics.

In 1967, Giap put large NVA units into the field, to see how the Americans would react to their presence. The US relished the idea that it would now be facing a conventional army, rather than guerrilla bands, believing that no regular army could resist its might. The NVA suffered huge losses, but still managed to kill Americans, often by fighting at such close quarters that the Americans were forced to bomb their own positions. The fact that the NVA could take the losses and continue fighting gave them a huge psychological advantage.

Giap knew if he could keep inflicting losses on US troops, whatever the cost in Vietnamese lives, America would get tired of the war and withdraw. He could lose every battle and still win the war. US Secretary of Defense Robert McNamara had already worked out that Giap was controlling the frequency and scale of engagements to keep his losses just below the birth rate – that way, the Vietnamese could fight forever.

In 1968, Vietnam exploded in the Tet Offensive. Even the US embassy in the South Vietnamese capital of Saigon was overrun and many Americans began to believe that the Vietnam war could not be won. The peace movement tore America apart and President Richard Nixon was forced to make peace and withdraw in 1973. After a 'decent interval', the war between North and South began again. Giap's forces were unstoppable and, on 30 April 1975, the NVA entered Saigon.

It is estimated that NVA losses were as high as 900,000 – over fifteen times those of the US and five times the South Vietnamese army's losses. That did not prevent it from invading Cambodia to end the genocidal regime of Pol Pot in 1978, nor from defending Vietnam's northern border against the Chinese in 1979.

VICTORIOUS COMMANDER

- *In November 1953, the French occupied the outlying town of Dien Bien Phu in an attempt to cut the Vietminh's supply line from Laos. Giap surrounded them there with an army of 40,000. Although the French had to be supplied by air, their well-equipped army remained confident of victory. But Giap surprised them by moving his heavy artillery 400 miles over rough terrain. The base was overrun on 7 May 1954.*

- *After the Tet Offensive, the Americans quickly re-established order. In the process, the Vietcong was decimated. This was a deliberate sacrifice and the North Vietnamese government did not want southerners challenging their power after they took over.*
- *After forcing the US to withdraw in 1973, Giap had his moment of glory. By 1975, he had already been eclipsed and his protégé Van Tien Dung led the final assault on Saigon.*

MOSHE DAYAN

1915–1981

1915 Born 20 May at Deganya, Palestine • 1929 Joins the Haganah • 1937 Joins Wingate's 'night patrols' • 1939 Imprisoned • 1941 Joins British Army; fights in Palestine • 1953–1958 Serves as Israeli chief of staff • 1956 Leads invasion of Sinai • 1965 Elected to Knesset • 1967 Appointed minister of defence; directs Six-Day War • 1974 Sacked from cabinet • 1981 Dies 16 October in Tel Aviv, Israel.

M OSHE DAYAN WAS ISRAEL'S best known soldier who, in a series of wars against its Arab neigh-bours, secured its borders.

Born on 20 May 1915 on Israel's first kibbutz at Deganya in Palestine, then a province of the Ottoman Empire, he was brought up on his country's first collective farm or *mostov*. After World

Moshe Dayan is considered the father of the Israeli Defence Force

War I the area came under British control. In 1929, he joined the Haganah, the Jewish militia, and was trained by the British officer Charles Orde Wingate who had been posted to Palestine. In 1937, he became one of the Mobile Guards of the Jewish Settlement Police.

▶ IMPRISONED

With the outbreak of World War II, Britain cracked down on the Haganah. Dayan was arrested and sentenced to five years in prison. In 1941 he was released and joined the British Army, fighting against the Vichy French in Syria where he lost his left eye.

By the end of the war, the Haganah had grown to 30,000 men and began a guerrilla war against the British for independence. In 1948, the British withdrew. Dayan took command in the Jordan valley, defending his birthplace. On 18 May 1948, his men defeated a vastly larger Syrian force there. He gained a reputation for his attacks on superior Arab positions. That August, he took part in the peace negotiations.

▶ THE SIX-DAY WAR

At the end of the Jewish War of Independence in 1949, he was a major-general leading the Southern Command in Beersheba. By 1953, he had risen to become chief of staff of the Israeli Defence Force. During the Suez campaign of 1956, he headed six infantry, three armoured and one parachute brigade which defeated the Egyptians in eight days.

Quitting the army in 1958, he was elected to the Knesset, the Israeli parliament, as a member of the Labour Party. He became minister of agriculture. On 1 June 1967, he was appointed minister of defence. Four days later the Israeli air force made a pre-emptive strike, destroying 200 Egyptian aircraft on the ground. Then 700 Israeli tanks, supported by mechanized infantry and artillery, thrust into Sinai, cutting off the frontline Egyptian forces from their bases. Three Israeli divisions, one headed by Ariel Sharon, faced seven Egyptian divisions and defeated them.

In the only crisis of the offence, one armoured division ran out of fuel and was surrounded. But a supply column broke through and relieved it. To the north the Israeli army also faced Egypt's allies, the Syrians and Jordanians, inflicting serious defeats on them. In just six days, Dayan's forces had defeated three other armies.

In 1973, Dayan was criticized for Israel's poor state of preparation when Egypt and Syria attacked again, on 6 October, starting the Yom Kippur War. He was dropped from the Cabinet the following year. In 1978, however, as foreign minister in the government of Menachim Begin, he became one of the chief architects of the Camp David Accords, but quit over Begin's plans to annex the West Bank. He formed a new political party, the Telem, which aimed to give back the territories that his army had taken in 1967. The struggle to achieve that continues.

He published his autobiography *The Story of My Life* in 1976. He died on 16 October 1981 in Tel Aviv, aged sixty-six, leaving a large collection of antiquities acquired from illegal digs.

CAREER HIGHLIGHTS

- *Dayan's media trademark was his black eye patch. In June 1941, he was observing enemy movements when a bullet struck his binoculars, driving glass and metal into his skull. The bone and tissue around the eye socket was too badly damaged to support a glass eye.*

- *During the Six-Day War in 1967, forces under Dayan's control took Sinai, destroying 200 Egyptian aircraft and taking 15,000 Egyptian prisoners. They also took the West Bank and Jerusalem from Jordan and Syria's strategically important Golan Heights.*

COLIN POWELL

B. 1937

CHRONOLOGY
1937 Born 5 April in New York City.
1958 Graduates from City College of New York.
1962–1963 Serves in Vietnam.
1968–1969 Second tour in Vietnam.
1972 Serves as White House aide.
1973 Commands battalion in South Korea.
1976 Commands brigade at Fort Campbell, Kentucky.
1983 Becomes senior military assistant to Secretary of Defense.
1987 Corps commander in West Germany; joins staff of National Security Council.
1989 Becomes chairman of the Joint Chiefs of Staff; plays leading role in invasion of Panama.
1990–1991 Leading figure in the first Gulf War.
1993 Retires from the military.
2001 Becomes Secretary of State.

distinguished career in the military.

Born in New York City on 5 April 1937 to Jamaican immigrant parents, he graduated from Morris High School in 1954. In 1958 he graduated with a Bachelor of Science degree in geology from City College of New York. At college Powell had joined the Reserve Officers' Training Corps and risen to the rank of cadet colonel.

'The discipline, the structure, the camaraderie, the sense of belonging were what I craved,' he wrote.

▶ MILITARY ADVISOR

After graduation Powell joined the United States army and took a commission as a second lieutenant. In 1962, he served as a military advisor in South Vietnam. He returned to South Vietnam in 1968, when the US was fully committed, as a battalion executive officer and became division

C OLIN L. POWELL WAS THE FIRST African–American to become the chairman of the Joint Chiefs of Staff, the highest military post in the US, after a

Powell came to international recognition as the architect of U.S. strategy in the Gulf War

operations officer. During this second tour, he survived a helicopter crash landing, returning to the smoking wreckage to pull out his commanding general and two others.

After his return to the United States, Powell attended George Washington University in Washington, DC, graduating with an MBA in 1971. In 1972, he became a White House aide, his first political job, then he served as assistant to Frank Carlucci, the deputy director of the Office of Management and Budget.

In 1973, Powell returned to the military as a battalion commander in South Korea: the rest of his career saw him shuttling back and forth between politics and the military. He graduated from the National War College in 1976 and became commander of 2 Brigade of the 101st Airborne Division at Fort Campbell, Kentucky. Then, in 1979, he became executive assistant to the Secretary of Energy and senior military assistant to the Deputy Secretary of Defense. From 1981 to 1983, he served as assistant commander of the 4th Infantry Division at Fort Carson, Colorado, then he became deputy commander of Fort Leavenworth, Kansas.

▶ COMMANDING GENERAL

From 1983 to 1986, he served as military assistant to the Secretary of Defense. In 1986, he went to West Germany as commanding general of the V Corps in Frankfurt. In 1987, he joined the staff of the National Security Council, again as deputy to Carlucci, then assistant for national security affairs to President Ronald Reagan. Later that year, Powell replaced Carlucci.

At the beginning of 1989 he took over the Army Forces Command. In April he was promoted to four-star general and in August he was nominated as chairman of the Joint Chiefs of Staff by President George Bush. After being confirmed in this position, he played a leading role in America's invasion of Panama in 1989. He came to international recognition as the chief architect of the successful Gulf War against Iraq in 1991. As ranking member of the US Armed Forces and senior military advisor to the President, he witnessed the fall of the Berlin Wall, the collapse of Soviet Union, the disastrous engagement in Somalia and the Bosnia crisis.

Powell retired from the Joint Chiefs of Staff in 1993. He wrote his memoirs *My American Journey* and embarked on a country-wide tour in 1995 to promote the book. During that tour there was widespread speculation that he would run as a candidate for the Republican nomination for President in 1996. But on 9 November 1995, he held a press conference and announced that he would not enter the race.

On 20 January 2001, he became Secretary of State in the administration of President George W. Bush. In that position, he played an active role in the second Gulf War which began in 2003.

CAREER HIGHLIGHTS

- *During his time in the military, Powell received numerous service medals, including the Purple Heart and the Bronze Star in 1963, Legion of Merit Award in 1969 and 1971, and the Distinguished Service Medal, Soldiers Medal and the Secretary's Award in 1988.*

- *Since Powell left the military, he has received civilian honours as well. In 1993, former President Ronald Reagan presented Powell with the Ronald Reagan Freedom Award. That same year, he received an honorary doctoral degree from Yeshiva University in Manhattan.*

COMMANDERS A–Z

PICTURE CREDITS

Picture Credits
All images © Getty Images Ltd

Arcturus Publishing Limited has made every reasonable effort to ensure
that all permissions information has been sought and achieved as required.
However there may be inadvertent and occasional errors in seeking permission
to reproduce individual photographs for which Arcturus Publishing Limited
apologizes.